Jane Austen, Virginia Woolf and Worldly Realism

Pam Morris

EDINBURGH
University Press

To Colin, with my love

Edinburgh University Press is one of the leading university presses in the UK. We publish academic books and journals in our selected subject areas across the humanities and social sciences, combining cutting-edge scholarship with high editorial and production values to produce academic works of lasting importance. For more information visit our website: edinburghuniversitypress.com

Edinburgh University Press Ltd
The Tun – Holyrood Road, 12(2f) Jackson's Entry, Edinburgh EH8 8PJ

First published in hardback by Edinburgh University Press 2017

Typeset in 11/13 Adobe Sabon by
IDSUK (DataConnection) Ltd, and
printed and bound in Great Britain by
CPI Group (UK) Ltd, Croydon CR0 4YY

A CIP record for this book is available from the British Library

ISBN 978 1 4744 1913 0 (hardback)
ISBN 978 1 4744 3769 1 (paperback)
ISBN 978 1 4744 1914 7 (webready PDF)
ISBN 978 1 4744 1915 4 (epub)

Contents

Acknowledgements

Material from earlier versions of Chapters 2 and 4 appeared in *Virginia Woolf in Context* ©, Cambridge University Press, 2012. I am grateful for permission to use this material. Material from an earlier version of Chapter 2 also appeared in *New Directions in the History of the Novel*, Palgrave Macmillan, 2014. I am grateful for permission to use this material.

I have been fortunate in having opportunity to discuss ideas on realism in the stimulating and congenial contexts of seminars, lectures and conferences at the universities of Freiberg, Zurich and Kent. I am much indebted to the challenging and wide-ranging discussions with staff and students at those institutions.

As always, a great many friends and colleagues contributed their wisdom and encouragement to the process of writing this book. In particular, I thank Jane Goldman for providing the initial impetus and encouragement to explore ideas on Woolf and realism. Martin Mülheim has generously shared with me his wide reading on realism. I also thank Angela Thirlwell who helped me think afresh about structure and has been unstinting in her enthusiasm. To Nancy Armstrong, I am indebted for many years of generous support, for late night talk over a convivial malt and for her inspirational insistence upon the limits of individualism. Elizabeth Allen and Jeannette King have, as always, sustained the long process of writing with their intellectual clarity, unceasing creativity of thought and unfailing warmth of friendship. My daughter Vicky's love of Jane Austen has been a source of certainty in moments of doubt about the project and Colin and Topes, together, have ensured, with love and solidarity, that the whole enterprise stayed afloat.

Introduction

Worldly Realism

> He . . . was driven by intellectual fervour, a burning belief in abstract nouns such as 'sovereignty' and 'freedom'. Those ideas are noble in themselves, of course they are. But not when they are peeled away from the rough texture of the real world. For when doctrine is kept distilled, pure and fervently uncontaminated by reality, it turns into zealotry.
>
> Jonathan Freedland,
> *The Guardian*, 2 July 2016

Jacob Flanders' room in Cambridge contains the works of only one woman writer among all the many male-authored texts scattered about; that writer is Jane Austen. Even so, her presence is there by default, in 'deference, perhaps, to someone else's standard'.[1] It is as if Woolf pays a quietly humorous tribute here, across the space of a hundred years, to her most important literary progenitor. Yet had Jacob availed himself of the pleasure of reading *Northanger Abbey* (1st drafts c.1798–9; pub. 1816), he might well have been struck by the similarities between its narrative, initiating Austen's mature style, and his own, in which Woolf, too, establishes her mature artistic form. In those two works, respectively, *Northanger Abbey* and *Jacob's Room*, both writers find the means and the voice to articulate the sceptical irreverence which constitutes the distinctive force of their artistic sensibilities and vision, a scepticism that is their shared inheritance from the tradition of Scottish Enlightenment.

In these early novels, both writers are consciously challenging the authority of previous representational modes. *Jacob's Room*, appearing in 1922, the same year as *Ulysses* and *The Waste Land*, has, not surprisingly, been largely considered as part of the modernist rejection of traditional literary forms. Yet, Alex Zwerdling is surely right when he suggests that critical commentary on the novel can only illuminate if it moves beyond a mere inventory of innovative techniques. Also required is consideration of why Woolf felt the need for a new kind of narrative.[2] Slotting writers into their generic pigeon hole can close off wider recognition of their artistic aims and achievements. Discussion of *Northanger Abbey* tends also to focus upon generic convention, especially Austen's debunking of the gothic novel. For some critics, like Alistair Duckworth, the novel ultimately fails because, while it makes fun of gothic form, the narrative remains too indebted to it to achieve its proposed moral vision.[3] By contrast, Claudia Johnson, among others, sees Austen's complex ironies as ultimately reinstating the value of the gothic imagination as a means of illuminating 'the ambiguous distresses, dangers, and betrayals of ordinary life'.[4] As with discussion of *Jacob's Room*, there is perhaps need to read the novel in broader terms than the generic, asking why Austen is challenging popular novelistic forms and what is the social perspective that informs her need to find a new mode of representation.

Despite the hundred odd years that separate them, both novels are centrally concerned to overturn concepts of heroic exceptionalism as portrayed in the protagonists of traditional literature. Both Catherine Morland and Jacob Flanders defy artistic convention in being resolutely ordinary. Despite her romantic response to gothic tales, Catherine lacks sensibility or even complicated interiority. Like most children she had enjoyed physical movement and games more than sentiment. Austen has been criticised for failing to provide convincing and sustained presentation of Catherine's growth in moral self-awareness. Yet, perhaps this is part of a deliberate, sceptical refusal of the heroic, a radical writerly commitment to people and things so normal as to remain beneath aesthetic notice. Jacob Flanders also lacks interiority. As has been recognised, Woolf writes not only against the form of the *Bildungsroman* but also against the traditional conventions of biography.[5] The narrative remains wholly external to Jacob's consciousness and lacks linear coherence. Given Jacob's death in the First World War, Woolf's totally unsentimental treatment sets itself provocatively against the prevailing reverence accorded the heroic dead. Before going up to Cambridge, Jacob accepts a present of Byron's writing and in his study he has the work of Thomas Carlyle (pp. 24, 49). The implication is that young men should be wary of the spurious attraction to heroes and hero-worship.

The title of the essay Jacob is writing, 'Does History Consist of the Biographies of Great Men?', with its obvious reference to

Carlyle's *On Heroes, Hero-Worship and the Heroic in History*, is darkly ironic given the premature, pointless deaths of so many young men in trench warfare. The title of the essay also forms part of Woolf's pervasive attack upon gender hierarchy throughout the text. Women are treated contemptuously by Jacob and his friends, regarded as lesser beings, lacking spirituality and necessary mainly for sexual pleasure. This presumption of masculine superiority is fostered by the cult of Hellenism that young men of Jacob's generation were immersed in at the public schools and Cambridge as part of a more general enthusiasm, in the early part of the century, for idealist philosophy. The effect was the elevation of the mind (invariably masculine) above the body (usually female). Woolf starkly ironises this idealising of disembodied rationality in her chilling account of death dehumanised by distance: 'Like blocks of tin soldiers the army covers the cornfield, moves up the hillside, stops [. . .] and falls flat, save that, through field glasses, it can be seen that one or two pieces still agitate up and down like fragments of broken match-stick' (p. 216). A hundred years earlier, Henry Tilney would find much common ground with Jacob as to women's lack of rationality and capacity for serious knowledge. Catherine's view of the history of great men as written by great men, however, is as sceptical as Woolf's: women are absent from their accounts and the male heroes all 'good for nothing' (p. 79). Henry Tilney's confidence in his capacity to educate and correct the female mind is ironically demoted by his serious failure of insight into his father's motives and conduct.

It is surprising to recognise how easily Woolf's representation of Betty Flanders, Captain Barfoot, Mr Floyd and most others in that circle of Jacob's childhood could be slipped unnoticed into Austen's village of Fullerton along with Mrs Morland and the Allens. There is a sense, moreover, that these rather complacent but respectable folk all belong to a way of life becoming outmoded and share a perspective that is no longer adequate, and this is so despite the hundred years between the two publications. The sceptical mockery of heroic endeavour, of individualist exceptionalism, and of gender hierarchy along with the ironic rejection of established literary forms are part of a larger agenda that Austen and Woolf share. Both writers are situated, at different historical points, within a continuing struggle of representation that constitutes the realms of art and of politics.

They both sense that a different possible world is struggling for perceptibility, a process engaging a new language and new forms. This is most obviously so for Woolf, writing in the aftermath of the

First World War that had thrown into disarray all the traditional certainties structuring social and political life: class and gender subordination, reverence for religion, national honour and law. It is the crisis of this ordered and authorised hierarchical perception of social reality that Woolf's narrative techniques aim to convey. Similarly, in *Northanger Abbey*, Austen interrogates and finds inadequate the available conventions of language and form. Failures of expression and understanding are characterised by a conflict between gothic and rational perceptions of realities. The occasions, moreover, involve reference to the forces of radical social change characterising the era of the French Revolution. When Catherine speaks enthusiastically of fresh horrors issuing from London, Eleanor Tilney mistakenly takes her to have news of political violence in the capital. Henry Tilney uses the opportunity to mock both women, informing his sister that any rational creature would relate Catherine's words to the circulating library not to 'a mob of three thousand men assembling in St George's Fields [. . .] the streets of London flowing with blood' (p. 82). But the unspoken challenge of the passage is that neither gothic melodrama nor pure rationality is adequate means to represent such actual social horror and turmoil as had indeed been recently experienced in London. Austen is in line, here, with British sceptical Enlightenment: pure rationality cannot fully comprehend the complexity of embodied experience.

The same irresolvable question of representation arises with Henry's lecture to Catherine as to the ungothic, law-abiding, Christian nature of England where atrocity would never be connived at or tolerated. Yet his moral and rational vision of English normality is overturned by the vicious brutality of his own father, General Tilney, whom he had rebuked Catherine for depicting as a gothic villain. Henry's rational picture of England leaves too much unnoticed and unspoken for. Yet to see the General's behaviour as vindication of the gothic mode is equally limiting. The General is not the exceptionalist villain of gothic horror. In his pursuit of greed and petty dictatorship he is all too ordinary; he represents the mundanity of secular evil. His competitive consumerism, his greed and concern with social status, moreover, typifies the powerful emergent force of aggressive individualism in British society and politics from the end of the eighteenth century onwards. As with Woolf, Austen's was a world in which the consensus was fracturing. The scepticism and lack of reverence that typify both writers facilitated a dissensual way of perceiving their changing worlds and forging the representational means adequate to their vision. I am terming that representational mode worldly realism, as distinct from psychological and social realism. As the words suggest, worldly realism conveys a materialist, non-hierarchical and encompassing perception of existence, a horizontal continuity of self, social world and physical universe.

It may seem surprising to suggest an artistic continuity between Austen, often seen as the originator of the British tradition of realism, and Woolf, who is generally understood to herald its end. Both, however, are the direct literary heirs of the sceptical tradition of British empiricism, and both are writing at moments of public debate as to the conflicting claims of materialism versus idealism. Derek Ryan, one of the few critics to recognise that 'throughout her writing Woolf theorises the materiality of human and non-human life' associates this artistic perspective with her wariness of the 'philosophical, ethical and political pitfalls of individualism'.[6] Austen similarly stresses the materiality of the self and regards with suspicion the consensual consolidation of an ideology of individualism.

In considering the work of both writers as constituted by a shared, dissensual perspective, albeit mediated by their very different worlds, the work of Jacques Rancière offers an insightful conceptual framework. Rancière challenges the poststructuralist orthodoxy, espoused by critics like Roland Barthes, that modernism marks a radical break with the foundational belief of realism that words can provide an account of the world. Modernism, such anti-realists assert, initiates an aesthetic practice of conscious self-referentiality, a disengaging of word from world. In opposing this view, Rancière argues that the radical break occurs around the end of the eighteenth century, when a new dissensual aesthetic regime came into conflict with the existing consensual regime of classical verisimilitude.[7] It is perhaps not coincidental that this is the moment at which Austen inaugurates her experimental novelistic practice, even though the British context of her work is different from that of the continental writers whom Rancière discusses.

The terms 'consensus' and 'dissensus' are central to Rancière's thinking both on art and on politics, which he sees as two facets of the same site of struggle, the struggle of representation. Consensus, for Rancière, is an order regulated by the logic of the proper. It constitutes a naturalised artistic and political hierarchy in which everyone has a proper place which defines the terms and domain of their speech and action. This classical order of representation systematises a facade of verisimilitude into a hierarchical totality comprising 'an affinity between characters, situations and forms of expression' (*Politics of Literature*, p. 153). Within this vertical hierarchy only certain people's speech is deemed significant and noteworthy and their actions rationally understandable in terms of values like honour, trust, ambition. These classical conventions constitute universal man as 'realistic' in the rational verisimilitude of congruous, meaningful speech, action and interpretation. This congruity of what is said, done and meant is held in place by the implicit guarantee of interiority, of the presence of capacity for mental willing. What is other to this proper realm of the classical regime is rendered unnoticed, unheard, without sense.

Politics and art, Rancière suggests, comprise a struggle over what is deemed deliberative, meaningful speech and what can be dismissed as mere expression of sensation, non-sense: 'Politics, before all else, is an intervention upon the visible and sayable.'[8] The cracking apart of the naturalised facade of the proper requires a writing practice as dissensus. This is the destructive/productive egalitarianism of the new aesthetic regime of representation that arises around the end of the eighteenth century. It produces a redistribution of the perceptible, bringing into visibility and audibility all that had been excluded as unworthy, improper and of no account. As opposed to the static, vertical hierarchy regulating the regime of the proper, the aesthetic regime is driven by the horizontal force of democratic energy. It is the 'tide of beings and things, a tide of superfluous bodies' that surges through the text of *Madame Bovary* (*Politics of Literature*, p. 39).

It is not the separation of the word from the world that typifies the aesthetic regime but its inclusivity. It redistributes 'space and time, place and identity, speech and noise, the visible and the invisible' (*Politics of Literature*, p. 4). Literary language is not a special elevated mode of poetics defining modernist writing, therefore, it is a new horizontal 'way of linking the sayable and the visible, word and things' (*Politics of Literature*, p. 9). It creates an egalitarian representational space in which anyone can say anything in any style of language whatsoever. Rather than textuality, the aesthetic regime replaces the idealism underpinning the classical regime by bringing into perceptibility the material continuity of 'the world-at-large that anyone can grab hold of' (*Politics of Literature*, p. 13). The usefulness of Rancière's concept of the perceptible lies equally in its materialism and its inclusivity. What is perceptible is that which is afforded by impressions gained through both the senses and the intellect but with a reversal of idealist emphasis from mind to what is physically present to ear, eye and hand. All the stuff of the world in which we have existence is thus comprehended within the struggle of representation that constitutes the political and aesthetic regimes.

Rancière sets out three relations of equality operating within the new dissensual regime of the perceptible. The first is that of 'the equality of subjects and the availability of any word and phrase to build the fabric of any life whatever' (*Politics of Literature*, p. 26). The second is the equality of mute things that are more eloquent than the most heroic orator. Finally, there is the 'molecular democracy of the states of things with no rhyme or reason' (*Politics of Literature*, p. 26). To illustrate this third equality he refers to Flaubert's claim that he was less interested in an individual beggar than in the mass of undifferentiated lice that lived off him (*Politics of Literature*, p. 25). Rancière claims that within the new aesthetic regime these three politics of equality are in tension, even conflict. Yet, what needs affirming as positive and productive in his account is the insistence upon things, upon the egalitarian tide of materiality that constitutes physical existence and the concomitant dethroning of human exceptionalism this necessarily entails. In a new regime of the perceptible, subjects and things and molecules are all equally noteworthy. It is this equality and inclusive horizontality that characterises the mode of writing I am terming worldly realism.

The conflict between a classical, vertical regime of the perceptible and the redistribution of what is visible and sayable within a new horizontal, egalitarian regime of representation has significant parallels with the central debate within Enlightenment thinking between the rational universalism of continental idealism and the material particularism of British empiricism. Classical verisimilitude underwrites the timeless values of universal man and erases from notice the embodied existence that renders humanity part of the changing physical world rather than the rational exception to it. British empiricism is sceptical of universal systems of knowledge, divorced from empirical particularity, and recognises the limitations of reason under the impress of habit and desires. It is, indeed, the promise of transcendence from an inconclusive, contingent everyday reality that constitutes the persuasive power of idealism as much as the rationality of its systems of thought.

The Hellenism flourishing among the young men of Jacob's generation in Woolf's text and in her actual world beyond fiction was part of a larger idealist reaction against what was seen as the spiritual aridity of nineteenth-century materialism. The smallness, ignoble detail and conventionalism of this way of thinking is the cause of Jacob's passionate rejection of H. G. Wells whose novels are exemplary, for him, of this narrow, provincial realism. Woolf, too, was critical of the writing of Wells, along with that of Arnold Bennett whom she accuses of aiming at such factual, empirical particularity that there is a stifling 'air of probability embalming the whole', so that there seems no possible alternative to the familiarity within which we live.[9]

This is the criticism still brought against realism by anti-realist critics from Roland Barthes to, more recently, Gabriel Josipovici. Realism as a genre, anti-realists claim, functions ideologically to consolidate the status quo; the seamless verisimilitude, in form and content, that insists there is no alternative, that this is just, naturally, how things are. In *Whatever Happened to Modernism*, Josipovici makes the same accusation as Woolf arguing that realist novels 'create a world and characters to inhabit that world that do not flout the laws of probability [. . .] Such narratives are easy to read [. . .] the smooth chain of sentences gives us a sense of security, of comfort even.'[10] Novels like this, Josipovici claims, make the world seem smaller and meaner. We could say that their consensual regime of the perceptible constitutes a meticulous facade that regulates too narrowly what and who can be seen and heard. It operates comfortingly rather like Henry Tilney's view of England.

Nevertheless, in a recent review article on J. Hillis Miller in the *London Review of Books*, Rachel Bowlby complains that in this kind of critique, as made by Hillis Miller and Josipovici, among others, 'realism tends to get identified with a demoted, simplified theory of language – a word for everything and everything consistently called by its name'.[11] As this suggests, underlying the attacks upon realism there is frequently a positivist correspondence theory of truth, a belief that words can offer a one-to-one match with things in the world. Anti-realists, like Josipovici and Hillis Miller, disdain such an over-simple view but, they imply, realist writers do not, or, at least, realists sell that reassuring belief to their readers. Realism, according to this view, perpetrates a naive sense of language of which Wittgenstein says, 'a picture held us captive'.[12] This comforting sense of identity between word and world is at odds with the epistemological scepticism that underpins David Hume's empiricism and equally with a view of language as inherently dialogic and communicative.[13] Such a narrowly referential view of representation, valorising accuracy and facts, is more usefully understood as actualist, as distinct from realist.

Georg Lukács makes a very clear distinction between realism and the reassuring consensual convention of actualism. 'But the more closely Balzacian method approaches objective reality,' he argues, 'the more it diverges from the accustomed, the average [. . .] Balzac's method transcends the narrow, habitual, accepted limits of this immediacy and because it thus runs counter to the comfortable, familiar, usual way of looking at things, it is regarded by many as "exaggerated"'.[14] Balzac's art, Lukács continues, moves completely beyond 'photographic reproduction' (p. 60). What Lukács is describing here seems very similar to what Rancière advocates as writing as dissensus, a shattering of consensual verisimilitude. Lukács' subsequent over-partisan defence of realism and attack upon modernism belongs to the Stalinist era, but the polarised controversies of that time initiated an unproductive, often misleading, binary opposition between realism and modernism that can too easily lead to an over-simplified, even caricatured version of one or the other, of which Josipovici's account of realism is an unfortunate example.

Modernism and realism are, in fact, far from incompatible; both are experimental and both can offer an open sense of the possibilities, as opposed to the factual probabilities, of human life. In his argument with Lukács, Bertold Brecht refuses to accept the polarisation of modernist experimentalism versus realist conventionalism: 'Formalism on the one side – contentism on the other. That is surely too primitive.'[15] Realism cannot be embalmed in any one form or style, he argues,

> Were we to copy the style of these [nineteenth-century] realists, we would no longer be realists. For time flows on [. . .] Methods become exhausted; stimuli no longer work. New problems appear and demand new methods. Reality changes; in order to represent it, modes of representation must also change. Nothing comes from nothing; the new comes from the old, but that is why it is new. (p. 82)

Conventional histories of the novel, such as Ian Watt's *The Rise of the Novel* (1957), have certainly associated its development closely with the influence of eighteenth-century empiricism.[16] Yet, anti-realists would be on firmer ground in recognising realist fiction's affiliation with and constitution of idealist conceptions of reality. It is in their underpinning of idealist values that many nineteenth- and twentieth-century realist novels are most open to criticism as serving a conservative consensus. Psychological realism has undoubtedly contributed in no small measure to the ideology of individualism, especially the elitist individualism that privileges interiority, intelligence and sensibility as indexes of moral, even human worth. Within this ideology, the acquirements resulting from cultural capital are taken as naturally endowed spiritual superiority. Literary criticism, too, has tended to prize fictions depicting the sustained and complex inner struggles, the conflicts of hope, doubt and suffering experienced by intensely individualised characters. Narrative trajectories, frequently tragic, show heroic protagonists crushed by the crass forces of materialism or their own failures of moral sensibility or by some combination of the two.[17] This common narrative pattern works against the democratic impulse that Erich Auerbach, in *Mimesis*, associated with the development of realism as a genre.[18] The main protagonists undeniably come from lower down the social scale than did earlier heroes and heroines, but novelists compensate by endowing them with exceptional inner nobility. The distinctive sensibility of a Dorothea Brooke, for example, elevates her as much above the mass of human kind as wealth and power separated earlier high-born protagonists. It is salutary to note that in all of Austen's fiction there is no Dorothea. Austen is always sceptical of exceptionalism.

Social realism, in addition, with its representations of detailed, particularised social worlds, frequently functions as the powerful, material 'other', against which the privileged interiority or 'soul' of the individual main character is defined. In this respect, it could be argued, realist fiction, in both its social and psychological forms, has frequently been inherently idealist rather than materialist, with plot structures maintaining the absolutism of the mind-matter hierarchical division. Moreover, plot structure, in conjunction with narrative technique, also functions as a model of universal knowledge in which mastery of particularity is brought intellectually into a unified systematised whole. Readers are interpellated into this fictitious position of panoptic omniscience and rewarded by the plenitude of certainty, justice and transcendence at the conclusion of even the most harrowing of stories.

It is not surprising this should be so. The modern novel takes its shape during the Enlightenment era. The struggles of representation that constitute that historical moment inevitably form part of the novel's generic DNA. From Austen through to Woolf and beyond novels play a major role in the ideological conflict between materialism and idealism. The consensual perception that came to dominate by the end of the nineteenth century was idealist, elevating mind over gross matter; bodily life retained visibility largely as the troublesome otherness of labouring people or alien races. A notable exception to this literary regime of the proper is Thomas Hardy's worldly realist fiction which explicitly thematises the continuity of human life with the physical world.

In 1918, just after Hardy gave up novel writing and before Woolf began writing *Jacob's Room*, in which young men aspire to Hellenistic ideals, scorning the materialism represented by writers such as H. G. Wells, Bertrand Russell published *Mysticism and Logic*. In this work, he argues that the greatest achievements in human creative thinking have been the result of a fusion of two contrary impulses driving a pursuit of knowledge, namely idealism and empiricism. The 'true union' of these, he says, produces the 'highest eminence' possible in the world of thought.[19] This understanding of two, often conflicting, forces shaping the comprehension of reality plays a key role in Woolf's view of the 'highest eminence' in literary art. She sets this out most explicitly in her essay on Ivan Turgenev where she claims the greatest novelistic achievement is to hold in balance the contrary truths of vision and fact, allowing neither to subordinate the other (*Essays*, 6.11). In the political worlds of her novels, however, those pursuing visions are frequently practitioners of a coercive will to dominate. In Austen's fiction, characters have to learn that their vision or wishes need to be subjected to empirical facts.

Russell was writing at a time when idealism was coming to dominate the teaching of philosophy in the universities. He and G. E. Moore, both members of the Bloomsbury group, wrote rigorous refutations of the foundational tenet of idealism that the only reality available was that of the mind.[20] Idealist modes of thought, however, were increasingly influential across wide sections of policy-making on public welfare, education and class legislation. Idealism was also shaping notions of national identity and the role of the state. Russell was highly critical of this political dimension of idealist thinking. For this reason, although he pays tribute, in *Mysticism and Logic*, to the power of the metaphoric mode of language he associates with visionary thinking, he is most severe upon systems of thought that elevate the mental or spiritual at the expense of the empirical. Even the meanest things, such as hair, mud and dirt are part of material existence, he insists, and the tendency to ignore such everyday reality, the thingness of the world, constitutes a failure of perception that renders so much of idealist thought 'thin, lifeless and insubstantial' (p. 14). Russell recognises the imaginative attraction of exorcising all that is mundane and messy in physical existence as unreal and to locate reality, instead, in the coherence and totality of rational systems of belief. But he warns that identification with the self-sufficiency of ideal mental worlds leads ethically and politically to 'absence of indignation or protest' (pp. 16–17).

Idealist philosophy no longer dominates the discipline within universities, in part due to Moore's and Russell's critiques. Nevertheless, idealist modes of thought are arguably more powerful and pervasive today across the globe than they were in Russell's time. Idealist assumptions underpin the consensus that regulates current regimes of the perceptible. The abstract mental and spiritual totalities of nationalism, religion and free-market neo-liberalism dominate much of human existence with coercive assertions that there is no alternative, rejecting any appeal to evidence and experience beyond the enclosure of system. According to David Harvey, in *Cosmopolitanism and the Geographies of Freedom*, for instance, neo-liberalism has become a universalistic mode of discourse, increasingly defining 'the common sense way many of us interpret, live in, and understand the world'.[21] In *Critical Realism*, the philosopher of science, Roy Bhaskar, claims that during his training as a mathematician and economist, it was 'totally taboo to talk about the real world' existing beyond the realm of mathematical models and macro systems.[22] In fact, as Katrine Marçal points out, there was remarkably little resistance to idealist economics. The abstract models were 'quite simply too elegant. Sexy [. . .] From Wall Street to university campuses: people wanted to believe in this dream. And so they did.'[23] We live now, it is claimed, in the era of post-factual debate.

At the other end of the spectrum from macro systems and models of reality, idealism equally underpins the ideology of individualism, by holding in place the subject-object hierarchy. This is the mental structure that determines most forms of social inequality. The elevation of reason and spirit above flesh has been, and still is, used to justify the subordination of women, the poor, the non-heterosexual and non-European. In addition, belief in the human capacity to master the object world has brought the planet close to ecological disaster. The persuasive charm of abstract perfection too frequently renders imperceptible its material costs. Human life would be immeasurably impoverished without dreams, aspirations beyond self and pursuit of expansive ideals. Yet, cut adrift from the empirical realities of actual lives, the rhetorical force of abstractions like freedom, sovereignty, civilisation, honour, can seem to promise a desired but dangerous simplicity.

Bertrand Russell's insistence that such 'lowly' physical things as hair and mud cannot be put aside in accounts of reality is, in effect, a call for the redistribution of the perceptible so as to recognise the hidden continuities and dependencies of the mental and the physical. It is a demand, in Rancière's words, for 'a new way of linking the sayable and visible, words and things' (*Politics of Literature*, p. 9). Acknowledging the egalitarian relation of people and things challenges the exceptionalist status of the human over the object world.

It foregrounds the fact that as physical beings we have our existence in a shared material space. The regime of the perceptible is reconfigured when things are recognised as constituting the actual stuff that mediates our lives and interactions with others. As Hannah Arendt points out, in *The Human Condition*, it is objects that 'guarantee a permanence and durability without which a world would not be possible [. . .] they give rise to the familiarity of the world, its customs and habits of intercourse between men and things as well as between men and men'.[24] Recent research into neurology and cognition has further erased the idealist hierarchical separation of mind from the object world, suggesting that the physical environment has to be thought of as part of our 'cognitive architecture'.[25] Andy Clark, in *Supersizing the Mind: Embodiment, Action and Cognitive Extension*, suggests the mind needs to be thought of as 'the productive interface of brain, body and social and material world'.[26]

In *The Social Life of Things*, Arjun Appadurai suggests that the powerful tendency to 'regard the world of things as inert and mute' should be exchanged for a view in which 'it is the things-in-motion that illuminate their human and social context'.[27] He quotes Nancy Munn's observation on an exchange system based upon shells: 'Although men appear to be the agents in defining shell value, in fact, without shells, men cannot define their own value; in this respect, shells and men are reciprocally agents of each other's value definition' (*Social Life*, p. 20). In his work on Actor-Network Theory, Bruno Latour takes this radical equalisation of people and things even further. He vigorously attacks the idealist tradition that elevates the mental and disregards matter. Things, he says, 'are much more interesting, variegated, uncertain, complicated, far-reaching, heterogeneous, risky, historical, local, material and networky than the pathetic version offered for too long by philosophers'.[28] Reversing the traditional notion of human agency as expression of mental willing, Latour claims, of things, 'they too do things, they too *make* you do things'.[29] This is what Jane Bennett, in *Vibrant Matter: A Political Ecology of Things*, refers to as 'thing power'.[30]

Latour takes from Heidegger the term 'gathering' to suggest the way meaning is collected in objects, extending the scope of the term well beyond Heidegger's usage. To consider a thing as a 'gathering' is to recognise all it brings together in its very substance: the range of materiality, the networks of people, institutions, social structures, past, future and present events, and so on, in an unclosable, horizontal chain of connection. For example, a camera 'gathers' within its material existence the scientific institutions that produce knowledge of its technology, industrial plants that bring the technology into being, commercial and advertising networks that promote its consumption; in addition, photography, professional and amateur, has shaped public and private rituals, and has reconfigured notions of aesthetics and realism, truth and identity.

Things, in this sense, can be seen as metonymies, as parts of larger structures, networks and social forces. Within literary criticism, however, things are more usually read as metaphors and symbols, valued especially within post-structuralist discourse as figuration that introduces ambivalence and playfulness into writing. Yet Jacques Derrida, in his essay, 'White Mythology', gives a more negative account, accusing metaphor of complicity with the whole tradition of Western idealist philosophy. Metaphor performs an illusionist trick, conjuring the abstract into the perceptible. Idealism, Derrida argues, deploys metaphor pervasively to elevate the transcendent and downgrade or erase from notice the physical. Concrete terms are imbued with spiritual values and with passage of time that figurative element is forgotten or reliteralised. 'Above all,' Derrida writes, 'the movement of metaphorization (origin and then erasure of the metaphor, transition from proper sensory meaning to the proper spiritual meaning by means of a detour of figures) is nothing other than a movement of idealization.'[31]

A simple example of this movement from concrete to spiritual by way of metaphor would be the use of physical terms like above/below, high/low, inner/outer as literalised metaphors to refer to non-spatial, immaterial relationships imputed to mental realms, like morality, consciousness and social relations.[32] Without such terms it is difficult to see how the metaphysical hierarchy of mind over matter could be thought, let alone articulated. Similarly, objects transformed into symbols like the cross or the national flag function to give figurative tangibility to abstract concepts like sacrifice and nation. In this way metaphor can imbue the non-existent with a powerful sense of referentiality borrowed from the actual non-metaphysical world, providing the visionary and spiritual with perceptibility to be felt upon the pulse.

Woolf's novels are thick with things, but it is perhaps surprising to recognise how few of these function as symbols. Jacob's boots are not metaphors of abstract values. On the contrary, they point poignantly to the embodied life that has been physically destroyed. Things, in Woolf's texts, are frequently metonymic, referring horizontally to larger material structures and forces, as Jacob's room stands for male-dominated cultural institutions and power relations. Woolf is, indeed, wary of the ideological functioning of symbolism and metaphor to impart a spurious reverence to questionable values, institutions and agendas. As Alex Zwerdling comments in his chapter on *Jacob's Room*, 'she had an instinctive distrust for reverence of any kind, treating it as a fundamentally dishonest mental habit that made symbols out of flesh-and-blood human beings' (*Virginia Woolf and the Real World*, p. 73). Things are, perhaps, less prolific in Jane Austen's fiction. Nevertheless, objects in her novels are far from being 'reality effects' in Roland Barthes' sense of functioning to guarantee verisimilitude. As with Woolf, things in Austen's writing are frequently metonymic, part of wider discursive networks, social processes and change. In this sense, certainly, the writing of both Austen and Woolf challenges the idealist regime of verisimilitude that relegates the material world below the mental. Their worldly realism makes perceptible the meaning systems articulated by mute things.

A representational regime that makes perceptible the egalitarian continuities and force fields linking the human world with the world of things radically challenges the exceptionalist status of the sovereign subject of interiority. Woolf's declaration of the necessity to kill the angel in the house is well-known. What is less recognised is that the whole project of her fiction from *Jacob's Room* onwards is to kill the angel within, the sovereign subject of privatised interiority. Austen, too, looks critically upon the developing individualistic ideology of self and subjects its illusions to ironic deflation. This scepticism towards the autonomous subject, by both writers, draws upon an anti-idealist understanding of self that develops in the eighteenth century.

Liberal individualism is frequently understood, by both detractors and supporters, as deriving unproblematically from Enlightenment thinking. It is important, therefore, to stress that David Hume is a major originator of an inherently social, as opposed to individualist, perception of self. The unity and sovereignty of the individual subject, deriving from Descartes's location of truth solely and innately in the rational mind, is dismissed by David Hume as 'unintelligible'.[33] The self, Hume argues, is nothing more than 'a train of different perceptions' (*Enquiry*, p. 142). Elsewhere, he exclaims, 'But what is man but a heap of contradictions.'[34] The passions, Hume claims, will always overrule reason. Instead of the autonomous, but lonely, individualism of the Cartesian interiority, Hume insists upon the priority of the co-operative process that constitutes social being and a shared world. 'The mutual dependence of men is so great, in all societies, that scarce any action is compleat in itself, or is performed without some reference to the actions of others' (*Enquiry*, p. 64). Even poetic vision, the *sine qua non* of idealist aesthetics, is regarded by Hume, as essentially a social process: 'it runs along the earth; is caught from one breast to another' (*Essays*, p. 114). The progress of the arts and sciences, he declares, is not due to 'the spirit and genius of the few, but concerns those of the whole people' (*Essays*, p. 114). Inevitably, this brings to mind Woolf's rather enigmatic assertion in *A Sketch of the Past*, 'But there is no Shakespeare, there is no Beethoven; certainly and emphatically there is no God; we are the words; we are the music.'[35]

Adam Smith saw himself as continuing the work of his friend, Hume. So it is not surprising that he, too, stresses the social constitution of the self only possible within a shared world, although this may be an unfamiliar idea to those proclaiming Smith as an original proponent of ruthless individualism. On the contrary, Smith insists that a notion of self is only possible at all through interaction with others. As Roy Porter has observed, for Smith, 'self was a construct of various force-fields of sympathy between individuals'.[36] Smith's notion of sympathy, at the heart of his *Theory of Moral Philosophy*, is based upon an almost novelistic understanding of perspective: the imaginative ability to shift across different viewpoints. For Smith, this is the necessary given of a shared world. He elaborates a concept of an 'impartial observer' – a far more productive idea than that of his one reference to an 'invisible hand' – as the basis of just and humane social relations.[37] When our opinion or interests come into conflict with another's, Smith argues, 'We must view them neither from our own place nor yet from his, neither with our own eyes nor yet with his, but from the place and with the eyes of a third person.'[38] This horizontal process of moving across perspectives offers an egalitarian expansion of the self, helping us to recognise 'that we are but one of the multitude, in no respect better than any other in it' (*TMS*, p. 158). Indeed for Smith there are no bounds to the expansive worldliness of the imagination: it is 'circumscribed by no boundary, but may embrace the immensity of the universe' (*TMS*, p. 276). This statement could well provide a summary of Woolf's aim in writing *The Waves*.

Austen is undoubtedly heir to the Enlightenment understanding of perspective as foundation of a shared world. The ideas of Hume and Smith were pervasive in the public sphere when Austen began to write, both in the form of their own essays and popularised in reviews and discussions in the periodical press. It is perhaps not surprising, therefore, that Austen developed such complex techniques for representing perspective. The innovative fluidity of point of view in her fiction constitutes the discursive grammar of a familiar common world which is the experience of reading her work. In her stories, it is those characters capable of achieving an observant impartiality, encompassing the viewpoints of others beyond their own, who embody the possibilities of progressive change. She initiates a transformation of plot structure, abandoning gothic plots and picaresque adventure to centre upon the ramifying social consequences of differing points of view. This experimental exploration of perspective projects focalisation to the heart of subsequent novel development. Opposing regimes of the perceptible become, in effect, the dynamic of narrative. From that transitional moment, at the end of the eighteenth century, the novel came to foreground perspective, the necessary condition of a shared world, in a way no other literary medium does. This defining emphasis upon point of view, within realism as a genre, has sustained a continuously experimental methodology into the present time.

Adam Smith's claim that a shared world of mutual justice depends upon the ability to enter into different viewpoints has considerable common ground with Jürgen Habermas's advocacy of a new 'paradigm of mutual understanding'.[39] A paradigm that he hopes can move philosophy beyond the sterile binarism of 'the transcendental and the empirical modes of dealing with issues'. Perspective is central to this project. Mutual understanding, Habermas claims, is 'structured upon the system of reciprocally interlocked perspectives among speakers, hearers and non-participants who happen to be present at the time' (*Philosophical Discourse*, p. 297). Going further than Smith, Habermas ties perspective to language structures, like, for instance, the ability of all competent speakers to use the grammar of personal pronouns. Anyone who has assimilated this practice has attained the performative capacity 'to take up and to transform into one another the perspectives of the first, second and third persons' (*Philosophical Discourse*, p. 297). One could go further and ask whether language as practice would even be possible in the absence of this intersubjective, shared world and equally whether self identity could be attained at all without the availability of such discursive positions.

An egalitarian understanding of perspective not only constitutes the condition of possibility for a shared social world. It also militates against the coercive imposition of a universalist system of belief. Classical idealism assumes a unitary mental elevation able to comprehend the particular as part of a totalised system of thought. Belief in a divine overview may be replaced by an ideal of science but the aim remains to impose order and meaning upon heterogeneous material existence by means of abstraction and distance. This is what Michel de Certeau, in *The Practice of Everyday Life*, terms an 'exaltation of a scopic and gnostic drive [. . .] a solar Eye, looking down like a god' that imposes regularity upon the swarming, disordered confusion of mass society.[40] It is the Olympic distance assumed by the narrator in *Jacob's Room* in which living and dying men become only numbers and unreal, twig-like figures. Hannah Arendt warns that 'The end of the common world has come when it is seen only under one aspect and is permitted to present itself in only one perspective.' Against this homogenising perspective, Arendt insists 'the reality of the public realm relies on the simultaneous presence of innumerable perspectives' (*Human Condition*, pp. 58, 57). This constitutes a good description of Woolf's radical use of multiple perspectives as in *Mrs Dalloway*, for example, where the varied passers-by on the street look up at a plane above London. This small episode crystallises the opposition of Olympic distance against an egalitarian horizontal continuity of 'innumerable perspectives'.

Well before twentieth-century experience of totalitarianism, David Hume issued a similar warning against the impulse to impose mental order upon the randomness of the world, 'lest we assign causes which never existed, and reduce what is merely contingent to stable and universal principles' (*Essays*, p. 113). In another essay, he comments, 'But would these reasoners look abroad into the world, they would meet with nothing that, in the least, corresponds to their ideas, or can warrant so refined and philosophical a system' (*Essays*, pp. 469–70). 'System' is a key term in Enlightenment critique of idealism; the imposition of conceptual schemes without due regard for the empirical, of vision at the expense of fact. Adherents of current neo-liberalism find it convenient to ignore Adam Smith's equally firm rejection of universal systems imposed upon human reality. 'Human society,' he writes, 'when we contemplate it in a certain abstract and philosophical light, appears like a great, an immense machine' (*TMS*, p. 372). But, he warns, 'The man of system [. . .] is often so enamoured with the supposed beauty of his own ideal plan of government [. . .] [that] He seems to imagine that he can arrange the different members of a great society with as much ease as the hand arranges pieces upon a chess-board' (*TMS*, p. 275).

Despite Austen's radical restructuring of narrative upon ways of seeing rather than upon action, her characters are very far from being disembodied points of view. Austen's people are always embodied, driven by physical vitality. David Hartley, very influential at the end of the eighteenth century, foregrounds what is largely absent from Hume's and Smith's accounts of self. To Hume's and Smith's considerations of the nature of human nature, Hartley contributed the notion of the embodied self, a self under the necessity of producing itself from the earliest physical sensations of pleasure and pain. For Hartley, therefore, self is always incomplete, emergent. As a complex of sensations and impressions, self is also, he says, '"factitious", i.e. generated by association; and therefore admit[s] of intervals, augmentations, and dimunitions'.[41] In *David Hartley on Human Nature*, Richard C. Allen explains that for Hartley 'the self, as a complex psychological structure of memories, thoughts, and, especially, dispositions, arises out of a ground of purely physical responses to one's circumstances'.[42] Hartley's materialist psychology foregrounds the long process of transformation from purely physical drives to the most highly cultural forms of self.

The account of self that prioritises social being, put forward by Enlightenment thinkers like Hume, Smith and, more recently, Habermas, can be criticised as overly optimistic. David Hartley is, if anything, yet more optimistic in his view of human nature. Nevertheless, his grounding of the self in the physical body makes perceptible the continuity of human life with that of the physical universe. There is nothing innately exceptionalist about the new-born child. On the contrary, Hartley's emphasis upon the fraught process that constitutes a factitious self from the primary physical sensations of pleasure and pain can lend itself to a darker psychology. For example, Judith Butler's understanding of identity as produced by reiterative practices that coerce the body into a gendered self shares common ground with Hartley's focus upon repetitive processes that constitute the factitious subject.[43]

Hartley's psychology was also developed in a much less optimistic way by Elizabeth Hamilton, Austen's contemporary. Hamilton's work did not and does not have the weight of major thinkers of the time but Austen knew at least some of her writing and spoke appreciatively of it.[44] Some recent studies of Hamilton have situated her on the conservative side of what Marilyn Butler termed the War of Ideas.[45] As I have argued elsewhere, this is surely mistaken. Hamilton's writing contains an acerbic critique of women's subordination to men and sets out in detail the ramifying evils that arise from that inequality.[46] The psychological insights she gains from this consideration of the human desire to dominate lead her to develop a remarkably modern account of a will to power that shapes individual identities, and social and national prejudices. Apart from William Godwin, there seems nothing comparable to its radicalism in the thinking of her male Enlightenment contemporaries. Although Austen most probably did not know Hamilton's later writing, it demonstrates the kind of insights into human relations that might well come more readily to a woman's perspective. Indeed, Austen's psychology shares significant similarities with Hamilton's.[47]

The basis of Hamilton's thinking is Hartley's embodied psychology. Like him, she accepts that the self is factitious, an identity that emerges from fleshly being. As such, the self is never complete, it has to be perpetually produced and sustained. It is this existential insecurity that engenders what Hamilton terms the 'primary motive' of human existence, prior even to self-love.[48] She calls this primal drive '*a propensity to magnify the idea of self*'. It is, she claims, 'the most active of all the principles inherent in the mind of man' (*Popular Lectures*, 1.279). Self as an 'idea' is a radical notion and Hamilton provides an illustration of what she means from primitive societies. In such a world, bodily strength alone would allow a person so endowed to enlarge their sense of self 'by multiplying into it all the human beings whom he has brought into complete subjection to his authority [. . .] The persons, the wills, nay the very thoughts of the multitudes whom he thus appropriates are considered by him as part of self' (*Popular Lectures*, 1.301). Although the example is from primitive societies, the application to modern social formations is clear and Hamilton points out that currently when women marry the ceremony 'annihilate[s] her legal existence which is at that moment merged in his' (*Popular Lectures*, 1.304).

What happens to the idea of self in all those who are forced into subservience to aggrandise the factitious identity of those with power? Hamilton's answer seems remarkably close to recent theorising of the 'willing' subordination of the subordinate. By identifying with those in authority, Hamilton argues, those without power find a 'species of gratification' by merging self in the greatness of their superiors. In this way 'the yoke is transformed into a badge of honour' and 'the wills of the many become not so properly subjected by, as incorporated with, the will of the individual who dominates' (*Popular Lectures*, 2.10). Hamilton extends this thinking to national identity and politics at a time when glorifications of Englishness and denunciations of the perfidiousness of France resounded in the public sphere. Love of country, Hamilton says, agreeing with Edmund Burke, constitutes one of the earliest benevolent associations. But the result of this in Hamilton's thinking is very different from that of Burke. Because of the strength of early associations there is no object more likely to be part of the idea of self than the land of one's birth. Where love of country becomes grafted to the propensity to magnify the sense of self, a zealous resistance meets any criticism and a refusal to contemplate change or reform. Where the idea of self depends upon the glorification of national identity, Hamilton warns, 'bigotry begets national hatred of all other countries with which the bigot is not identified' (*Popular Lectures*, 1.412). The primal need to magnify the idea of self can lead to similar intolerance when the idea of self is derived from identification with party or class or religion. For Hamilton the fleshly neediness for a self is the given for any understanding of identity or social relations.

What Hamilton recognises is the complex interrelationship between abstract belief systems and the desires and needs of the embodied self, a materiality that idealism disavows. A dissensual regime of the perceptible brings into visibility this inseparable interdependence of the mental with the physical realm, radically overturning the foundational distinction of idealist ideology. It foregrounds, equally, the constitutive continuity of self with others and with the world of things as the necessary basis of a shared world and language. It replaces the subject-object hierarchy with a relationship of equality between the embodied self and physical universe. This anti-idealist, egalitarian, horizontal regime of representation I am terming worldly realism. It is an order of the perceptible that, I shall argue, underlies the sceptical irreverence of Austen's and Woolf's views of reality and which drives their aesthetic innovations and achievements.

I have organised the book so that chapters on Austen alternate with chapters on Woolf. The idea is to allow for recognition of the similar areas of engagement between them. I would not wish to overemphasise this; they are writing from very different worlds. Placing chapters by Austen and Woolf alongside each other also makes the point that realism and modernism are not incompatible. Both are experimental and both can constitute a regime of the perceptible that is radically at odds with the consensus. If preferred, however, the chapters on Austen may be read first before moving on to those on Woolf. This would allow for greater sense of the chronological development and continuity within each writer's fiction. In *Sense and Sensibility*, *Emma* and *Persuasion*, for example, Austen positions each of her young female protagonists as a prime focus of change. In each case they move from place as location of idealist time-resisting values out into a more mobile, heterogeneous social space. This narrative pattern grows increasingly pronounced and overt from *Sense and Sensibility* onwards, culminating most radically in the unfinished novel, *Sanditon*. In a similar narrative trajectory, Woolf's main female protagonists move out from the domestic regularity of the private drawing room into the public world.

In *Sense and Sensibility*, Austen registers a transitional moment, in the wake of the French Revolution, when consensual notions of the self begin to shift. Earlier traditions of sociability, of self as primarily social being, come under challenge from emergent individualistic values centred upon an idea of self as superior sensibility, understood as a unique interiority, or upon competitive acquisition of wealth and possessions as aggrandisement of identity. Both of these ideas of self are subject to Austen's irony, as they continue to be throughout her work. Woolf, writing in the period of social upheaval following the First World War, also sets out to dismantle the ideology of individualism. In overturning the idealist belief in human exceptionalism, both writers reconnect an embodied self to the physical world and to the world of things in a relationship of equality. In *Persuasion*, Austen ridicules aristocratic claims of exemption from fleshly vulgarity, emphasising the vulnerability of the physical body. In *The Waves*, Woolf reorders the distribution of the perceptible, evoking the bodily movement of nerves alongside the currents of tides and seasons. In all six novels, material things, like fireplaces and flowers, connect the lives of characters into larger networks of social change.

Alongside this redistribution of the self from a vertical to a horizontal relationship with material existence, both writers warn of the dangers inherent in the disconnection of ideas and beliefs from empirical reality. Elevated mental systems, each writer shows, are often driven by embodied desires for mastery, perfection and from fears of dissolution. Emma Woodhouse's sweeping confidence when she declares 'there can be no doubt' causes pain and harm to individual lives in her community. Woolf shows the devastation wrought by idealised systems of belief nationally and internationally.

In all six novels, narrative perspectives are subject to constant experimentation as determined by each writer's worldly comprehension of social and physical continuities. For both Austen and Woolf, fluidity of point of view is the creative condition of community, of the common life we have as part of physical existence. It is the rigorous refusal of mysticism and deference that allows them to treat what is revered with irreverent comedy and to look sceptically at whatever and whoever claims authority. Considering Austen and Woolf together, in this way, allows for a fuller recognition of just what an impressive, intelligent, artistically ambitious body of work these two women writers achieved. Above all, their writing constitutes an aesthetic regime that makes perceptible the vision and the fact of human life as primarily that of embodied creatures sharing all the vicissitudes of our material existence in a common physical world. In its ethical and political implications, there can be no greater dissensual challenge to the consensual order of things.

Notes

1. Virginia Woolf, *Jacob's Room*, p. 49.
2. Alex Zwerdling, *Virginia Woolf and the Real World*, p. 64.
3. Alistair Duckworth, *The Improvement of the Estate: A Study of Jane Austen's Novels*, p. 83.
4. Claudia L. Johnson, 'Introduction', Jane Austen, *Northanger Abbey, Lady Susan, The Watsons and Sanditon*, p. xxiii.
5. See, for example, Michael H. Whitworth, *Virginia Woolf*, p. 106; Lindon Peach, *Virginia Woolf*, pp. 69, 73.
6. Derek Ryan, *Virginia Woolf and the Materiality of Theory: Sex, Animal, Life*, p. 4.
7. Jacques Rancière, *The Politics of Literature*, pp. 10–12; see also, *Aisthesis: Scenes from the Aesthetic Regime of Art*, pp. ix–xvi, 1–20; *The Aesthetic Unconscious*, p. 24.
8. Jacques Rancière, 'Ten Theses on Politics', reprinted in *Dissensus: On Politics and Aesthetics*, p. 37.
9. *The Essays of Virginia Woolf*, 4.160.
10. Gabriel Josipovici, *Whatever Happened to Modernism*, p. 164.
11. Rachel Bowlby, 'Waiting for the Dawn to Come', *London Review of Books*, 11 April 2013, vol. 35, pp. 32–4.
12. Ludwig Wittgenstein, *Philosophical Investigations*, 48e.
13. I outline this communicative view of language with reference to Wittgenstein, Jürgen Habermas and Donald Davidson in *Realism*, pp. 142–62.
14. Georg Lukács, *Studies in European Realism*, p. 58.
15. Bertold Brecht, 'Against Georg Lukács', *Aesthetics and Politics*, p. 71.
16. Ian Watt, *The Rise of the Novel: Studies in Defoe, Richardson and Fielding*.
17. Jeannette King, *Tragedy in the Victorian Novel*, demonstrates the conscious espousal of classical ideals by nineteenth-century novelists.
18. Erich Auerbach, *Mimesis: The Representation of Reality in Western Literature*, p. 497.
19. Bertrand Russell, *Mysticism and Logic*, p. 11.
20. G. E. Moore, *Philosophical Studies*, pp. 1–30.
21. David Harvey, *Cosmopolitanism and the Geographies of Freedom*, p. 57.

22. Roy Bhaskar, with Mervyn Hartwig, *The Formation of Critical Realism: A Personal Perspective*, p. 36.
23. Katrine Marçal, *Who Cooked Adam Smith's Dinner?: A Story about Women and Economics*, p. 79.
24. Hannah Arendt, *The Human Condition*, p. 94.
25. 'Cognitive Architecture' is a term widely used in theories of the structure of the mind, especially in relation to how long-term memory patterns are established.
26. Andy Clark, *Supersizing the Mind: Embodiment, Action and Cognitive Extension*, p. 219.
27. Arjun Appadurai, ed., *The Social Life of Things: Commodities in Cultural Perspective*, pp. 4, 5.
28. Bruno Latour, *Reassembling the Social: An Introduction to Actor-Network Theory*, p. 21.
29. Bruno Latour, 'Why has Critique Run Out of Steam: From Matters of Fact to Matters of Concern' in Bill Brown, ed., *Things*, p. 168.
30. Jane Bennett, *Vibrant Matter: A Political Ecology of Things*, p. 6.
31. Jacques Derrida, 'White Mythology: Metaphor in the Text of Philosophy', in *Margins of Philosophy*, p. 226; in *The Philosophy of Rhetoric*, I. A. Richards makes a similar point, 'As it [philosophy] becomes more abstract we think increasingly by metaphors that we profess *not* to be relying upon', p. 92; for a brilliant and positive discussion of metaphor's dependence upon a universalising function, see Paul Ricoeur, *The Rule of Metaphor: The Creation of Meaning in Language*, p. 101.
32. For further discussion of literalised metaphors, see George Lakoff and Mark Johnson, *Metaphors We Live By*.
33. David Hume, 'An Abstract of a Book lately published; Entitled a *Treatise on Human Nature, Etc*', reprinted in *An Enquiry Concerning Human Understanding*, p. 142; see also, *A Treatise*, p. 300.
34. David Hume, *Essays, Moral, Political and Literary*, p. 188.
35. Virginia Woolf, *Moments of Being*, p. 85.
36. Roy Porter, *Flesh in the Age of Reason*, p. 336.
37. Adam Smith, *An Inquiry into the Nature and Causes of the Wealth of Nations*, p. 292. Several recent commentators have criticised over-emphasis of Smith's concept of the 'hidden hand': Roy Porter, *Enlightenment*, claims that to understand the term in a purely economic way is 'myopic and shallow', p. 395; James Buchan, *Capital of the Mind: How Edinburgh Changed the World*, notes that the view of Smith as apostle of modern capitalism has been under attack in Scotland for some years, adding that 'by the end of his life [Smith] was expressing the most profound misgivings about the moral complexion of commercial society', pp. 120–1; Nicholas Phillipson, *Adam Smith: An Enlightened Life*, records that, in his later years, Smith declared he had always considered *The Theory of Moral Sentiments* as 'a much superior work' to *Wealth of Nations*, p. 274.

38. Adam Smith, *The Theory of Moral Sentiments,* p. 157. Further references to this book will be given as *TMS*; Amartya Sen, *The Idea of Justice*, invokes Adam Smith's thinking on the 'impartial spectator', pp. 44–6, 134–8.
39. Jürgen Habermas, *The Philosophical Discourse of Modernity: Twelve Lectures*, p. 296.
40. Michel de Certeau, *The Practice of Everyday Life*, p. 92.
41. David Hartley, *Observations on Man, his Frame, his Duty and his Expectations* [1791], 1.3.3.370.
42. Richard C. Allen, *David Hartley on Human Nature*, pp. 265–6.
43. Judith Butler, *Bodies that Matter: On the Discursive Limits of 'Sex'*, pp. 93–119.
44. When Austen learned that *Sense and Sensibility* had been attributed to Hamilton, she responded that it was a pleasure to be identified with such a respectable writer, *Jane Austen's Letters*, p. 251.
45. For accounts of Hamilton as conservative, see Kathryn Sutherland, 'Hannah More's Counter-Revolutionary Feminism', in Kelvin Everest, ed., *Revolution in Writing: British Literary Responses to the French Revolution*, p. 42; William Stafford, *English Feminists and their Opponents in the 1790s: Unsex'd and Proper Females*, pp. 32–3.
46. See my Introduction to Hamilton's *Letters on the Elementary Principles of Education* [1801], rpt in *Conduct Literature for Women 1770–1830*, 3.1–18; Gary Kelly, *Women, Writing and the Revolution*, aligns Hamilton's politics with those of Godwin and Wollstonecraft, p. 26.
47. In a letter to her sister Cassandra, Austen expresses a view of the embodied, feeling self as a process of continuous change that shares striking similarities with that of Hartley and even that of Hume: 'But seven years I suppose are enough to change every pore of one's skin, & every feeling of one's mind', *Jane Austen's Letters*, p. 99.
48. Elizabeth Hamilton, *A Series of Popular Lectures* [1813] 2 vols, 1.272.

Part I

Systems and Things

Chapter 1

Sense and Sensibility: Wishing is Believing

Sense and Sensibility (1st drafts c.1795–7; pub. 1811) opens with a wrenching moment of change and loss as the Dashwood women are forced to leave their home. Yet the pressures and insecurities of lives caught up in processes of change seem barely to figure in popular screen adaptations of Austen's novels which serve largely to perpetuate an idealist consensus. Visually beautiful and nostalgic in tone, these versions of her stories offer viewers entry into a charmingly organic English world of pretty young women, safely comic idiosyncrasy, wealthy young men and country estates. This is a popularised idealism of eternal verities, benign hierarchy, predictable plots, all untouched by historical forces and seeming to have existed always in a sunny clarity of the imagination. Such depictions represent what Raymond Williams has criticised as 'idealised abstractions' of Austen's novels.[1] Yet this bland popularism belies the critical seriousness with which Austen's writing was received by some, at least, of her first readers. Walter Scott, for example, immediately recognises that Austen is doing something new in fiction. Not only is she dealing with characters and feelings taken from ordinary life as opposed to the nobility, it is the innovative quality and detail of this ordinariness in her writing that is interesting and illuminating for Scott.[2] What Scott appears to grasp here is that Austen is shifting the field of the perceptible, to use Jacques Rancière's term, making visible and audible a familiarity which was nevertheless previously below the horizon of notice, deemed inappropriate to the dignity of representation. Rancière locates this shift of representational regime at around the end of the eighteenth century.[3]

The potential insights contained in Scott's assessment of Austen had dissipated by the mid-nineteenth century. George Henry Lewes condescendingly concurred with those like Bishop Whately who, in 1822, praised the Shakespearean realism of Austen's dramatic dialogues;[4] for Lewes, however, the smallness of scale and limited social range of her work denied it serious artistic stature.[5] This view of an unhistorical, unchallenging Austen was reinforced by her family's posthumous emphasis upon her retiring, lady-like demeanour.[6] Although she remained steadily popular through into the twentieth century, there was no early critical reappraisal of the importance and scale of her work. Only Virginia Woolf, in her essays, consistently asserts a far more appreciative view. For Woolf, Austen is a highly significant writer, undoubtedly the more so for being a woman. She figures among those writers that Woolf regards as achieving the highest levels of novelistic art. She belongs with Defoe, Dickens, Hardy and Conrad, writers certainly not thought of as limited in scale or ambition. Woolf largely ignores Austen's story matter, recognising her rigorous artistic impersonality and capacity to light upon that detail which 'expands in the reader's mind and endows with the most enduring form of life scenes that are outwardly trivial'.[7]

In *The Rise of the Novel* (1957), Ian Watt sought to position Austen at a pivotal moment in literary, cultural and social history. Watt claims Austen is heir to eighteenth-century philosophical and social developments and, as such, must be recognised as the initiator of a modern tradition of realism. Austen combines Richardson's psychological focus upon individual subjectivity with Fielding's social objectivity, Watt asserted.[8] Despite this recognition of Austen's heritage in eighteenth-century empiricism, the predominantly idealist understanding of Austen's art remained; as a supreme ironist she was concerned to express a classic moral, rather than a historical, vision. In 1963, Watt summed up the consensual view of her art in ahistorical, universalist terms: 'the current view of Jane Austen is that she is first and foremost a critical observer of humanity'. Her novels, he concluded, are now seen as 'a microcosm of some larger moral universe'.[9] It was not until Marilyn Butler's groundbreaking *Jane Austen and the War of Ideas*, published in 1974, that Austen's fiction was fully considered within a historical perspective. Butler's scholarly account of the polarisation of British politics in the era of the French Revolution and her readings of Austen's novels as partisan products of these polemics broke completely with earlier reverential accounts of the fictions as timeless masterpieces. While opening up Austen studies to invigorating historical research, Butler nevertheless imposed a new orthodox view of Austen as morally, socially and politically conservative.[10] Butler banished the moral idealist and superb ironist, but she banished, too, Austen as heir to the Enlightenment. Butler's Austen is unattractively pious and illiberal.

From the 1970s, feminist critics began to engage with Austen's texts from a historical perspective, that of the woman writer in the early nineteenth century, but none directly challenged Butler's thesis. Important early feminist studies, like those of Gilbert and Gubar and Mary Poovey tended to interpret her as a female artist hemmed in by repressive patriarchal structures and ideologies.[11] Such a perspective inevitably slants the readings towards negative discoveries of what Austen cannot do or to ways in which she is complicit with masculine hegemony. It also tends to preclude awareness of other social and cultural forces beyond those of gender. Even Claudia L. Johnson's undoubtedly radical readings in *Jane Austen: Women, Politics and the Novel* (1988) and *Equivocal Beings* (1995) avoid direct confrontation with *The War of Ideas*. Although Johnson situates Austen within a discussion of the influence of Locke's liberalism upon end-of-century women writers, the focus is still upon her representation of marriage and family rather than any wider national forces and structures.[12] As such, Austen's realism has only a slightly wider scale of reference from that allowed her by early critics like George Henry Lewes.

Recently, Butler's argument in *Jane Austen and the War of Ideas* has been more seriously challenged. Edward Neill, for example, in *The Politics of Jane Austen*, is undoubtedly right when he points to 'a certain theoretical naivety' in the way Butler presents her case, and the lack of all consideration of language, techniques of representation and subjectivity in Butler's readings of the novels.[13] In *The Historical Austen*, William H. Galperin also convincingly overturns the Butler view of Austen as wholly conservative and supportive of regulatory structures.[14] However, these studies by Neill and Galperin, and others like them, are informed by New Historicism and poststructuralist critical perspectives. Thus they look for progressive elements within Austen's novels only in terms of the uncanny or of a resistant otherness. Their theoretical positions disallow any recuperation of a more radical Austen by linking her in positive ways to either the Enlightenment or to realism. Indeed, in addition to refuting Butler, their stated aim is to deny Ian Watt's recognition of Austen as originator of the modern tradition of realism. According to Galperin, Austen's 'historical role as realism's most important progenitor has been grossly exaggerated' (*Historical Austen*, p. 6).

Only Peter Knox-Shaw, in *Jane Austen and the Enlightenment*, attempts to answer Butler in her own historicist terms. He refutes the accusations of religious conformity and conservative politics, demonstrating instead Austen's many allegiances to Enlightenment thinking and 'more particularly [to] that sceptical tradition within it that flourished in England and Scotland during the second half of the eighteenth century'.[15] Knox-Shaw's scholarly and detailed account of the whole Austen family's pervasive cultural engagement with many aspects of Enlightenment thinking provides an authoritative counterbalance to Butler's over-polarised interpretation of post-revolutionary England. The limitation of his study lies in its concern entirely with ideas and cultural context. Readings of individual novels provide few insights into how the techniques and form of the fictions are shaped by Austen's immersion in Enlightenment views of self, social reality and structures of knowledge. Without this dual perspective of Austen's formal innovations and the determining social vision that requires them, it is impossible fully to appreciate either her experimental realism or her political progressivism.

In fact, the narrative form of all three novels that I shall discuss here, *Sense and Sensibility*, *Emma* and *Persuasion*, articulates a contested process of emergence as an old order begins to yield to new possibilities of an order not yet fully resolved. It is thus a moment of dissensus in which contesting regimes of representation, both artistic and political, strive for dominance. The writing practice Austen forges from this transitional context articulates a worldly realist aesthetic and perspective, emphasising the horizontal continuity of self with social and bio-physical worlds. In each of these three novels, the central character or characters track a movement from a stable, hierarchical order of life out into a world of horizontal social plurality. Moreover, the primary concern of the fiction increases in scope from novel to novel; widening from contested representations of self to those of nation and finally to the commonality of all creaturely life. In each story, the central protagonist, who mediates the energies of social change and shifting values, is a woman. It is through her young women that Austen looks to the possibilities of a more progressive social order. This movement enacted by the plot structure of these three novels can also be understood, in Michel de Certeau's terms, as a shift from place as metaphor, symbolising time-denying values, to space as metonymic process and flow.[16] Equally, it can be seen as a shift of representational regime from what Jacques Rancière denotes as the vertical classical order of the perceptible to a new horizontal democratic distribution of the seen and heard, of people and things, of self and other (*Politics and Literature*, p. 10).

A representational struggle over what constitutes the self is always at issue in any emergence of a new social order. Roy Porter remarks that there was no single Enlightenment view of what constituted human nature 'but rather difference, debate and dialogue'.[17] Austen's novels enter into these debates by dramatising conflicting representational regimes of self. Hence the prevailing impression, in her fiction, that characters are in some sort performing their identity, their idea of self. The predominant view from the eighteenth-century Enlightenment tradition of David Hume, Adam Smith and David Hartley is of the self as a factitious, embodied, social being; an identity produced as physical sensation is wrought upon by social sympathies and mutual interests. This eighteenth-century notion of embodied sociability has roots in an earlier tradition in which the shared needs of physical existence – shelter, warmth and food – provided the common basis of celebrations, rituals and festivals like Christmas, harvest, weddings and so on, that punctuated the yearly calendar.

By the end of the eighteenth century, however, the ideal of sociability was challenged by two emergent forms of individualism, both of which situated the self within a newly conceptualised private realm. One version of the individualistic private self is produced by identification with competitive possession. Wealth, land and consumer goods all function to magnify the imagined idea of self, to utilise Elizabeth Hamilton's term,[18] by the ceaseless expansion of material ownership, of the realm of what is mine as opposed to yours. Subjective individualism, on the other hand, augments the idea of self by imposing its own abstract system of values, its mental universe, upon the external world. In giving dramatic form to these two factitious versions of self, Austen seems to recognise, like Hamilton, the powerful embodied energies that relentlessly impel such self-projections. For Austen, both self-interest and subjective idealism are driven not so much by rationality as by the self's desires and insecurities.

Austen's worldly realism is evident in her recognition of the interactive dynamics between self and things. In Austen's novels material objects are inseparable from the emergence of new social formations and from the self's ability to objectify its own imagined identity. This horizontal interdependency between social structures, self-consciousness and things is most apparent in the realm of taste, in which objects of consumption constitute emerging and residual representational regimes. On the one hand, conspicuous consumption denotes, materially and competitively, the extent and substance of wealth and hence the importance, power and amplitude of self. On the other hand, and equally competitively, things act as signifiers of inner sensibility. In this regime, the substance and materiality of things is disavowed as they become symbols of abstract values. This paradoxical, idealist conversion of the objective world into the subjective is directly opposed to eighteenth-century empiricism in which material things are taken as evidence of the order of the physical world.

There is an earlier still representational tradition in which things function both materially and symbolically to refer to the necessities of creaturely life: they are, in this sense, literally objects of consumption. Food and fires, for example, contain rich residual connotations of older communal life and values. In all of these ways, things, in Austen's texts, traverse various, often antagonistic, networks of residual, dominant and emergent discourses, institutions and practices. Things, for Austen, as for Bruno Latour, function as gatherings.[19]

Despite the binarism of its title, the opening of *Sense and Sensibility* plays upon a different opposition: the constitution and visibility of a shared world versus the restrictions and possessiveness of the private realm. The first two paragraphs trace an alternation between expansion and contraction of the social identity and sympathies of the Dashwood family. Having previously lived expansively on the family estate of Norland in 'the general good opinion of their surrounding acquaintance', the late owner retrenched to a less outgoing social style with only his sister as companion and housekeeper. Her death, however, brought into his life 'the society of his nephew and niece, and their children'.[20] 'Society' is a much used term in the text. Marvin B. Becker has noted how the meaning of the word shifts during the course of the eighteenth century. It is a shift that denotes the loss of value of the social and public realm to the private. Whereas the older designation had been that of fellowship, it increasingly came to denote 'an entity both distant and abstract'.[21] Austen uses the term 'society' here in this first chapter and elsewhere in the older sense of 'fellowship' underlining this by emphasising the comfort of social sympathies the elder Mr Dashwood gains from the goodness of heart of his nephew and wife and the relish added to his life by the cheerfulness of the children. Yet, despite this experience of expanded social being, his death seals a contraction of identity around a strictly bounded notion of possessive self. He secures the whole of his estate to the nominal male line, a child of four years old. As a result, the Dashwood women are propelled out from the settled security of place into an interactive space of unpredictable social processes and events.

'A world without property was almost inconceivable to eighteenth-century Englishmen', according to Paul Langford.[22] In a very real sense, property, for the upper classes, was self. Certainly, for a great many of the characters in *Sense and Sensibility* it is their foremost concern. Characters almost invariably accompany a person's name with an account of their property, as if the two are inseparable. At times the text almost reads like a property catalogue, or indeed, the front page of national dailies, like the *Morning Chronicle*, taken by the Austens, which were wholly given up to advertisements of properties for sale, with detailed inventories of furniture, china, domestic and outdoor goods of all kinds. Late eighteenth-century society was intensely concerned with wealth and money. The frequent wars during the century had exponentially increased the national debt resulting in higher taxation demands, a grievance constantly featuring in the newspapers. It also enhanced riches for wealthy capitalists able to loan money to government at high returns.

John and Fanny Dashwood represent a propitious union, not at all uncommon in Austen's actual world, of landed wealth with city wealth. It suggests an early stage of what Raymond Williams, in *The Country and the City*, terms 'a developing capitalist order of the land' (p. 139). Mrs Ferrars' desire that her son, Edward, make a figure as an orator in Parliament is driven by no ideal of civic duty to promote national interests. Men 'no more dreamt of a seat in the House in order to benefit humanity than a child dreams of a birthday cake that others may eat it', Lewis Namier writes.[23] Edward's success as a public figure would certainly have gratified his mother's vanity but more importantly it would have opened the way to further wealth-getting. According to Namier, a parliamentary seat was always regarded as a means to self-making and self-enrichment (p. 2). Banking, merchant and political hierarchies were thoroughly interrelated during the last decades of the eighteenth century.[24]

If Edward eschews the path of self-interest, John and Fanny Dashwood are exemplary in their obsessive and competitive acquisitiveness. While all their passions are invested in wealth-getting, their sense of social extension into a shared world of fellow-feeling is practically non-existent. John Dashwood is 'cold hearted, and rather selfish', epithets used throughout the text to indicate those lacking social sympathies and pursuing self-interest. The second chapter of the novel, in which John is only too ready to accept Fanny's arguments against keeping his promise to his father to provide for his step-sisters, offers a comic drama of the contraction of sympathies to exclude all but self. Fanny's language repeatedly foregrounds the possessive pronouns of the private individualist self as she contrasts the projected impoverishment of 'our poor little boy', John's 'own child' against the claims of Elinor and Marianne who are nor '*really* his sisters [. . .] only half blood' (p. 7). Further contraction of social sympathies is exemplified in Fanny's example of her mother being 'clogged' by her husband's will with the payment of annuities to old superannuated servants so that 'her income was not her own' (p. 8). The chapter closes with Fanny's possessive indignation that her mother-in-law, Mrs Dashwood, has been left all the china, plate and linen from the former household. Again her language emphatically opposes 'our' and 'own' to 'theirs' and 'them' as the discursive structure of competitive, acquisitive individualism.

Land enclosure reached a peak at the end of the eighteenth century, funded in part from increases in landed wealth due to high grain prices and also from investment from merchant and capital sources.[25] In the long term, land enclosure and improvement increased food production but at the time the most obvious result was the impoverishment of many small land-holders, tenant farmers and the agricultural poor who depended on common land for grazing and foraging. Land enclosure provides a materially literal example of the exclusion of others in order to magnify the idea of self by means of possessions. John Dashwood details a typical pattern of enlargement of his property by the 'inclosure of Norland Common' and the purchase of East Kingham Farm, so immediately adjoining his own land 'that I felt it my duty to buy it' (p. 196). 'Duty' here functions typically as an abstract moral euphemism for competitive materialism since 'I might have sold it again the next day, for more than I gave' (p. 197). That the Dashwood's use their property and wealth to compete in the stakes of conspicuous consumption is indicated by a newly fashionable greenhouse and garden Fanny is planning for Norland. Their factitious notion of self as substantiated and magnified by competitive possession demands a continual expansion of their acquisitions of material things. 'English landowners were a class of consumers', Professor Habakkuk notes.[26]

Originally the notion of 'taste' was aligned to Adam Smith's idea of sympathy as responsiveness of feeling extended to the aesthetic realm. By the turn of the century, however, it was increasingly associated with more socially restricted notions of refinement and consumerism. Taste, as a subjective attribute of the refined interiority, came to be substantiated in the competitive purchase of material things. In *Sense and Sensibility*, those who most ostentatiously pride themselves on their displays of taste, like Lady Middleton, Fanny Dashwood and Mrs Ferrars, are also represented as those most concerned with purely conventional forms of civility as opposed to 'society' as fellowship. Throughout the text, this type of civility is linked to coldness, self-centredness and especially to lack of social sympathies. Fanny is 'narrow-minded and selfish', Lady Middleton 'piqued herself on the elegance of her table' but is 'reserved' and 'cold' and they are attracted to each other by mutual 'cold-hearted selfishness [. . .] [and] an insipid propriety of demeanour' (pp. 3, 27, 200).

Initially Willoughby seems to represent an opposing view of taste, one based upon sympathy and warmth of feeling rather than conspicuous consumption and elegant civility. He enters fully into Marianne's enthusiasms and shares her romantic tastes in music, literature and art. Yet his predatory attitude to women reveals a drive to expand self by means of possession. His callous disregard for the trail of misery he leaves in the wake of his sexual conquests and his loveless marriage to gain a fortune are alike indicative of his ruthless self-interested individualism. Elinor rightly judges him extravagant, 'cold-hearted and selfish' (p. 290). Lucy Steele is another character dominated by competitive self-promotion. As a means of magnifying her own sense of self, she clearly relishes the thrill of power she gains from wounding Elinor. She is even more cold-hearted than Willoughby in swapping lovers purely for financial gain. She earns an unusually direct comment from the narrator, 'The whole of Lucy's behaviour [. . .] and the prosperity that crowned it, therefore, may be held forth as a most encouraging instance of what an earnest, an unceasing attention to self-interest, however its progress may be apparently obstructed, will do in securing every advantage of fortune' (p. 331). Were its irony to pass unnoticed, this statement could be read as a comprehensive summary of the moral myth of individualist self-making by struggling against adversity as disseminated or 'held forth' by numerous early nineteenth-century clergymen, moralists, politicians, economists and novelists. Throughout her novels, Austen's hostility to the emergent values of possessive individualism remains unambivalent.

Her representation of subjective individualism is also consistently critical but more complex and nuanced. Marianne, for example, might seem to represent an idea of self derived from a notion of sensibility and taste more closely aligned to Adam Smith's view of sympathy, based upon fellow feeling. Marianne's sense of her self expands around an imagined identity as unique sensibility. For her, sympathy is demonstrated primarily in reciprocal enthusiasm for favourite music and poetry. 'I could not be happy', she declares, 'with a man whose taste did not in every point coincide with my own. He must enter into all my feelings; the same books, the same music must charm us both' (p. 14). Austen's irony here is easily noted: Willoughby '*must* enter into all *my* feelings' (emphasis added).

It is no accident that Austen represents Marianne's especial accomplishment to be piano playing and Elinor's to be drawing. In *Essays on Philosophical Subjects*, published posthumously in 1795, and extensively reviewed in 1796–7, Adam Smith contrasts the pleasures arising from both arts. Drawing and painting give delight by the skill of rendering objects in the three-dimensional world in a two-dimensional form as if they are indeed three-dimensional. The aesthetic satisfaction is thus outward-looking, deriving from attentiveness to the empirical world. The pleasure of music, on the other hand, derives not from imitation of external objects, 'but [from] the power of exciting and varying the different moods and dispositions of the mind'.[27] In *Jane Austen's Possessions and Dispossessions*, Sandie Byrne points out that of the possessions unpacked on arrival at Barton Cottage the 'pianoforte is described as Marianne's particular property, but Elinor's drawings are fixed to the walls to become the decoration and property of all'.[28]

Marianne equates knowledge, in the mode of idealist philosophy, with the self-revealed, intuitive truth of the sovereign mind, scorning any reference to an objective social world. For her, truth is a matter of inner feeling and emotional response. She boasts that despite the very short time she has known Willoughby, she is better acquainted with him than with any other creature in the world. 'It is not time,' she claims, 'it is disposition alone' (p. 50). When Elinor criticises her impropriety in driving off alone with Willoughby, she insists that she would have known intuitively if she had been acting wrongly (p. 59).

By the end of the eighteenth century, it had become a commonplace in women's conduct writing across the political spectrum, from Hannah More to Mary Wollstonecraft, to attack the dangers that excessive sensibility posed to vulnerable young women. Undoubtedly, *Sense and Sensibility* shares this concern and Marianne's treatment by Willoughby exemplifies the risk. The satiric treatment of sensibility by Austen also provides a central part of Marilyn Butler's argument for Austen's political conservatism. Austen's critique of Marianne's claims to sensibility, however, derives from a social, even a radical perspective, and is forward-looking in its historical significance rather than inhering in the narrow evangelical partisanship of revolutionary era politics. Austen's position originates in the sceptical empiricism of Hume and Smith in their quarrel with idealism as imposing totalising systems of thought regardless of evidence from the material world.

Austen uses one of the key terms of Smith's accusation against idealism's totalising tendency when Elinor criticises Marianne's enthusiasm for her 'systems' of thought which are based upon an 'ignorance of the world' (p. 48). Conceptual systems, according to Hume, rely upon imagination and the exclusion of external reality. Adam Smith warned against 'the man of system'.[29] Idealism, its critics claimed, facilitates the expansion of subjective self by disavowing or rendering imperceptible anything contrary to a wished for mental reality. When Marianne declares she could love no man whose taste did not in every point coincide with her own, it is not fellow feeling she is affirming but the desire to subsume the world into her own subjective identity. Marianne, with all her excellent abilities and disposition, says the narrator, 'expected from other people the same opinions and feelings as her own, and she judged of their motives by the immediate effect of their actions on herself' (p. 175). As David Hume pointed out, one of the dangers of this subjectivism is the imaginary association of ideas into coherent mental systems so that wishes and illusions come to seem reality. Colonel Brandon says, 'Where the mind is perhaps rather unwilling to be convinced, it will always find something to support its doubts' (p. 150). Mrs Dashwood comically demonstrates this truth in reverse; where the mind is willing, rational doubt is easily excluded. Once she learns of Brandon's love for Marianne she is immediately 'carried away by her imagination' and her 'active fancy [. . .] fashioned every thing delightful to her' as to her daughter's future (p. 295).

This easy transition of ideas and wishes into firm systems of belief is facilitated by an assumed contempt for materiality. Like most idealists, Marianne pretends to scorn worldly things. 'What have wealth and grandeur to do with happiness', she proclaims romantically. When Elinor mischievously enquires what she considers a moderate establishment, Marianne produces a very material list: servants, one or two carriages and hunters. In a similar way, she accepts Willoughby's offer of a horse without the least consideration of the enormous additional expense this would involve for her mother: 'Most unwilling was she to awaken from such a dream of felicity, to comprehend all the unhappy truths which attended the affair' (p. 49).

A regime of perceptibility structured vertically by the dominance of mind over matter renders the physical realm inconsequential, of no account. The socially divisive effect of contempt for the material world is its tendency to downgrade the commonality of embodied human existence which forms the basis of fellowship and sympathy. The high esteem placed upon private interiority, mediated as refinement of individual taste, functions as a mechanism of social exclusion, justifying disregard, even contempt, for others. While Marianne is narcissistically charmed by Willoughby because he 'acquiesced in all her decisions, caught all her enthusiasm', she dismisses Colonel Brandon as possessing 'neither genius, taste, nor spirit' (p. 44). These perceived imperfections of Brandon's mind, Elinor suggests, rest upon 'your own imagination'. Marianne similarly projects her intolerance upon the kindly if loquacious Mrs Jennings. Despite all the objective evidence of Mrs Jennings's compassionate sympathies, Marianne insists upon excluding her from any possible fellowship, 'she cannot feel. Her kindness is not sympathy; her good nature is not tenderness. All she wants is gossip' (pp. 174–5). As her last sentence here suggests, Marianne is actually making a judgement based upon a system of social prejudice and passing it off to herself as a matter of her own superior innate sensibility and the other's lack of the same delicacy of feeling.

Yet once convinced that some fellow humans have no feelings of value, it becomes possible to treat them as beings without a self worthy of note. A vertical, idealist regime of the perceptible constitutes the labouring poor, the uneducated, superannuated servants and those to be cleared away for land enclosure, as wholly insignificant existences. Marianne, comments the narrator, 'had never much toleration for any thing like impertinence, vulgarity, inferiority of parts, or even difference of taste from herself' (p. 109). Far from being implicated in revolutionary ardour, as Butler claims, sensibility, as productive of a notion of self constituted as refined interiority, became, especially as the nineteenth century progressed, a powerful means of social exclusion.

A new distribution of the perceptible rendered the polite, private bodies of the respectable invisible, while the bodies of the poor became the focus of public attention as indices of troubling inferiority. Roy Porter comments, 'The representatives of gross corporeality were the vulgar, the labouring poor; élites upheld their own superiority as creatures of mind rather than base matter.'[30] He concludes,

'The doctrine of mind over matter stood for power over the people' (p. 474). As Rancière notes, changes in the regime of the perceptible are always political. At the turn of the eighteenth century, it is Austen's prescient insight that both emergent ideologies of self, acquisitive individualism and subjective individualism, entailed an expansion of the idea of self upon the world and, at the same time, a radical retraction of sympathies, and of any horizontal sense of self as part of extended social and embodied being. The respectable self is privatised. Commonness becomes synonymous with the vulgar.

Sir John Middleton and Mrs Jennings, his mother-in-law, are the two characters in the novel who most exemplify an earlier tradition of self as both social and embodied. Indeed, Sir John represents his sense of sociability almost entirely in terms of food. On the Dashwoods' arrival at Barton Cottage he sends the family a large basket of garden stuff, followed by a gift of game (p. 25). Their comfort, as this unsolicited generosity suggests, is 'an object of real solicitude to him' and he is vociferous as to 'his earnest desire of their living in the most sociable terms with his family' (p. 25). His gregarious enthusiasm offends current notions of civility as upheld by his wife. Inclusive sociability was becoming old-fashioned in a culture increasingly valorising the more restricted virtues of the private and domestic. By contrast, 'Sir John's satisfaction in society was [. . .] real; he delighted in collecting about him more young people than his house could hold [. . .] in summer he was forever forming parties to eat cold ham and chicken out of doors' (p. 27). In this passage, as throughout the novel, Austen is again using the words 'sociable' and 'society' in the older sense to suggest fellowship and social being. While Lady Middleton enjoys entertaining in order to show off her domestic elegance, Sir John is frequently planning informal outdoor meals. Austen repeatedly stresses Sir John's *real* feelings in opposition to what is recurrently described in the text as 'cold civility', a politeness without fellow feeling.

Mrs Jennings is introduced as 'a good-humoured, merry, fat, elderly woman, who talked a great deal and seemed [. . .] rather vulgar' (pp. 28–9). Judging by this description, refined readers might well expect her to be a figure of fun. Yet, over narrative time, it becomes apparent that her sterling qualities are far more important than any deficiencies in civility. Objective judgement, based upon evidence, corrects first opinion. Mrs Jennings is one of those characters in Austen's fiction who seems to reach back into much older popular traditions, associated as she is with those carnival qualities of birth, food and merriment. Mrs Jennings has affinities with a character like Juliet's nurse in *Romeo and Juliet*. She has the same robust interest in marriage and procreation, proclaiming enthusiastically of her pregnant daughter, Charlotte, 'I warrant you she is a fine size by this time' (p. 141). She regales Elinor with all the details of her husband's last illness and death (p. 46). As this suggests, Mrs Jennings has no notion at all of the self as private; she is a wholly social being. For her, relationships and alliances are warp and woof of a communal sphere of sociability and her desire to know all that is going on provokes her to question acquaintances without the least sense of indelicacy at encroaching upon a private realm. Believing Colonel Brandon to have been involved in matters concerning what she has termed 'a love child', she accosts him, 'Come, come, let's have no secrets among friends' (p. 141). The many secrets in the text are, in fact, an index of the encroachment of the private upon the social.

In the story, it is Mrs Jennings who represents the antithesis of idealist disavowal of the flesh. Her earthy understanding of people as embodied beings rather than interior sensibilities determines her practical expressions of fellowship and kindness. In contrast to her daughter-in-law's fastidious disavowal of the fleshly, her satisfaction, like Sir John's, comes from providing creature comforts. On the journey to London she is solicitous for everything that could ensure Elinor's and Marianne's ease and enjoyment, insisting upon a choice of salmon, cod, boiled fowls or veal cutlets when they stop for dinner (p. 138). In London, once she learns of Marianne's unhappiness she treats her 'with all the indulgent fondness of a parent towards a favourite child', ensuring she has 'the best place by the fire' and is tempted 'to eat by every delicacy in the house' including some of 'the finest old Constantia wine' (pp. 167, 171). She refuses to leave Elinor alone to tend Marianne in her illness, declaring that by her attentive care she will supply the place of their mother. This 'kindness of heart [. . .] made Elinor really love her' and in all the fatigues of the sick-room she found in Mrs Jennings 'a most willing and active helpmate' (p. 269). The final biblical word, here, is a forceful and striking term to express sympathetic fellowship.

Mrs Jennings meets all of life with the same material practicality, disregarding the mores of new civility. When she believes that Lucy and Edward will start upon an impoverished married life, she cries, 'Aye, we all know how *that* will end [. . .] they will have a child every year! And Lord help 'em!' Her immediate response, in sharp contrast to the mercenary deliberations of Mrs Ferrars and Fanny and John Dashwood, is 'I must see what I can give them towards furnishing their house', declaring of Mrs Ferrars, 'I have no notion of people's making such a to-do about money and greatness' (pp. 241, 225). The earthy vigour of Mrs Jennings's discourse derives much of its force from roots in demotic speech. Deploring the imminent departure of Elinor and Marianne home to Barton, she exclaims to Colonel Brandon, 'Lord! We shall sit and gape at one another as dull as two cats' (p. 245). In the redistribution of the perceptible, imposed by a new regulatory regime of privacy, the vigorous insistence upon life as embodied, as represented by Mrs Jennings's voice, would become mute.

In the representation of Sir John and especially Mrs Jennings, therefore, Austen elegises the ethos of sociability that would be sacrificed in a culture dedicated to private individualism, whether in the form of materialist possessiveness or idealist interiority. The perceptibility of embodied existence that underwrites extended sympathies and fellow feeling drops out of sight. This is not to suggest that Austen is indulgently nostalgic in her treatment. Both Mrs Jennings and Sir John are the objects of her ironic comedy. Their constant, undiscriminating geniality can seem inappropriate and even tedious. More damagingly, their refusal of any space for a private self is shown to lead to insensitivity that can be wounding. While Austen clearly views the coming order of acquisitive individualism with dismay and dislike and the development of idealist values with concern and scepticism, she does not turn away from change as such. For the Dashwood women, the loss of Norland impels them into processes that cause insecurity and pain but their lives are opened up to wider experiences and to new possibilities that are ultimately empowering.

In Elinor, Austen explores the tensions arising from the conflicting claims of the private and the social self. As such, Elinor represents Austen's projection of a potentially progressive modern sensibility. In contrast to the acquisitive self that desires to possess ever more of the world and the subjective self intent upon shaping the world to its own desires, Elinor's sensibility expresses a worldly sense of self as horizontally part of the larger social whole. Her behaviour is grounded in toleration of others even if their values differ from her own. She tells her mother, 'I will not raise objections against anyone's conduct on so illiberal a foundation, as a difference in judgement from myself, or a deviation from what I may think right and consistent' (p. 70). This does not constitute a collapse into relativism, however. When Marianne accuses her of advocating subservience to the judgements of neighbours, Elinor's response is firm and unequivocal.

'My doctrine has never aimed at the subjection of the understanding,' she insists, 'I confess [. . .] often having wished you to treat our acquaintance in general with greater attention; but when have I advised you to adopt their sentiments or conform to their judgements in serious matters?' (p. 81).

The irony, of course, is that this is precisely what Marianne *does* insist upon from others, that they conform to her sentiments and judgements. Elinor's principles, outlined in these two statements above, place her centrally in the Enlightenment tradition of David Hume and Adam Smith in their insistence on tolerance and sympathetic fellowship, their hostility to idealism as an imposition of self and systems of belief. Often in the story, Elinor occupies a position like that of Smith's impartial observer, able to enter into a much wider range of perspectives than those characters enclosed in self-interest or their own interiority. Elinor's artistic ability is drawing, an art that Adam Smith praises for its comprehensiveness of observation.

Critics have pointed to Austen's sustained use of forensic language in the story where terms like 'proof', 'evidence', 'grounds' and 'conviction' abound. In fact, this linguistic preoccupation was quite common within the general discourse of the time due to the exponential increase in empirical experiments and observations. This was not a specialist discourse conducted only within a small scientific community; it constituted a shared account of the common world. The investigations were discussed at length in the literary quarterlies aimed at a wide readership among the whole of the educated class. In 1794, the *Monthly Review*, for example, carried a substantial article on Thomas Beddoes, *Observations on the Nature of Demonstrative Evidence* (1793).[31] Every issue of the journal throughout that decade carried articles evaluating the observations and evidence put forward in published works on electricity, chemistry, medicine, agriculture, mathematics, mineralogy and many other empirical studies.

In contrast to most other characters who nourish secrets and subjective illusions, Elinor consistently attempts to order her judgements and behaviour upon empirical evidence. In so doing she asserts her realist faith in a shared world. Rather than elevating mind over matter, Elinor respects the substance of materiality, the things, that constitute the common world. When Lucy reveals her secret engagement to Edward, Elinor 'dared no longer doubt; supported as [Lucy's claim] was too on every side by such probabilities and proofs, and contradicted by nothing but her [Elinor's] own wishes [. . .] the picture, the letter, the ring, formed altogether such a body of evidence, as overcame every fear of condemning him unfairly, and established as a fact, which no partiality could set aside, his ill-treatment of herself' (p. 119). Like a true empiricist, Elinor challenges wishes with things and facts. When she begins to doubt the honesty of Willoughby's intentions she resolves to gain 'every new light as to his character which her own observation or the intelligence of others could give her' (p. 137).

Although Elinor accepts the challenge of empirical evidence, the novel does not subscribe to naive actualism. In the tradition of David Hume's epistemological scepticism, the text foregrounds the unpredictability of events and the partiality and fallibility of human perspectives. Indeed, Austen gains much of her comedy from the incongruous mismatch between characters' desiring interpretations and conflicting actuality, often in the shape of other people's desires and interpretations. The innovative narrative technique of free indirect speech she develops to exploit these comic fallibilities owes much to Adam Smith's novelistic exposition of interactive shifts of perspective through first, second and third person points of view. Yet, in contrast to her characters' attachment to their own systems of belief, authorial omniscience is denied totalising knowledge. Understanding of people and things is certainly asserted to be possible and sharable, but never final. In each Austen novel there comes a moment or moments when the narrator admits to lack of knowledge or of words that can adequately convey a state of affairs.

In *Sense and Sensibility*, when Edward is told by Elinor of Colonel Brandon's offer of a living that will allow him to marry Lucy, the narrator comments, 'What Edward felt, as he could not say it himself, it cannot be expected that anyone else should say for him' (p. 252). At the end of the story, when Elinor's future prospects are even more radically transformed, the narrator asks, 'But Elinor – How are *her* feelings to be described?' (p. 318). The explicit and implicit semantics of those two sentences are, as always with Austen, complex. Clearly, they mark out a space of interiority as private, an acceptance that the press of memories, impressions, hopes and fears can be so intense and fluid as to be knowable to no-one but the experiencing self, and perhaps not even fully by them.

Yet the interpellative logic of Austen's sentences draws the reader into a communicative space with the narrator in which the implicit norm *is* of shared communication of feelings, of distributed consciousness. It is only the existence of this norm that gives force to the exceptions of these two cases. Indeed, without such a norm there could be no shared life. The constitution of intersubjective consciousness between narrator and reader is a pervasive means by which

Austen produces that sense of an interactive familiar community that is the experience of reading her novels. Austen's innovative prose foregrounds the linguistic structures of a shared world paradoxically at the very moment when the notion of it comes under attack from an ethos of privacy.

Partly the sense of inclusivity is achieved by the innovative motility of Austen's language, its fluid ability to slide horizontally across linguistic temporalities as well as different consciousnesses. The sudden movement into the present tense, as in 'How are *her* feelings to be described', provides a good example, bridging as it does the past tense of the story and a present narrative moment shared by implied teller and implied listener/reader. The effect of immediacy, in her prose, is further strengthened by Austen's frequent use of deictics, especially 'now'. 'I come now to the relation of a misfortune', the narrator directly informs the reader, implying a shared temporal space. When Chapter 5 opens, 'The Dashwoods were now settled at Barton' the reader is effectively brought into the time and space of the story as well as that of the narrator. By such means Austen gives linguistic substance to the intersubjective experience that is communal reality.

This writerly constitution of consciousness as shared and fluid contributes equally to a sense of self as non-bounded and inconclusive. David Hartley saw the self as always emergent and factitious. Austen's characters convey a very similar sense. Frequently, they seem at one and the same time wholly familiar yet startling and unpredictable. Character speech not only suggests unspoken currents of thought but equally the force of non-verbal energies. Self, for Austen, is an embodied performance, like that of the Steele sisters and Marianne, for example, but a performance driven by needs and passions. There are those, moreover, like Mr Palmer and Fanny Dashwood, who seem to exist at the edge of performative excess. These qualities are perhaps those that earlier critics were recognising when they refer to Austen's dialogue as Shakespearian. The effect is a sense of identity as resistant to any final interpretive closure.

The social self, for Austen, is also inseparable from the world of things. Her novels mark the initiating moment in which consumer goods of all kinds become active forces shaping individual identity and social structures. In *Sense and Sensibility*, shops and purchases feature prominently in the text. Shops can be understood as metonymies of a public sphere largely structured upon consumption. On the very first day of their stay in London, Elinor and Marianne accompany Mrs Jennings and Mrs Palmer on a shopping trip. Thereafter they make several other trips to shops in Pall Mall and Bond Street. These occasions are represented by Austen as social events in the public sphere as much as they are purchasing opportunities. Women do not shop singly, friends are met and gossip and news exchanged. These interactions are shown to be part of the interdependent dynamics of the public and private spheres, in that they lead to further social events, opinion forming and the circulation of rumour and information as well as cash.

Consumer goods also function as metonymies for the public constitution of self. Miss Grey's wedding clothes are put on display in a fashionable warehouse (p. 187). Men, too, use things to signify their identity as wealthy connoisseurs of taste. Robert Ferrars exploits the public purchase of a toothpick to demonstrate the 'correctness of his eye and the delicacy of his taste' (p. 192). Willoughby contemptuously dismisses Colonel Brandon as the kind of man who only buys two suits a year, while Marianne insists that the Colonel's flannel waistcoats are attributes of age and ailment (pp. 44, 32).

It is ironic that Marianne, who insists upon the priority of mind over matter, should be so quick to judge Brandon's person by his clothing. What the text shows, comically, is that the most sublime and intense experiences of the subjective self depend upon common things for substantiation. Even moments of romantic intimacy require the banal mediation of material objects as catalogued by Margaret's account of seeing Willoughby take up Marianne's scissors, cut off a long lock of her hair, and fold it 'in a piece of white paper, and put it into his pocket book' (p. 51). When Willoughby leaves abruptly without explanation, Marianne would have thought herself inexcusable if she had been able to sleep or eat (p. 71). Yet despite rejection of what is offensively material to her emotional state, she turns to objects that are just as material to express her grief. She spends hours playing the pianoforte and reading the books they had shared. Taste, as a means of expressing transcendent sensibility, is, moreover, just as inseparable from the economics of consumption as is taste as conspicuous display. Austen is typically astute as to the hard cash necessary to substantiate and maintain the inner life. Edward fantasises on the 'magnificent orders' that would flow to London booksellers, music-sellers and print-shops should the family come into a fortune. Knowing Marianne's 'greatness of soul', Edward claims, 'there would not be music enough in London to content her' (p. 79). How else is the soul to know its greatness or estimate its qualities if not substantiated by material things and practices?

It is undoubtedly significant that Edward, Elinor and Colonel Brandon all disclaim at various moments what the Colonel calls 'pretensions to connoisseurship', a term newly current in the eighteenth century (p. 205). They do not use things either to extend the acquisitiveness of the competitive self or to substantiate interior sensibility. Brandon listens attentively to Marianne at the pianoforte but without 'being in raptures' (p. 30). Elinor, too, makes no claim to musical taste, and is unrestrained 'by the presence of a harp and violoncello', from turning her eyes to 'other objects in the room' (p. 218). Edward stubbornly refuses to associate things with sensibility and his interchange with Marianne brings to the surface the opposing politics of the material versus the ideal, empirical facts versus an abstract system of belief. 'How can you think of dirt, with such objects before you?' Marianne exclaims. Edward replies, 'Because [. . .] among the rest of the objects before me, I see a very dirty lane' (p. 76). He goes on to insist that he prefers tall, flourishing trees to crooked, blasted ones, he dislikes tattered cottages, nettles and thistles, and takes pleasure in a troop of tidy, happy villagers (p. 84). This last image of contented poor may suggest patrician complacency. Yet, that negative judgement needs to be balanced with recognition that tattered cottages and weeds indicate the poverty of tattered, ill-clad, undernourished inhabitants and of neglect by landowners. During the peak of the enclosure movement at the end of the eighteenth century, and with rural hardship and unrest increasing, Edward's preference does not seem reactionary. Romantic rapture at 'tattered cottages' provides as little to ameliorate pressing material needs as does indulgence in extravagant display.

Political ideologies are also at stake in a material site of even greater import for self, sensibility and taste than that of landscape, namely, the ideology of home, of domesticity. This prime location of the private self is, of course, constituted by things, common objects. When the Dashwoods move into Barton Cottage they endeavour, 'by placing around them their books and other possessions, to form themselves a home' (p. 25). Again, material things produce the subjective values. 'Home' is an important and recurrent term in the text. The idealisation of domesticity and the shift of values from the public to the domestic, occurring from the latter part of the eighteenth century and into the nineteenth is a well-documented aspect of British patriotic and moral discourse. There is an easily recognisable metaphoric transformation of the concrete into the ideal in the movement from hearth to home to domesticity to Englishness. *Sense and Sensibility* is undoubtedly participating in this discursive domain. The ideology of the home as a privileged sanctuary that sustains the competitive struggle in the public sphere underwrote the increasing privacy of the family and its individualistic ethos. In *Englishness Identified*, Paul Langford notes that even foreigners and overseas visitors to Britain commented upon the fervent belief in home life that most English people espoused. Yet, visitors also noticed the devaluing of more general sociability and fellowship. Festive days based upon commonality beyond the home were neglected in England. Langford quotes an Austrian diplomat who concludes, 'it proves how little the English feel it necessary to give proof of their good feeling to each other'.[32]

Where does *Sense and Sensibility* position itself within the shifting semantic-political field of domestic values? It is certainly not privacy that is stressed in the text. Mrs Dashwood's first thought on settling in Barton is of enlarging the cottage so that they can accommodate 'such parties of our friends as I hope to see often collected here' (p. 24). In the meantime, she hopes they can make themselves 'tolerably comfortable'. The notion of comfort is much associated with the word 'home' in the narrative, as in national discourse. Elinor recognises that Edward's mother does not make 'his home comfortable' to him and Edward himself later repeats this phrase (pp. 18, 318). When Mrs Jennings is praising Delaford as Marianne's future home if she marries Colonel Brandon, she calls it a 'nice, old-fashioned place, full of comforts and conveniences' (p. 170). Willoughby comes to love Barton Cottage 'as his home' (p. 61). In his discussion of English domesticity, Langford points out that the 'idea of comfort was a subject of endless debate both at home and abroad', the more so since there existed no obvious synonym for comfort in other languages (*Englishness*, p. 117).

Part of the semantic field constituting the ideology of English domestic comfort was the idea of warmth, a notion that moves effortlessly from the material basis of life to the metaphorical, subjective domain. Within *Sense and Sensibility* almost all the characters are categorised as either cold-hearted or warm-hearted. Not surprisingly, fires and fireplaces are among the domestic things referred to in the text. Warmth and creature comforts were quintessentially associated with the open fire typical of English domestic interiors as opposed to the stoves in continental countries (*Englishness*, pp. 116–17). In national discourse and in its physical substance 'the hearth' undoubtedly operates as a 'gathering' in Bruno Latour's sense of a point of intersection of many meaning systems ('Why has Critique', p. 170). Both in the public sphere and in *Sense and*

Sensibility 'the hearth' resonates across the discursive domains of traditionalism, patriotism, reaction and reform.

The emotional leverage of the hearth within domestic ideology, for example, was intensified by nostalgic connotations of older, partly mythic, traditions of a merry England in which peasantry and nobility gathered in fellowship around Yule logs blazing in the squire's feudal halls. The character in *Sense and Sensibility* most closely associated with a comforting fire is Mrs Jennings. After a three-day journey to London, Elinor and Marianne are grateful to enjoy 'all the luxury of a good fire' (p. 138). When she learns of Marianne's unhappiness, Mrs Jennings makes sure that she has 'the best place by the fire' (p. 167). This association with both physical warmth and sympathetic warmth accords with Austen's depiction of Mrs Jennings as not only representative of an older ethos of sociability, as opposed to privacy, but also of an earlier way of envisaging human life as shared and embodied.

It is not only Mrs Jennings who is associated with fireplaces and sociability. Mrs Dashwood wants to put a new grate into the spare bedroom in readiness for guests (p. 33). Her plans to enlarge the cottage, however, meet with passionate resistance from Willoughby. He declares he would not sacrifice one sentiment of local attachment for all the improvements in the world. In response, Elinor asks him whether he finds even 'a kitchen that smokes' desirable (p. 62). This is almost certainly a reference out to the world of things beyond the text. In particular, it alludes to Count Rumford's invention of a stove that eliminated the smoky fires of traditional building. Count Rumford was much in the news during the years Austen was writing the novel. There were lengthy discussions of his ideas in *Monthly Review* throughout the 1790s. The *Review* praised him as a man who was practical as well as philosophical and who had made a real improvement to the comforts of ordinary life.[33]

Not everyone was in favour of Rumford, however. In a politically factional world, innovation was regarded at best with suspicion by conservatives. One reactionary commentator expresses his opposition in terms not so unlike those of Willoughby, 'Rumford, by his *philosophical* chimneys, is likely to destroy the comforts of our firesides. When will reformers and sciolists meet with that contempt which they deserve!' (Langford, *Englishness*, p. 117). There is no doubt that, at the time, the reference to philosophy would bring to many English minds thoughts of the French *philosophes* whose scepticism and anti-religious sentiments were held by many in Britain to have precipitated the Revolution.

Indeed, it was not just chimney innovations that accounted for Rumford's unpopularity among those of conservative opinion. One of his publications, *Essays, Political, Economical and Philosophical* (1796), provides an account of his administration of poor relief in Munich. The *Monthly Review* quoted a lengthy passage that would have offended all those insisting that the indigent must be made to espouse the moral discipline of sturdy individualism. Rumford writes, 'To make vicious and abandoned people happy, it has generally been supposed necessary, *first*, to make them virtuous. But why not reverse this order? Why not make them first *happy* and then virtuous? If happiness and virtue be *inseparable*, the end will be as certainly obtained by the one method as by the other [. . .] [therefore] Every thing was done that could be devised to make the poor people I had to deal with comfortable and happy in their new situation.'[34] On 21 October 1800, the Austens' daily paper, the *Morning Chronicle*, printed a letter to the editor advocating the adoption of Count Rumford's system for ameliorating the condition of the poor.[35]

It is, of course, impossible to know what Austen would have made of such comments if she read them. They do, however, provide an intriguing gloss on Edward's preference, like Rumford's, for 'happy villagers' over 'tattered cottages' and on Willoughby's defence of nostalgic sentiment despite the consequent discomfort to servants in a smoky kitchen. What is certain is that when homes are re-formed at the close of the novel the emphasis is upon social being not individualistic privacy. Mrs Jennings, the text's representative of sociability, is the first to visit Elinor and Edward at their parsonage. Once Marianne has married Colonel Brandon there is 'constant communication' between Barton and Delaford (p. 335). The ending of the novel, and especially Marianne's marriage, have left some readers disquieted. What is less noticed is that it indicates a rejection by Marianne of the narcissistic subjectivism that sought to impose self and its systems upon the world. This critical blindness to Marianne's blindness on the part of present-day readers is, perhaps, an index of the still powerful charm of the ideology of individualistic interiority.

True to the realist grounding of the story, however, Marianne finally accepts that her passionate opinions and principles have been tested by experience and observation and proved false. She acknowledges the empirical reality that constitutes a shared world. For modern readers, however, there is a further jarring note to the description of her 'submitting to new attachments, entering on new duties, placed in a new home, a wife, mistress of a family, and the patroness of a village' (p. 333). Undoubtedly, an element of the condescension of the lady of the manor is evoked by the term 'patroness'.

Austen's plot structures articulate a movement of social change from a settled world to one that is more socially fluid and open. Nevertheless, Austen never conceives a world that is not ordered by rank. Yet, in the context of the novel's critique of the self-expansionism of acquisitive individualism and the imposition of self upon the world by subjective idealism, one should perhaps also recognise the emphasis upon the outgoing social inter-activeness of Marianne's new roles. The text perhaps implies that Marianne will be more passionately concerned with the happiness of the village in terms of material needs than with its supply of picturesque, blasted trees.

There is also a gender inflection in the outline of Marianne's new position. She does indeed enter on new duties as a wife, but the terms 'mistress of a family' and 'patroness of a village' seem to emphasise empowerment rather than conventional feminine submission. The submission, if there is one, is of the private interiority to the social self. *Sense and Sensibility* opens by expelling its two young female protagonists from the security of the patriarchal home. By its conclusion, both Elinor and Marianne have moved into a larger material world. They have, however, retained a sense of self as social being, rejecting both privatised interiority and acquisitive competitiveness. As so often in Austen's fiction, the close of the narrative hints at the formation of a new, potentially dissensual, social order, worldly rather than idealist, horizontal rather than vertical, and one in which women have an active and intelligent public role to play.

Notes

1. Raymond Williams, *The Country and the City*, p. 141.
2. Walter Scott, 'Unsigned Review of *Emma*', *Quarterly Review*, vol. 14 [1816], in Ian Littlewood, ed., *Jane Austen: Critical Assessments*, 4 vols, 1.287–8.
3. Jacques Rancière, *The Politics of Literature*, pp. 3–30; *Aisthesis: Scenes from the Aesthetic Regime of Art*, pp. ix-xvi, 1–20.
4. Richard Whately, 'Unsigned Review: *Northanger Abbey* and *Persuasion*', *Quarterly Review*, vol. 24 [1821], in *Critical Assessments*, 1.318–19.
5. George Henry Lewes, in B. C. Southam, ed., *Jane Austen: The Critical Heritage*, p. 166.
6. James Edward Austen-Leigh, *A Memoir of Jane Austen and Other Family Recollections* [1870], pp. 9, 140–1.

7. *Essays of Virginia Woolf*, 4.149.
8. Ian Watt, *The Rise of the Novel*, p. 338.
9. Ian Watt, ed., *Jane Austen: A Collection of Critical Essays*, p. 2.
10. Marilyn Butler, *Jane Austen and the War of Ideas.*
11. Sandra M. Gilbert and Susan Gubar, *The Madwoman in the Attic: The Woman Writer and the Nineteenth-Century Literary Imagination*, pp. 146–83; Mary Poovey, *The Proper Lady and the Woman Writer: Ideology as Style in the Works of Mary Wollstonecraft, Mary Shelley and Jane Austen.*
12. Claudia L. Johnson, *Jane Austen: Women, Politics and the Novel*, pp. 13–14; *Equivocal Beings: Politics, Gender and Sentimentality in the 1790s.*
13. Edward Neill, *The Politics of Jane Austen*, p. 4.
14. Wm H. Galperin, *The Historical Austen*, p. 1.
15. Peter Knox-Shaw, *Jane Austen and the Enlightenment*, p. 5.
16. Michel de Certeau, *The Practice of Everyday Life*, p. 101.
17. Roy Porter, *Enlightenment: Britain and the Creation of the Modern World*, p. 171.
18. Elizabeth Hamilton, *A Series of Popular Lectures*, 1.279.
19. Bruno Latour, 'Why has Critique Run Out of Steam: From Matters of Fact to Matters of Concern', p. 170.
20. Jane Austen, *Sense and Sensibility*, p. 1.
21. Marvin B. Becker, *The Emergence of Civil Society in the Eighteenth Century: A Privileged Moment in the History of England, Scotland, and France*, p. 2.
22. Paul Langford, *Public Life and the Propertied Englishman 1689–1798*, p. 1.
23. Lewis Namier, *The Structure of Politics at the Accession of George III*, p. 2.
24. For an account of the various interests see Richard Price, *British Society 1680–1880: Dynamism, Containment and Change*, pp. 67–75.
25. For an account of this see Edward Royle, *Modern Britain: A Social History 1750–1985*, pp. 1–3.
26. H. J. Habakkuk, *American and British Technology in the Nineteenth Century*, quoted in Raymond Williams, *The Country and the City*, p. 144.
27. Adam Smith, *Essays on Philosophical Subjects*, 2. 22.198; Smith also describes the utility of music to those, like Marianne, who seek to 'either indulge the ecstasy or give way to the agony' of passionate feelings (2.12.191).
28. Sandie Byrne, *Jane Austen's Possessions and Dispossessions: The Significance of Objects*, p. 34
29. Adam Smith, *Theory of Moral Sentiments*, p. 275.
30. Roy Porter, *Flesh in the Age of Reason*, p. 472.
31. *Monthly Review*, 1794, vol. 13, pp. 1–7.

32. Paul Langford, *Englishness Identified: Manners and Character 1650–1850*, p. 109.
33. *Monthly Review*, Review of Count Rumford, *Essays, Political, Economical and Philosophical*, 1796, vol. 21, pp. 66–70; *Monthly Review*, Review of Count Rumford, *Experimental Essays, Political, Economical and Philosophical*, 1794, vol. 24, pp. 319–32; Austen refers explicitly to Rumford in *Northanger Abbey* as part of her negative depiction of General Tilney's hypocritical posturing as an enlightened property owner. See Marilyn Butler's editorial note in *Northanger Abbey* (London: Penguin, 1995), p. 252.
34. *Monthly Review*, Review of Count Rumford, 1796, vol. 21, p. 68.
35. *Morning Chronicle*, 21 October 1800.

Chapter 2

Mrs Dalloway: The Spirit of Religion was Abroad

'We think back through our mothers, if we are women', Woolf famously said.[1] If Woolf has a literary mother it must surely be Jane Austen. The recurrent references to Austen throughout Woolf's critical writing express a fascination with and admiration for her artistic achievements.[2] In the essay devoted to Austen in *The Common Reader*, Woolf's language constitutes Austen's writerly effect in terms that seem almost identical to her own aesthetic. From out of the stream of the commonplace in Austen's narrative, Woolf claims, a moment is suddenly full of meaning, 'It fills itself; it shines; it glows; it hangs before us, deep, trembling, serene for a second' (*Essays*, 4.152). Had Austen not died young, Woolf suggests, her art would have continued to develop. She seems to draw Austen into a continuity with modernism, predicting she would have 'devised a method [. . .] for conveying not only what people say, but what they leave unsaid [. . .] She would have been the forerunner of Henry James and of Proust' (*Essays*, 4.155). *Persuasion* marks the beginning of a shift in Austen's sensibility, Woolf claims, 'the observation is less of facts and more of feelings' (*Essays*, 4.152–3). Yet despite the apparent dichotomy here between facts and feelings, what Woolf most pervasively shares with Austen is an aesthetic of worldly realism and an antipathy to idealist modes of thought. As against a world ordered vertically and hierarchically, Woolf, like Austen, perceives self, social world, the world of things and the physical universe as a horizontal, material continuum.

Nevertheless, the emphasis upon subjective interiority rather than facts would certainly have seemed, to many of Woolf's first readers, wholly applicable to Woolf's own art. Early criticism of Woolf's novels interpreted them within an idealist perspective as privileging inner states of mind rather than an object world. According to idealist inflected readings, Austen was held to deal with universal and timeless moral values, albeit in a limited domestic sphere, whereas Woolf was read, yet more negatively, as a writer only concerned with a nebulous and class-privileged inner life. Again, as with Austen, Woolf's own family helped seal the negative image. In his biography, her nephew, Quentin Bell, wrote, 'Her gift was the pursuit of shadows, for the ghostly whispers of the mind and for Pythian incomprehensibility.'[3] The only striking exception to early readings of Woolf as inward-looking and soulful, by both detractors and admirers, was Erich Auerbach's groundbreaking account of her narrative techniques in *Mimesis: The Representation of Reality in Western Literature* (1946).[4] *Mimesis* was not published in an English translation until 1956, but even then it had surprisingly little impact within Woolf studies in terms of realism as opposed to appreciation of her formal methodology.

During the 1950s and 1960s, serious scholarly studies of Woolf tended to consider her work from philosophical, Jungian and Freudian perspectives.[5] Yet, while enhancing her status as a major writer, they did not challenge the idealist perception that her concern was with the inner life rather than the body and with universal abstractions like time rather than history. It was feminist studies, as with Austen, which began to situate Woolf's novels within the particularities of the time in which she was writing. Many of the feminist studies of Woolf published from the 1970s onwards took a psychoanalytic approach to the novels.[6] While this focus did not directly undermine the dominance of idealist concentration upon interiority, the concern with gender identity and especially with issues facing a woman novelist in the early twentieth century did redirect Woolf studies to cultural realities. Undoubtedly, it was this earlier feminist work that gave impetus to the current recognition of, and scholarly investigation into, Woolf's concern as a writer with many of the most urgent cultural, political and social issues of her own time.[7] The most recent scholarly edition of her work, for example, provides a mass of textual information relating each work in complex ways to Woolf's social and political world.[8]

Surprisingly, though, despite this detailed and rich body of studies demonstrating Woolf's imaginative and intellectual response to her world, there has been almost no concomitant re-examination of her views on realism. The critical consensus that, as a high modernist, Woolf was unquestionably intent upon a wholesale rejection of past forms, especially realism, remains veritably unchallenged. Linden

Peach, for example, in his illuminating study of Woolf's historical imagination, reiterates the critical orthodoxy, '*The Years*, despite its apparent concessions to social realism [. . .] can be seen in terms of her quarrel with realism in her essay "Modern Fiction".'[9] Peach's dismissive phrase 'concessions to social realism' is typical of the pejorative attitude to realist writing that continues to inform much current critical discourse written from a modernist perspective.

In *Virginia Woolf and the Real World*, Alex Zwerdling, one of the few critics to offer positive readings of Woolf's realism, asks why this aspect of her work has been so largely ignored. By way of answer he suggests that one cause is the smokescreen Woolf herself created in her classic essay 'Mr Bennett and Mrs Brown'.[10] The quotation above from Linden Peach indicates that we should also include the other classic manifesto of modernist intent, 'Modern Fiction' as contributing to the misunderstanding. Peach's comment, however, equally indicates that it may be critics themselves in their selective reading of these two seminal essays that have created the smokescreen, not Woolf herself. As Jacques Rancière points out, it is a mistake, made by Barthes and similar critics, to understand a modernist aesthetic as a rejection of world for word, as a move to self-referential textuality.[11] Rather, Rancière argues, it is a new aesthetic regime, originating around the end of the eighteenth century, that opens up the text to the proliferating flood of people and things that constitute existence; a disorder that challenges the dominant hierarchical consensus.

Woolf's two essays, 'Modern Fiction' and 'Mr Bennett and Mrs Brown' are so often and so confidently cited as articulating the break of modernism with realism that it comes almost as a shock to realise that in them Woolf nowhere uses the words 'realism' or 'realist'. The only terms of distinction she uses to characterise different conventions of novelistic writing are the 'Edwardians' and the 'Georgians', adding that the Edwardians, such as Bennett, Wells and Galsworthy, are 'materialists' while the Georgians, represented by the younger generation of Joyce, Lawrence and Forster, are 'spiritual' (*Essays*, 4.159, 161). She does, undoubtedly, express strong dissatisfaction with the novelistic aims of Bennett and his contemporaries to 'embalm' probability within a mass of factual detail, but this constitutes a criticism of what I suggest is actualist writing rather than realist. Indeed, in both essays she explicitly praises realists like Austen, Thackeray, Hardy, Chekov and Tolstoy. 'Our quarrel [. . .] is not with the classics', she says in 'Modern Fiction' (*Essays*, 4.158).

Woolf takes the oppositional terms 'materialists' and 'spiritualists' from her father's usage. Leslie Stephen refers to materialists as those subscribing to the doctrine that matter is the ultimate reality, while spiritualists, he defines as those who believe that mind is the only reality.[12] In other words, spiritualists subscribe to idealism, a mode of thought to which Woolf is largely hostile. In this she follows her father but equally she is engaging with the public debates and contention of her own generation. This explains the ambivalence of her account of Joyce's writing in 'Modern Fiction'. Certainly, the famous injunction to 'Look within' seems to demand a shift of focus away from the material world of realist texts into the subjective states of consciousness that typify so much modernist fiction (*Essays*, 4.160). The declaration in favour of interiority in 'Modern Fiction' is undermined, however, as the essay continues. She singles out James Joyce as pre-eminent among the younger generation of writers in being 'concerned at all costs to reveal the flickerings of that innermost flame'. He does 'undoubtedly come so close to the quick of the mind', she affirms. Yet, she goes on, the experience of reading him is not one of imaginative expansion. Rather, there is a 'sense of being in a bright yet narrow room, confined and shut in [. . .] *centred in a self* which, in spite of its tremor of susceptibility, never embraces or creates what is *outside itself and beyond*' (*Essays*, 4.162, my emphasis). The final sentence here constitutes the essential critique of idealism by opponents.

Woolf does, at times, although rarely, seem explicitly to reject realist forms. In her positive review of Dorothy Richardson's experimental stream-of-consciousness novel, *The Tunnel* (1919), she exclaims, 'We want to be rid of realism' (*Essays*, 3.12). Yet, characteristically, the review constantly shifts position so that the viewpoint oscillates between seeming to yearn for the new while adhering to tradition. Although she welcomes Richardson's ambitious experimental representation of interiority, she also admits 'the old method seems sometimes more profound and economical' (*Essays*, 3.12). The review concludes with a plea that the new be fashioned into 'the shapeliness of the old accepted forms' (*Essays*, 3.12). The implication of these oscillations of opinion that structure the review, seems to be that while a new generation of writers must be impatient with and critical of earlier forms of writing, they should retain, in some way, what is artistically powerful in the old. In her biography of Roger Fry, she says of him, 'he could explain that it was quite easy to make the transition from Watts to Picasso; there was no break, only a continuation. [The post-impressionists] were only pushing things a little further'.[13]

She also quotes Fry's vigorous anti-idealism, 'I elaborated a good deal on my empiricism [. . .] So the scientific spirit really had the last word and a great triumph over the abstractionists and metaphysicians' (*Fry*, p. 268). Woolf does not, perhaps, seek a 'great triumph' over idealists but, as her critical comments on Bennett's and Joyce's writing suggest, she does believe that neither a wholly idealist nor a crudely materialist perspective is adequate for the writer. Rather, what is required is a disciplining balance of the two forces, as she explains in her essay on Turgenev. The great writer, like Turgenev, she claims in that essay, has that rare quality of being able to combine fact and vision, '[he] is never allowed to mount unchecked into the realms of imagination; again the observer pulls him back and reminds him of that other truth, the truth of fact' (*Essays*, 6.11). In 'Phases of Fiction', she warns that the 'two powers fight if they are brought into combination. The most complete novelist must be the novelist who can balance the two powers so that one enhances the other' (*Essays*, 5.83). As well as Fry, Woolf's thinking here is undoubtedly influenced by Bertrand Russell's assertion, in *Mysticism and Logic*, that the greatest achievements in human thought have been produced by a fusion of vision with empiricism.

Russell's quarrel with idealism was part of a widespread public debate over the relative social, political and epistemological merits of idealism as opposed to empiricism. In this sense, Woolf was writing within a strikingly similar intellectual context to that of Austen at the end of the eighteenth century. By the 1870s, idealism was becoming a powerful force in British intellectual, cultural and political circles. Publications by leading figures within the movement, like F. H. Bradley, T. H. Green and Bernard Bosanquet, offered a unified spiritual account of self and world that was welcomed by those late Victorians reacting against what they saw as the aridity and materialism of philosophies that had determined public thinking for much of the century: empiricism, utilitarianism and Darwinian naturalism.[14] The idealists re-asserted the vertical hierarchy of spirit over matter, and gave priority to those concomitant virtues of reverence, obedience and duty towards authority and tradition. As idealists, they denied the possibility of a reality independent of mind, elevating purely rational sciences like mathematics over empirical observation. They propounded a revisionary theory of evolution, insisting that explanations of existence must necessarily move from higher forms of life down to the lower. It was impossible, they argued, for inferior matter to give rise to more elevated beings. For them, evolution was the progress towards greater spiritual perfection and unification of ideal self with ideal world.

British idealists attacked utilitarianism for purveying a notion of self as atomistic and of society as merely an aggregate. They argued that the individual has no reality but as part of the ideal organic unity that is the collective mind and will of the nation inherited down the generations. By subordinating themselves to the ideal of the state or nation, individuals become one with the common Good and the common Will that constitutes its and their perfection. This hierarchical view of society was expounded most fully in a highly influential essay by F. H. Bradley, entitled, 'My Station and its Duties'. 'We have found ourselves when we have found our station and its duties', Bradley declares.[15] In a later essay he asserts that a person's best self consists for the greater part in 'his loyalty, and according to the spirit, in performing his duties and filling his place as a member of a family, society and the state' (Boucher, *British Idealists*, p. 103).

The thinking of the British idealists became influential across a wide range of political opinion during the early part of the twentieth century. Some of the major idealists like T. H. Green and Bernard Bosanquet were active figures in the fields of education, welfare and social policy. Many of their students from Oxford became prominent in public life.[16] British idealist thinking constituted an important force in British life until at least the 1930s and remains an influential strand of thought within modern conservative understanding of public policy. Undoubtedly, the identification of the mental with the spiritual, the mind with the Good, reinforces social class conservatism. It underpins a representational regime in which material indications of deprivation are transformed into symbols or symptoms of inner states, thereby losing their perceptibility as physical actuality. T. H. Green saw poverty as indicative of a moral deficiency of character (Boucher and Vincent, *British Idealism*, p. 115). Bernard Bosanquet argued that poverty was a breakdown of the will (*British Idealism*, p. 118). State intervention to relieve hardship, therefore, could be deemed injurious in increasing feebleness of character rather than self-reliance. If the fullest expression of the self was manifest in spiritual perfection, then the corollary cast those whose feebleness of will left them bereft of even the decencies of life into an underclass perceived as barely human. This representation of the poor as trapped by mental wretchedness shifts attention away from, renders imperceptible, those material inequalities of insanitary housing, endemic unemployment and chronic ill health that actually determined the conditions of the labouring population in early twentieth-century Britain.

The philosophers G. E. Moore and Bertrand Russell, both members of the Bloomsbury group, published elaborate logical refutations of the idealists' claim that there was no reality independent of mind.[17] Bertrand Russell additionally extended his arguments into a comprehensive political critique. In *Mysticism and Logic* (1918), he begins by castigating idealism's elevation of individual inwardness and denial of value to the shared material life of existence. Anyone who has experienced 'absorption in an inward passion', he suggests, has felt the strange sense of 'unreality in common objects, the loss of contact with daily things'.[18] In its assertion of the priority of the individualist mental realm, idealism passes over the thingness of the world as beneath notice; common objects that give substance to a shared common life are rendered effectively imperceptible and insignificant. In *Problems of Philosophy*, Russell repeats this charge that idealism demotes from notice all that constitutes the material world. There is currently a widespread philosophical tendency, he claims, towards the view that 'Man is the measure of all things, that truth is man-made [. . .] and that, if there be anything not created by the mind, it is unknowable and of no account to us.'[19]

This denigration of material life is frequently driven, Russell claims, not by rationality as idealists like to think but by 'passion'. It is fleshly distaste for the messiness of life that leads idealists to seek otherworldly perfection, whether mental or religious. A system of thought promising unity, harmony and coherence produces 'a feeling of infinite peace', and such quietism goes along with an 'absence of indignation or protest' (*Mysticism and Logic*, p. 17). Social ills can be unnoticed or rendered inconsequential when perfection is sought in transcendence. There is a further, more active, danger present within idealist modes of thought, Russell asserts. The passion driving idealists is not only the desire for perfection, he argues, it is, not infrequently, the will for self-assertion and aggrandisement, the urge to impose self upon the world. What is claimed as knowledge in such cases, he says, is nothing 'but a set of prejudices, habits and desires, making an impenetrable veil between us and the world' (*Problems*, p. 93). This is precisely the folly of subjective idealism that Austen satirises throughout her fiction. It is also the passion of the man of system who, Adam Smith warns, will seek to enforce his will upon others as if they are merely pieces upon a chess board.[20] Idealist dismissal of empiricism ensures that inconvenient facts are excluded as evidence against the system of thought. 'A man who finds pleasure in such a theory of knowledge is like the man who never leaves the domestic circle for fear his word might not be law', Russell declares (*Problems*, p. 93). Woolf takes this insight much further, suggesting that the will to impose authoritarian systems of belief is often domestic tyranny writ large.

That Woolf shared much of Russell's criticism of idealism is made clear in an extended passage near the beginning of *Mrs Dalloway* (1925), the novel in which she sets out to attack the 'social system and to show it at work, at its most intense'.[21] The word 'system' occurs frequently in anti-idealist critiques. In the passage in question, the narrator offers an account of the thoughts and feelings of an unnamed figure, 'an atheist perhaps'.[22] The language and details provided are remarkably similar to those of Bertrand Russell. The 'solitary traveller', as he is called, experiences what Russell terms an 'inward passion' as moments of 'extraordinary exaltation'. These convince him that 'Nothing exists outside us except a state of mind' (p. 48).

That he is perhaps an atheist is Woolf's way of suggesting that it is not only the conventionally religious who seek otherworldly perfection and unity; unbelievers, scientists and others can equally experience that desire. Typically, this impulse felt so strongly by the 'traveller' in *Mrs Dalloway* is driven by distaste for actual fleshly life, a desire for 'something outside these miserable pigmies, these feeble, these ugly, these craven men and women' (p. 48). In seeking relief from such unwanted realities, he reassures himself that if he can only 'conceive' of a solacing perfection, 'then in some sort [it] exists' (p. 48). He proceeds to imagine an idealised image of majestic womanhood, showering down 'from her magnificent hands, compassion, comprehension, absolution' (p. 49). Woolf is clearly having fun here at the expense of all those male thinkers who deify women as abstract virtues and ideals while frequently denying dignity and value to their actual material lives.

There is a darker irony also in that even while bestowing a kind of religious reverence upon abstractions like compassion and comprehension, the traveller is turning away from actual people as contemptible and beneath regard. Idealism disavows the material conditions of human existence that could give substance to the values it claims to pursue. 'Such are the visions', the narrator comments, 'which ceaselessly float up, pace beside, put their faces in front of, the actual thing [. . .] taking away [. . .] the sense of the earth' (p. 49). No novelist is more aware of the actual thingness of the world than Woolf, and in *Mrs Dalloway* things are represented as essential anchors holding the individual within shared social existence. But the 'solitary traveller' does not hanker for a shared, common world; his longing is to lose himself in a 'general peace, as if [. . .] all this fever of living were simplicity itself; and myriad things merged in one thing' (p. 49). This is desire for vision unchecked by fact.

Mrs Dalloway opens with a totally opposite view of 'this fever of living'. We are presented with Clarissa Dalloway's celebratory identification of the pulsing energy of London streets with the vitality of life itself. City streets, in all of Woolf's London novels, are represented as complex locations of multiple social forces. At the beginning of *Mrs Dalloway*, they evoke a surging space of possibilities, a heterogeneous flood of people and things, vividly suggestive of the demotic realism that, Rancière claims, challenges the vertical orderliness of classical representational modes. The 'bellow and uproar' of London makes audible as well as visible the teeming, random disorder of 'carriages, motor cars, omnibuses, vans, sandwich men shuffling and swinging; brass bands; barrel organs [. . .] the triumph and the jingle and the strange high singing of some aeroplane overhead' (p. 4). This is a new regime of the perceptible, a seen and heard material, horizontal, egalitarian continuity of being, the audibility of the common life.

Woolf's writerly style is equally fluid and inclusive, preferring non-subordinate conjunctions and constantly shifting perspectives. Yet, despite the motility of viewpoints, Woolf retains a third person narrator. She thereby reserves a space that is formally non-subjective to avoid the enclosure within subjective imagination that she criticises in 'spiritual' writers like James Joyce. The narrator's position, however, is never Olympian; it stays at the level of life in the streets. Woolf's representation of self is equally open and fluid. Sally Rosseter's exclamation that we are imprisoned in self and can only scribble on the walls of our separate private cells is treated ironically for its melodramatic egoism (p. 163). Clarissa Dalloway's sense of self as metonymic is underwritten by Woolf's own stylistic horizontal fluidity. Travelling up Shaftesbury Avenue by bus, Clarissa explains that 'she felt herself everywhere; not "here, here, here"; and she tapped the back of the seat; but everywhere [. . .] so that to know her, or any one, one must seek out the people who completed them; even the places [. . .] some woman in the streets [. . .] even trees, and barns' (p. 129). This passage well illustrates the worldly realism of Woolf's artistic imagination; it evokes the egalitarian perception of a material continuity between self, social world, the world of things and the physical universe.

There are, however, forces represented in the text that are hostile to disorder and heterogeneity, forces that are intent upon imposing systems of discipline and conformity on any unregulated form of existence. It is salutary that immediately after she has exulted in the common life of the streets, Clarissa Dalloway encounters Hugh Whitbread with his government-stamped dispatch box and his mission to take his cowed wife 'to see doctors' (p. 5). Yet the streets themselves contain impulses that run contrary to diversity and nonconformity. Woolf uses the episode of the imposing car, with blinds drawn down, that gets stalled in Bond Street to illustrate a general willingness among people of all classes to coalesce emotionally around idealised abstractions, and more especially around things metaphorically elevated into symbols of such abstractions. The mysterious car quickly becomes an object of veneration as the location of 'greatness', 'the majesty of England', 'the enduring symbol of the state' (p. 14). Caught up in this sense of awe for a power beyond themselves, 'faces which a second before had been utterly disorderly' are stilled. The heterogeneity of those in the street is erased: 'they had heard the voice of authority; the spirit of religion was abroad' (p. 12).

Woolf's mocking language to describe this mass emotional religiosity – 'mystery had brushed them with her wing' – undoubtedly pokes fun at idealist veneration of a spiritual or mystical common will that binds people under the 'voice of authority' into a cohesive organic state. What the episode demonstrates is that reverential passion is easily triggered by something, as the text says, 'so trivial'. The feeling, far from emanating from a communal best self, is merely irrational emotion sweeping through the crowd. Yet the effect is sinister and threatening. Just as the car has blinds drawn to shut out the world beyond its privileged enclosure, so the passions aroused are blind to actuality: 'the spirit of religion was abroad with her eyes bandaged tight and her lips gaping wide' (p. 12). The urge of the crowd to become one with an imagined majesty and greatness is 'formidable' the text concedes; the emotional fervour is dangerous to those so caught up but also to anyone perceived to dissent. The nationalist zeal aroused by the trivial incident of the car leads to xenophobic brawls in a public house and to a desire to sacrifice self 'in the cannon's mouth' (pp. 15, 16).

Not all of those influenced by a religious spirit of idealism are anonymous. Indeed *Mrs Dalloway* is peopled with characters who are idealists. This takes a variety of forms but they all share a desire to impose a more orderly vision upon the imperfections of human existence. They seek to escape the 'fever of living' in a non-material realm. Doris Kilman's religious faith, expressed in her fondness for metaphor, is perhaps the most traditional form of idealism (p. 110). She is drawn to the 'bodiless' light of Westminster Abbey as escape from 'the infliction of her unlovable body' and all the pains of the flesh, the anguish of the hates and loves of earthly life it brings upon her (pp. 103, 109). Part of the misery she suffers is at the hands of Clarissa Dalloway. Woolf uses their fraught relationship to illustrate the power of abstract ideas when they become visions or veils blocking out actuality. Clarissa fears Doris Kilman is stealing her daughter's affections and under the influence of that passion of jealousy the tutor becomes a figment of her hatred rather than a real person, so that when 'the body of Miss Kilman was not before her, it overwhelmed her – the idea' (p. 107). Clarissa, however, just as Woolf demands in her essay on Turgenev, brings the truth of metaphor into contact with the truth of fact. When she makes herself look at the actual embodied person, there is a complete 'dwindling of the monster' (p. 107). Clarissa's response to this shift from imprisoning idea to observed reality is to laugh at the comic mismatch of vision to fact.

The carnage of trench warfare leaves Septimus Warren Smith with an overwhelming repugnance for embodied life. He recoils in horror from 'the sordidity of the mouth and the belly' and the 'filth' of copulation (p. 75). Yet Septimus is acutely sensitive to the materiality of the physical world, responding intensely and sensuously to the texture of sounds and sights. But he elevates these out of the horizontal realm of physical matter into a system of symbols to be interpreted as 'the birth of a new religion' (p. 19). Sir William Bradshaw deems this a highly dangerous symptom, indicative of insanity, unaware apparently of his own resort to metaphysics in worshipping the abstract Goddesses of Proportion and Conversion (pp. 84–5). Septimus's poignant moment of release from metaphysical delusion is brought about by material things. To use Woolf's terminology from the Turgenev essay again, Septimus stops interpreting and starts observing. He becomes a realist, shifting from the vertical metaphoric mode to the horizontal metonymic. 'And so, gathering courage, he looked at the sideboard; the plate of bananas; the engraving of Queen Victoria and the Prince Consort; at the mantelpiece, with the jar of roses. None of these things moved. All were still; all were real' (p. 120). Once grounded in this material thingness of actuality, he realises that the voices of the dead that have been coercing him are nothing more than his own imposition of transcendent meaning upon mundane things like a curtain rustling, a mouse squeaking (p. 123). In this space of empiricism, recognising the comic incongruity of things as just things, Septimus, like Clarissa, begins to joke and laugh. 'He had become himself then,' Rezia thinks, 'he had laughed then' (p. 122). Contrary to idealism, self is produced in active relationship with the things that constitute a common daily life.

All of Woolf's novels bring perceptibility to things. In *Mrs Dalloway* there are two kinds of things in particular that recur on almost every page: cars and flowers. The two things are brought together at the start of the novel when Clarissa is in Miss Pym's flower shop selecting blooms for her party. She is startled by 'a violent explosion' (p. 12). The noise comes from the car outside in Bond Street, but Woolf's language links it metonymically with the violence of the first fully mechanised world war. The example of Septimus and of the idealist interpretations that passers-by so readily impose on the car, suggest that symbolic readings of these recurrent things in the text are best avoided. This is so, even though the description of Sir William Bradshaw's opulent grey car with silver-grey rugs, is clearly intended to evoke the highly prestigious Rolls Royce Silver Ghost and thereby point ironically to Bradshaw's boasted concern with souls while actually enhancing his own wealth and power.

The extended series of references to cars and flowers constitute a metonymic structure connecting Woolf's text dialogically to political, cultural and scientific forces in the world of 1920s Britain. Cars figure as metonymies for the whole transport revolution and increased mobility that constitute modernity. In 1924, the London Traffic Act was passed in response to public debate and concern about the threat posed by the ever-increasing volume of traffic on the streets of the capital. *Mrs Dalloway* contains references to every form of modern traffic: not just cars but buses, taxis, vans, an ambulance, a plane and the tube. Cars also serve as metonymies for the process of mass industrialisation, known metonymically as Fordism, which had become a determining force shaping the modern world. Methods of mass production also brought about transformation in means of warfare.

Flowers, understood metonymically as part of the whole biological system of life, might seem to assert a deliberate textual opposition to industrial mechanisation. Yet in the 1920s, horticulture was being transformed by advances in biological sciences into a mass production industry. Human biology and reproduction were equally becoming the focus of scientific 'engineering'. Both industrial mechanisation and biological science were coming to be recognised as efficient means of managing potentially troublesome populations. While the conformist spirit of religion was much abroad in public rhetoric transposing material things like cars into symbols of abstract ideals, real politics was only too aware of the actual continuum of embodied selves, the social world and the physical universe. The two metonymies of cars and flowers in *Mrs Dalloway* are thus much over-determined, they are 'gatherings' bringing together multiple intersecting networks of meaning.

Peter Walsh is another of the text's idealists. Seeing the ambulance carrying Septimus Warren Smith's body, he thinks admiringly, with unwitting irony, that it is a symbol of 'civilization' which he associates with the further progressive-sounding abstractions of 'efficiency' and 'organisation' (p. 128). All these intangible ideals are substantiated for him by the busy yet orderly traffic in the streets of London. In her representation of characters like Peter Walsh, Woolf suggests that the religiously inflected idealism of her father's generation is in process of shifting into the new discourses of science and progress. With his belief in the abstract concept of 'civilization', Peter prides himself on his progressive idealism. His identification of futuristic efficiency and technology with a vision of glamorous and powerful modernity is illustrated as he stops to admire the 'great motor cars' through the plate-glass windows of a car sales room. 'How many miles on how many gallons?' he wonders (p. 41). Peter would have been at Oxford University when it was dominated by idealist thought and his approval of the 'communal spirit of London' suggests his affiliation with idealist social organicism (p. 128). Although he was sent down from Oxford for being a Socialist, he yet complacently assumes, 'with their love of abstract principle [. . .] the future of civilization lies in the hands of young men like that' (p. 43).

Immediately following this self-congratulatory thought (if I can think it then it must in some sense exist), Peter sees a troop of working-class boys marching to the Cenotaph. The 'weedy', ill-nourished condition of their physiques passes him unnoticed, a materiality rendered imperceptible within an idealist regime of representation. To Peter, their faces appear stamped with those abstract principles of 'duty, gratitude, fidelity, love of England' (p. 43). It is 'a very fine training', he thinks as they march by him. The principles he mentally imposes on the boys' faces are precisely those that

British idealist F. H. Bradley invoked in his essay 'My Station and its Duties' as expressive of the best self. Yet Peter's use of the term 'training', here, indicates that it is the force of authority and discipline that has wrought this effect, not any spiritual recognition of the Common Good. Indeed, the impersonal narrator makes explicit the subordination of particularity and diversity, whether of class or person, that underpins the pursuit of idealised national unity. It was 'as if one will worked legs and arms uniformly, and life, with its varieties, its irreticences, had been laid under a pavement of monuments and wreaths and drugged into a stiff yet staring corpse by discipline' (p. 44). Not only have the young men been put into uniform, they have been transformed from the heterogeneity of living beings into an almost mechanistic force. Their faces are 'unmixed with sensual pleasure or daily preoccupations', fleshly life has been converted into the will of duty and conformity (p. 43).

Peter's admiration for the 'fine training' of the working-class boys follows on from his admiration of the power and efficiency of 'great cars'. This suggests he would equally admire the kind of discipline that Henry Ford was imposing upon his industrial workforce in the name of efficiency and organisation. Another group of marching men also appear in the novel. They are the unemployed seen by Elizabeth Dalloway (p. 117). By the 1920s, the end of military conscription was resulting in rising unemployment and increasing political and industrial unrest and protest. With military training at an end, the disciplinary regimes imposed by new mass production methods were looked to in the British press and in governing circles as an alternative means of inculcating a regulated and productive labour force, 'one will working arms and legs uniformly', the body subordinated to the mind.

An article in *The Times*, in 1923, for example, the year in which *Mrs Dalloway* is set, advocated the adoption of Henry Ford's methods to address the problem of the unruly poor in Britain.[23] Ford also had many admirers within the growing Nazi party in Germany, including Adolph Hitler. He had opened his first British car plant in Manchester in 1911, and by 1923 the *Times* estimated that the plant was selling 40,000 to 50,000 cars a year in Britain. What particularly appealed to British authorities, though, was the systematic and rigorous regime of discipline Ford imposed upon his work force. Not only did he resort to brutal strong-arm tactics to prevent unionisation, he also employed a department of investigators to check that his employees were adhering to the strict standards of personal behaviour the company prescribed. These applied not only while at work but also governed all aspects of behaviour outside the factory. Advocates of Ford's industrial relations couched their arguments in the abstract ideals of efficiency, progress and productivity, but what they sought in material terms were docile working bodies disciplined to the regulated order of machinery. J. B. S. Haldane, a leading British scientist, asked in 1923 whether 'the machine minder engaged on repetition work [is] the goal and ideal to which humanity is tending'.[24] Antonio Gramsci described Ford's production methods as 'the biggest collective effort to date to create, with unprecedented speed, and with a consciousness of purpose unmatched in history, a new type of worker and a new type of man'.[25]

Mr Bentley is another idealist in *Mrs Dalloway* who admires machines as symbols of abstract values. This is, perhaps, unsurprising given the illustrious reputation of the Bentley car. Like Peter Walsh, the character of Mr Bentley also suggests that, by the 1920s, idealism was shifting its dominant location into the realm of science and visions of modernity. Not only does Mr Bentley see the plane over London as a symbol of human aspiration, of man's desire to 'get outside his body [. . .] by means of thought', the systems of thought he names are largely the abstract sciences: 'Einstein, speculation, mathematics, the Mendelian theory' (p. 24). To many people in the early part of the twentieth century, Einstein's theories seemed to offer conclusive scientific validation to idealism, since his work set out a field of knowledge that could only be comprehended by the intellect and was not, it was claimed, susceptible to empirical verification. The science of mathematics was expanding forms of knowledge derived entirely from closed-system abstract models of the sort that have come to dominate the present-day systems of macro-economics.

But why does Woolf include Mendelian theory in this list of speculative knowledge that Mr Bentley associates with the desire to leave the body for a realm of greater mental perfection? Mendel's genetic work on pea plants in the 1860s only came to prominence in the early part of the twentieth century when the scientist William Bateson recognised the significance of the work for agriculture. Bateson coined the term 'genetics' in 1905. He became director of the John Innes Institute, set up by a wealthy businessman of that name, who astutely recognised the vast commercial potential of the new science. The institute was soon at the forefront of international genetic research.

Bateson's successor at the John Innes Institute was J. B. S. Haldane, whose radical politics and enjoyment of controversy ruffled the establishment but ensured him a public platform. In 1923, the year in which *Mrs Dalloway* is set, as we have noted, Haldane delivered a widely-published lecture to the Heretics Society at Cambridge. One year later, Woolf read a version of 'Mr Bennett and Mrs Brown' to the Heretics. The title of Haldane's paper, 'Daedalus, or Science and the Future', suggests a more questioning view of the ideal of intellectual flight from material concerns than that of Mr Bentley in the novel. Haldane's starting point was the horrific destructive power witnessed in the First World War which had largely been made possible by scientific knowledge. Despite this, Haldane expresses cautious optimism that scientific research would lead to significant improvement in human life. Yet it would not be Einstein's theories that would achieve these benefits, he predicted. It would be advances in the science of biology, in particular, genetic research, that would transform the conditions of future existence by its revolutionary progress in the fields of food production, human reproduction and the eradication of diseases (*Daedalus*, pp. 57–68). When Elizabeth Dalloway is stimulated by her exciting first bus ride, to reject her mother's traditional woman's world and enter upon a career, her intention is to pursue this either in farming or medicine (p. 116). These were the fields of knowledge, agriculture and medicine, about to be radically transformed by Mendelian theory; the fields of genetic knowledge that Haldane believed would, in their turn, transform human life.

Throughout *Mrs Dalloway* there is an unobtrusive trail of references to plant breeding, at times explicitly related to Darwinian theory. Clarissa's aunt, old Miss Parry, who went botanising in Burma, was part of that generation, facilitated by imperial conquest, who scoured the world for exotic plants to enhance English estates. Her book on orchids was commended by Charles Darwin (p. 152). Sally Seten, who shocked Miss Parry by floating the heads of flowers in bowls, turns up years later as Lady Rosseter who breeds 'hydrangeas, syringas, very, very rare hibiscus lilies that never grow north of the Suez Canal' (p. 161). Part of the social satire here is that the rebel Sally, who chopped off heads, now aspires, by means of her husband's industrial wealth, to imitate the aristocratic pursuits she used to mock. Plant breeding, however, had become popularised since Miss Parry's time. Peter Walsh elicits approval from fellow diners in his hotel simply because he asks for a specific breed of pear, a Bartlett (p. 135). The family he impresses, the two-car-owning Morrises (another non-coincidental name; Morris was an early British popular car company), have travelled down from Leeds to attend the Westminster flower-show (p. 136). The many different kinds of flowers in Miss Pym's shop that, left to nature, would bloom at different seasons, also point to the commercialisation of plant breeding.[26] Even Moll Pratt, a street flower seller, has bunches of roses, not the traditional violets, to sell. She is tempted to throw a bunch after the mysterious car, thinking the passenger may be the Prince of Wales (p. 16). The Prince's mistress, the Countess of Warwick, aptly nick-named 'Daisy', founded one of the first agricultural colleges for women at Reading. It may perhaps be another aspect of Woolf's humour with names in the novel that Peter Walsh's most recent conquest is named Daisy!

The war imposed a pause on the popularisation, among all classes, of flower cultivation and breeding. The government encouraged patriotic gardeners to turn their land over to vegetable production to help feed the nation. Royalty set an example by replacing the geraniums from the flower beds in front of Buckingham Palace with potatoes.[27] The end of hostilities heralded a renewed burst of enthusiasm for flower cultivation. Civic and domestic displays of colour in public parks and gardens seemed appropriate to the general celebration of peace. The Chelsea Flower Show and other municipal ones reopened to showcase the latest plant species produced by large-scale commercial producers like Suttons. In 1923, the novelist, Marion Cran, began broadcasting radio's first gardening programme (Uglow, *Little History*, p. 257). In *Mrs Dalloway*, post-war London is bright with flowers, in public areas, in hanging baskets, and bought in large bunches as gifts (pp. 46, 56, 79, 88, 97). The statue of Queen Victoria in front of the palace is again bedecked with geraniums (p. 16). Geraniums were, indeed, one of the earliest successes of plant hybridisation programmes.[28]

However, not all references in the text to improved breeding by scientific means, and certainly not those in public discourse outside the text, were so innocuous. Septimus Warren Smith looks forward to a world entirely changed 'after all the toils of civilization – Greeks, Romans, Shakespeare, Darwin' (p. 57). Darwinian ideas clearly influence his religious vision of evolutionary improvement in which dogs become men and flesh melts from the body leaving only nerve fibres. In Septimus's madness Woolf dramatises the fusion of idealist religiosity with scientific modes of thought. Septimus repeatedly insists that his vision of future redemption of the flesh, given only to him, must be understood 'scientific[ally] above all things' (p. 58). It is, he presumes, the effect of the heat wave 'operating upon a brain made sensitive by eons of evolution' (p. 58). Public discourse in the non-fictional world of 1920s Britain was much pre-occupied with a redemptive vision of the future proffered by Social Darwinism, or, as it was increasingly called, eugenics. The rediscovery of Mendel's work in the 1900s seemed to offer scientific credence to the project of Social Darwinism with its dream of human perfectibility. The Eugenic Society was formed in 1907 and its journal, *The Eugenic Review*, in 1909. The movement mounted a high profile public campaign in support of the Mental Deficiency Act of 1913. Opponents of the Act described it as the first attempt 'in the scientific breeding of the poor'.[29] As here, the language of the eugenics debate drew heavily upon the popularised scientific discourse of horticulture; it combined that with the other new discourse of mass production processes.

In the 1920s, the Eugenic Society raised the stakes by campaigning for legislation that would permit the voluntary mass sterilisation of the feeble-minded poor. In addition to utilising the familiarised discourses of breeding and mass production, proponents of eugenics also made use of emotive abstractions such as 'Civilisation', 'Nation' and 'Nature', invariably capitalised, to impart a sense of threat to the physical integrity of national identity. On 20 June 1922, *The Times* printed a review entitled 'Civilization's Danger. The Revolt of the Underman'. The author of the reviewed book, *The Revolt against Civilization*, was American journalist and eugenicist, Lothrop Stoddard. *The Times* quotes him as warning that 'racial misfits' and 'the congenitally unfit' would seek to destroy what they cannot understand, namely the superior, more intelligent classes. On 21 October 1922, *The Times* reported the speech of William Inge, Dean of St Paul's Cathedral, to the Society of Medical Officers of Health. To the cheers of his audience, Inge declared it mistaken philanthropy to allow those to survive whom Nature 'might have preferred to die [. . .] The only way to eliminate [some diseases] was to discourage the propagation of infected stocks.' Similarly, on 18 January 1922, an article in *The Times* declared 'We may not agree on what is "best" but we can agree that the mental defective, the blind, the dumb are not the "best" and we can largely limit our production of them.'

In *Mrs Dalloway*, figures from the lowest stratum of social life appear fleetingly but recurrently at the margins of the narrative. They represent an encroaching otherness at the perimeter of the privileged community of those deemed the superior, more intelligent classes. From the woman who sits drinking in a doorway, to the pub brawl with broken glasses, to Moll Pratt selling flowers, to Mrs Dempster with her knobbed lumps for feet, to the seedy-looking unemployed man at St Paul's, to the battered woman at the tube station, to the superfluous youth Lady Bruton intends to ship abroad, to the costermongers and prostitutes harassed by the police, to the female vagrant Richard Dalloway smiles at, to the unemployed men noticed by Elizabeth Dalloway, to the shindy of brawling women, all of these figures are perceived as troublesome or threatening to social order (pp. 4, 15, 16, 23, 24, 69, 93, 98, 99, 117, 139). Many of these unruly characters are women. One of the emotive anxieties driving support for the Mental Deficiency Act was the belief that feeble-minded women were invariably promiscuous, hence responsible for the increased breeding of defective children. After the Act was passed any poor, unsupported woman suspected of sexual misconduct was liable to be judged mentally defective and as such institutionalised for life. In the novel both Clarissa and Richard Dalloway express concern about the welfare of vagrant women they notice in the streets (pp. 4, 99). Clarissa is sure they cannot be dealt with by Acts of Parliament.

In the text there are idealists who find the messiness of unregulated fleshly life repugnant, especially that of 'miserable pigmies, these feeble, these ugly, these craven men and women' (p. 48). For Peter Walsh, the discipline imposed upon the troop of weedy youths converts their ugly feebleness into an image of patriotic nobility. In the 1920s world of Britain beyond the text, feeble, ugly life was repeatedly associated with vagrants, prostitutes, the mentally deficient, the poor, the insane, homosexuals and the racially degenerate. Psychiatrists were closely involved in public debates, campaigns and legislation concerning mental deficiency, vagrancy and insanity, categories which lacked any clear dividing distinctions. In the early twentieth century there was unease among psychiatrists that their professional discipline lacked the prestige of other branches of medicine.[30] As part of their campaign to raise their social and professional status, psychiatrists had a vested interest in working with government and legislators. Their science, they claimed, offered objective knowledge of mental disorder and their theory-based practice the means to control those whose deficiencies posed a threat to the common good of the nation.

In *Mrs Dalloway*, Sir William Bradshaw is gratified to be seen in consultation with those in power. With his worship of the Goddess of Proportion, Bradshaw is undoubtedly the most sinister idealist in the text. He ruthlessly feeds his desire for power by forcing all those who fall into his hands to submit to his authority, including his own wife. Once she had caught salmon freely, but 'quick to minister to the craving, which lit her husband's eye so oilily for dominance', she had 'gone under' (p. 85). Bradshaw is one of those frightening types of idealist, as described by Bertrand Russell, who insists their word is law. In *Mrs Dalloway* and elsewhere in her fiction, Woolf represents this bullying insistence upon conformity as a coercive continuum from the domestic sphere to the public and political domains. In *Mrs Dalloway*, this desire for domination is termed 'Conversion', sister goddess to Proportion. It is a force that 'feasts on the wills of the weakly, loving to impress, to impose, adoring her own features stamped on the face of the populace' (p. 85).

Some such submissive process as this is illustrated in the rapt faces of the youths that Peter Walsh admires and in the faces, transfixed with veneration, of those who behold the large car as symbol of 'the majesty of England'. While the aim is to impose conformity of will upon the populace, the force of Conversion is equally ready to 'smite out of her way roughly the dissentient, or dissatisfied' (p. 85). Clarissa Dalloway, who insists she would never try 'to convert anyone', feels instinctively that Bradshaw is 'capable of some indescribable outrage – forcing your soul' (pp. 107, 157). 'Conversion' is primarily a religious term; it is to renounce the world for the spirit, to subdue the body for the sake of the soul. Woolf's choice of the word suggests the intolerant and fanatical zeal with which those like Bradshaw seek to force upon others their systems of belief, whether secular or religious. It points, also, to the idealist desire to transform the disordered imperfection of embodied life into a docile unity of conforming souls or wills, into what could be thought of euphemistically as the common Good.

Septimus Warren Smith also has religious visions of a brave new world in which flesh has melted away leaving only the nerves or will. It is a religion that, he insists, is based upon science above all. It is his duty, he believes, to communicate his knowledge to the Cabinet (p. 57). Sir William Bradshaw, 'priest of science', shares that vision of flesh brought under control of the will (p. 80). The parallels between Septimus's insane delusions and the social visions of Bradshaw are deliberate, yet there is an important difference. Bradshaw seeks to impose his subjective prejudices as objective knowledge just as Bertrand Russell accused idealists of doing. Unlike Septimus, but like leading idealists in the real world, Sir William has access to the Cabinet and the legislative means to impose his will on all those who are in any way disempowered and vulnerable. 'There was no alternative. It was a question of law', he says relentlessly to Septimus (p. 82). Yet while his rhetoric is that of the irresistible authority of science and law that have 'made England prosper', his methods are the technologies of eugenics, practised upon the flesh. He 'secluded [. . .] lunatics, forbade childbirth, penalised despair, made it impossible for the unfit to propagate their views' (p. 84). Such measures are justified by his 'scientific' belief that all 'unsocial impulses [are] bred more than anything by lack of good blood' (p. 86).

For Woolf, any form of subjectivity or system of beliefs that avoids confrontation with the materiality of bodies and things risks succumbing to a will to power: the attempt to impose prejudices and passions upon others in the name of 'higher' values. In *Mrs Dalloway* she demonstrates the paradoxical regime of the perceptible that holds idealism in place. On the one hand, idealist rhetoric, whether of the nation's common Good or of the rational power of science and progress, depends upon the metaphorical functioning that allows things to provide tangibility to abstractions like nation, duty, civilisation. On the other, idealist emphasis upon the 'will' as the defining value of self and nation renders inconsequential, beneath notice, the physical suffering and damage inflicted on embodied persons and population by the brutalities of war, poverty and legalised coercion.

Elizabeth Hamilton, living through factional post-Revolutionary politics, suggested that the factitious self frequently shores up its precarious idea of self by imaginative identification with the nation or a system of values. Any challenge, criticism or perceived harm to these mental projections that enlarge and empower the idea of self will be experienced as a threat to the self's very existence. Woolf similarly suggests that those enjoying class privilege and power are wholly unable to distinguish between self and an ideal of the nation that sustains and reflects back their own imaginary 'best self'. Not surprisingly, anything or person that does not subscribe to the regulated homogeneity of that imaginary order has to be either excluded or compelled to conform. Peter Walsh excludes from the civilised efficiency that he imagines is England the otherness that he terms the chaos of India. There are moments when 'civilization' seems to him 'a personal possession' as, too, does 'pride in England' (p. 47). Lady Bruton's glorification of a mythic England of Shakespeare energises her ruthless drive to exclude, by means of emigration, 'the superfluous youth of our ever-increasing population'. This project has become an 'object round which the essence of her soul is daily secreted' (p. 92). It is for her a 'sublime conception', an abstract idea in other words, but one which she, nevertheless, intends to impose upon those whom she never conceives as actual people with particular lives, hopes and incongruities. Her term 'superfluous' precisely registers the idealist regime of the perceptible in which those without status are denied the right even to material existence.

British idealists were accused by their critics of justifying the subordination of the subject to an ideal of the state as a spiritual unity. Instead of the horizontal mobility and heterogeneity of space, as Woolf represents London, with its democratic blare and uproar, idealists desire a controlled and bounded place structured vertically by lines of obedience to rank and duty, just as the clocks of Harley Street counsel 'submission, upheld authority, and pointed out in chorus the supreme advantages of a sense of proportion' (p. 87). The many idealists in the text of *Mrs Dalloway* do not by any means share the same vision of order, even though they all desire the imposition of the will upon what they see as the waywardness of physical being. The object of Woolf's attack is not any one specific school of idealism or even on any one form of social or political tyranny underwritten by it. Rather her critique is aimed at idealism as a pervasive ideological structure, sustaining a regime of the perceptible that allows visibility to the mass of the population only at the price of disciplined conformity. In just this way, Peter Walsh screens out from his view of the marching boys evidence of their malnutrition, seeing only disciplined uniformity. The novel suggests, moreover, that idealist systems of thought follow the discourses of power. From the moral and religious conceptions of the state and the self that dominated Woolf's father's late Victorian world, idealism, with its zealous spirit of religion, has moved into those modern forms of knowledge that operate from an Olympian perspective. From that disembodied distance, heterogeneity and diversity can be homogenised into a mass, or be conceptualised into abstract regularity.

In opposition to that imposed conformity from above, Woolf's writing fluidity offers a common horizontal world teeming with people and things. Only a democratic regime of the perceptible, as a shared world in which everyone and everything is visible and heard, can create a dissensus that resists totalising systems of thought. It is the non-reverent, secular, non-vertical visibility of a comic incongruity, so often prevailing between the vision and the fact, that allows monsters to be destroyed by laughter before the idea or abstraction takes substance through infliction upon actual bodies. As Woolf argues in her essays, the idea must always be brought back to the truth of empirical fact. *Mrs Dalloway* suggests there are hugely crucial political imperatives at stake in this necessary adherence to empiricism. This is the insight underlying her aesthetic practice of worldly realism. The metonymic structures and stylistics of *Mrs Dalloway* enact an egalitarian recognition of the multiple interdependent force fields constituting self, social structures, things as 'gatherings' and the physical world. Her inclusive aesthetic lays bare the brutal coercion of 'the social system at its most intense'. Equally, it constitutes a radical dissensus to the authoritarian vertical regime of the perceptible imposed by idealist ideology.

Notes

1. *Room of One's Own*, p. 57.
2. See, for example, *Essays of Virginia Woolf*, 2.9–16; 3.331–5; 4.41, 146–57, 390–3, 513; 5.59–63; 6.439. For a less sympathetic account of Woolf's fascination with Austen see Janet Todd, 'Who's Afraid of Jane Austen', in *Jane Austen: New Perspectives*, pp. 107–27.
3. Quentin Bell, *Virginia Woolf: A Biography*, 2.186.
4. Erich Auerbach, *Mimesis: The Representation of Reality in Western Literature*, pp. 548–53.
5. See, for example, Jean Guiguet, *Virginia Woolf and her Works*; James Haffley, *The Glass Roof: Virginia Woolf as Novelist*; Shiv K. Kumar, *Bergson and the Stream of Consciousness Novel.*
6. Among influential studies see Elizabeth Abel, *Virginia Woolf and the Fictions of Psychoanalysis*; Nancy Topping Bazin, *Virginia Woolf and the Androgynous Vision*; Rachel Bowlby, *Feminist Destinations*; Jane Marcus, ed., *New Feminist Essays on Virginia Woolf*, *Virginia Woolf and the Languages of Patriarchy*; Makiko Minnow-Pinkney, *Virginia Woolf and the Problem of the Subject*; Sue Roe, *Writing and Gender: Virginia Woolf's Writing Practice.*
7. See, for example, Gillian Beer, *Virginia Woolf: The Common Ground*; Melba Cuddy-Keane, *Virginia Woolf, the Intellectual and the Public Sphere*; Mark Hussey, *Virginia Woolf and War: Fiction, Reality and Myth*; Anna Snaith, *Virginia Woolf: Public and Private Negotiations*; Michael Whitworth, *Virginia Woolf.*
8. Cambridge University Press edition of the Works of Virginia Woolf (launched 2011).
9. Linden Peach, *Virginia Woolf*, p. 169.
10. Alex Zwerdling, *Virginia Woolf and the Real World*, p. 15. Other discussions of Woolf and realism include Susan Dick, 'Literary Realism in *Mrs Dalloway*, *To the Lighthouse* and *The Waves*', in Sue Roe and Susan Sellers, eds, *Cambridge Companion to Virginia Woolf*,

pp. 50–71; Hintikka Jaakko, 'Virginia Woolf and Our Knowledge of the External World', *Journal of Aesthetics and Art Criticism*, Fall 1979–80, vol. 38, pp. 5–14; S. P. Rosenbaum, 'The Philosophical Realism of Virginia Woolf', in S. P. Rosenbaum, ed., *English Literature and British Philosophy*.

11. Jacques Rancière,*The Politics of Literature*, p. 38.
12. Michael Whitworth makes this point in his chapter on 'Philosophical Questions', p. 119.
13. Virginia Woolf, *Roger Fry: A Biography*, p. 152.
14. In what follows I am indebted to the accounts of British idealism offered in David Boucher and Andrew Vincent, *British Idealism: A Guide for the Perplexed*; David Boucher, ed., *The British Idealists*; Peter P. Nicholson, *The Political Philosophy of the British Idealists*; Andrew Vincent and Raymond Plant, *Philosophy, Politics and Citizenship: The Life and Thought of British Idealists.*
15. F. H. Bradley, *Ethical Studies* [1876], pp. 160–213.
16. Boucher and Vincent (pp. 102–30) and Vincent and Plant (pp. 132–62) offer informative accounts of the widespread social, political and educational activities of idealist affiliates.
17. G. E. Moore, *Philosophical Studies* [1922], pp. 1–30.
18. Bertrand Russell, *Mysticism and Logic* [1918], p. 15.
19. Bertrand Russell, *Problems of Philosophy* [1912], p. 92.
20. Adam Smith, *Theory of Moral Sentiments*, p. 275.
21. *The Diary of Virginia Woolf*, 2.248.
22. Virginia Woolf, *Mrs Dalloway*, p. 48.
23. *The Times*, 28 November 1923; for an account of the expansion of mass assembly production from its inception at Ford's Dearborn factory, see Mark Rupert, *Producing Hegemony: The Politics of Mass Production and American Global Power*, pp. 63–7 and Douglas Brinkley, *Wheels for the World: Henry Ford, his Company and a Century of Progress*, pp. 134–60.
24. J. B. S. Haldane, *Daedalus, or Science and the Future*, pp. 4–5.
25. Quoted in David Harvey's chapter on 'Fordism', in *The Conditions of Postmodernity: An Enquiry into the Origins of Cultural Change*, p. 126. Aldous Huxley makes a similar point in *Brave New World* (1932) where time in the futuristic world state is referred to as AF – After Ford.
26. Elisa Kay Sparks, '"Everything tended to set itself in a garden": Virginia Woolf's Literary and Quotidian Flowers: A Bar-Graphical Approach', in Kristin Czarnecki and Carrie Rohman, eds, *Virginia Woolf and the Natural World*, comments that the number of flower references in *Mrs Dalloway* 'towers over other texts' p. 44.
27. Jenny Uglow, *A Little History of British Gardening*, p. 255.
28. Maggie Campbell-Culver, *The Origins of Plants: People and Plants that have Shaped Britain's Garden History since the Year 1000*, p. 356.

29. Quoted in Matthew Thomson, *The Problem of Mental Deficiency: Eugenics, Democracy, and Social Policy in Britain c. 1870–1959*, p. 47. Thomson provides an excellent bibliography of the extensive number of books concerned with mental deficiency and with eugenics that were published during the early decades of the twentieth century.
30. Thomson, pp. 120–4; Edward Shorter, *A History of Psychiatry: From the Era of the Asylum to the Age of Prozac*, pp. 65–6, 143.

Part II

Nation and Universe

Chapter 3

Emma: A Prospect of England

Emma (1815) is one of those literary works which can seem to exist within the timeless glow of its own perfection. For many readers, Emma's world evokes an ideal of England. Of all Austen's novels it is perhaps the one that most lends itself to what Roger Sales calls the promotion of a 'particular idea of Englishness'.[1] The 'association between Austen and Englishness is currently a very strong one', he says. The perception of timeless, quintessential national values is, however, an illusion largely imposed on Austen's text by an idealist regime of interpretive practice. Rather than depicting a pastoral England that never was, *Emma* is a novel that proclaims, from its very first page, the inevitability of change. As in *Sense and Sensibility*, this process is enacted as a shift away from the settled order of inherited place to the motility of social space. A vertical regime of the proper gives way to horizontal recognition of those previously regarded as below notice. Again, as in the earlier novel, the focus of change is a young woman, Emma Woodhouse. The transition that Emma makes in the novel continues Austen's social critique of subjective idealism, as an imposition of self upon the world. Equally, the narrative trajectory explores the changing identity of the English nation, challenging the consensual acceptance of hierarchical social exclusiveness with the possibility of greater horizontal inclusivity.

Questions as to the proper nature of social relations and political settlements were central concerns within eighteenth-century British Enlightenment. Austen was rooted in that interrogative mode of thinking but she was writing in the aftermath of the French Revolution, and, importantly, after the publication of Edmund Burke's influential *Reflections on the Revolution in France* (1790). Burke's romantic idealism produced a powerfully imagined vision of an immemorial England, sustained by hierarchical traditions of patrician and religious ideals.

National sentiment, Burke claimed, is nurtured in the small 'platoon' of childhood and that early reverence for local attachments expands and cements the ties of gratitude, benevolence and obedience that secure the unity of the nation.[2] This ideal appealed powerfully to public reaction and anxiety in the wake of the Revolution and has retained a central place ever since in conservative concepts of English national identity.[3]

A sense of privileged English destiny was much enhanced during the time Austen was writing *Emma* by the defeat of Napoleon in 1814 and the conclusion of a quarter of a century of continental wars. It was a momentous event. It requires an act of historical imagination now to comprehend what the removal of that constant threat to national safety must have felt like at the time to all shades of public opinion. The *Edinburgh Review* expresses something of the immense relief to people's spirits and the sense of renewed social possibilities for the nation when it speaks of 'the enchanting prospect of long peace and measureless improvement' at last opening up.[4] The journal goes on, this scene that has 'burst on our view' has arrived 'like the balmy air and flushing verdure of late spring after the dreary chills of a long and interminable winter'.

The *Edinburgh* plays here upon both the literal meaning of the word 'prospect' as an expansive view of English landscape and the metaphorical elevation of this primary, material sense into a mental image of some future possibility or hope. It thus operates across the matter–mind, empiricist–idealist dualism. 'Prospect' is also a word that resonates in the text of *Emma*, articulating its thematic concern with processes of transformation, the movement from the fixture of 'here' to an emergent or possible 'there', from the vertical order of metaphor to the horizontal movement of metonymy. In particular, there is a striking use of the term, prospect, in which Austen, too, plays across the material and metaphoric meanings. Her imagery and language are not only similar to that used in the *Edinburgh Review*, they also trace, at Emma's personal level, the same emotional transformation of hopeless stasis into delighted possibilities of 'measureless improvement'. The moment of release from the paralysis of misery occurs when Emma's spirits are at their lowest as she contemplates the closing off of her future due to her own class arrogance and blindness. 'The prospect before her was threatening [. . .] Hartfield must be comparatively deserted; and she left to cheer her father with the spirits only of ruined happiness.'[5] The physical prospect outside offers added gloom 'with cold, stormy rain' and a 'despoiling' wind (p. 459). Yet the following morning, with the wind changed into a softer quarter, 'it was summer again' and the view of the garden warm and brilliant. Emma is experiencing bodily release from physical enclosure even as Mr Knightley makes an unexpected appearance that will totally transform her hopes for expansive change (p. 362).

The celebratory spirit marking the end of the Napoleonic wars gave powerful impetus to popular rhetorical representations of England as a united community or family, but these imagined identities were always politically inflected. Two opposing ideas of national identity struggled for legitimacy of representation. The conservative *Gentleman's Magazine* rejoiced that bread, meat and drink were so distributed that in every town and almost every village, people were able to participate 'in the general joy and to keep the feast of peace, as one united family'.[6] The naturalising image of nation as a family constitutes the country as a benign organic hierarchy. Patronage of the poor by the rich, in the form of food and drink, was seen by conservatives as engendering those feelings of gratitude and benevolence that cemented the bonds of social unity. Within this ideal of nationhood, the privilege of rank and its bestowal of favours were viewed as essential for the maintenance of civility, cultivation and social order. In 1814, for example, the *Gentleman's Magazine* published a letter deprecating the violent changes that had occurred to the internal structure 'of ranks in old England'.[7] As the nostalgic reference to 'old England' suggests, the writer is hostile to what he sees as the growing importance of commerce and the City fostered by the administration of William Pitt. The new men, the writer claims, have 'ousted the old Country gentlemen [. . .] and shoved them into insignificance'. Another writer to *Gentleman's Magazine* even blamed a rise in suicide on 'this attempt to overthrow the bounds of society that have hitherto kept ranks of society distinct, and to confound and mix all that ought to have been kept separate'.[8] Those who feared such social and political confusion tended to look to Edmund Burke's powerful advocacy of rank and deference as the only sure foundation of national identity and as bulwark against social anarchy.

Not all imaginings of the nation as a unity were so opposed to change. As the *Edinburgh Review* claimed, peace brought with it possibilities of 'measureless improvements'. Progressive opinion welcomed the ending of war as offering the opportunity for a widening of participation in the public and political activities that, in effect, constituted a more inclusive ideal of national identity. In *British Society 1680–1880*, historian Richard Price writes, 'The French Revolution allowed the unthinkable to be imagined in politics.

It was for this reason that from the 1790s the boundaries of the politically (and socially) possible were continually tested and stretched.' The revolution, Price argues, put reform irrevocably on the agenda, 'largely because the French Revolution had extended the possibilities for the role of "the people" in the political nation'.[9] The question of who was recognised within perceptions of England as a nation became a matter of contestation. It was a moment of potential dissensus, to use Jacques Rancière's term, when Burke's vertical exclusivity of rank was challenged by an emergent horizontal regime making visible and audible those formerly regarded as beneath notice.[10] The Liberal *Edinburgh Review*, for example, argued that the whole revolutionary period had demonstrated that national prosperity and security rest upon 'expressing and giving effect to the general sense of the community'.[11] The question of Catholic emancipation much debated in the public sphere during 1813 was also expressed, by those in favour of reform, as encouraging 'expanded affections which embrace the whole community in one system of fair and equal legislation, by which the several parts of the social body shall be as it were amalgamated into an harmonious whole'.[12]

Both the above quotations are implicitly drawing upon a widely recognised sense that a literate public opinion had developed rapidly during the latter part of the eighteenth century and was continuing to extend its social boundaries. This expanding community of the informed and literate, 'the people', was a strengthening presence within national life. In *Emma*, the young tenant farmer, Robert Martin, provides a fictional illustration of the new class of citizen. Emma dismisses Robert Martin as having nothing to do with the public realm of books although he is actually well-informed and well-read. Emma's initial response, here, in refusing to 'notice' Martin, voices the traditional regime of the perceptible in which those of lower rank are rendered mute and invisible within a tightly-circumscribed, elite perception of who constitutes England.

Nevertheless, in the real world, despite reactionary views like those of Emma, there were increasing voices in the public sphere, warning of the damaging effects of patronage as the dominant form of social relations. Critics argued that rather than maintaining national stability, patronage was exerting a deadening influence on the country's energies, holding back necessary change. In early 1814, the *Monthly Review*, a moderate liberal journal, was rehearsing the evils of government by patronage.[13] Maria Edgeworth contributed to this critical discourse in her novel appropriately titled *Patronage* (1814), which contrasts the fortunes of two families, one relying only on their own energetic endeavours and the other resting upon hope of influence. A reviewer in the *Edinburgh Review* explained that the book offered 'a picture of miseries resulting from a dependence on *Patronage*, in every form and degree, and throughout every station in society'.[14] The strongest critics of patronage and privilege were those advocating the ideology of competitive individualism. They were, in effect, the spokespeople for the aspiring middle class. The pernicious effects of influence are also at the centre of *Emma*, and Austen, like Edgewood, sees patronage as damaging those who bestow favour as much as those who are recipients. Nevertheless, Austen's representation is more nuanced in terms of social class. Austen recognises that patronage was a source of influence and power that many of the middle class were willing, even eager, to exploit in their own interests.

As this suggests, it is a mistake to understand the conflict between traditional values like patronage and the new competitive ethos of individualism in unambiguous binary terms of old ruling elite against new commercial middle class. The main aim of the aspiring middle class was elevation into the elite, to become part of those recognised as the perceptible nation. Richard Price argues that, 'Competition and convergence describe the relationship between the middling classes and the patriciate. It is helpful [. . .] to imagine middle-class consciousness as a spectrum bounded at one end by emulation of the landed elite and at the other end by competition with its styles and politics' (*British Society*, p. 311). In particular, Price claims, the middle class consolidated its hegemonic visibility and audibility by emulating and competing in the assertion of economic, cultural and social patronage. One of the main locations in which the middle class was able to challenge the traditional elite in the exercise of influence and patronage was within the cultural realm demarcated as taste. Taste is a pre-eminent means of rendering status visible. The other sphere of competition was patriotism. Any real or perceived threat to the nation was seized upon as an oratorical and practical opportunity to display public patriotism. Middle-class women vied with aristocratic ladies in proclaiming loyalty as English women.

During the early years of the nineteenth century, there was indeed plenty to alarm even those less timid than Mr Woodhouse as to the precariousness of social order. Luddism was still a threat, and a series of bad harvests had exacerbated the hunger and suffering of the poor, resulting in bread riots, attacks upon property, and an increase in burglary and housebreaking. Even those living in unaffected areas of the country could have their fears aroused by the frequent reports of law-breaking and disorderliness in the lower classes that featured prominently in all the daily, weekly and monthly journals.[15] In 1811, the *Gentleman's Magazine* carried an appeal to the Women of England to concern themselves with the plight of the poor by teaching the bible, presumably with the aim of preserving deference.[16] Emma certainly concerns herself with helping the poor, but the emphasis is upon her practical administration to physical needs and well-being rather than to their minds or souls. She also inadvertently benefits when Mr Woodhouse's fear of housebreaking persuades him to look more favourably on the change her marriage will bring.

The opening paragraphs of the novel, however, play not upon threats of disorder, but upon fairy-tale motifs that evoke an arrested, spell-bound world. Emma is the youngest daughter, her mother died while she was still a child, and like all princesses she is handsome, clever and imperious. Her doting father allows her full sway over their small kingdom or platoon, to borrow Burke's term. Yet the language hints that the stasis of this select community is precarious. The use of the conditional 'seemed' in the first sentence hints that the idyllic existence may lack reality. This suggestion is reinforced three paragraphs later by the deictic phrase 'at present'. Even more than Austen's recurrent use of 'now' in her narratives, 'at present' foregrounds temporality, the inevitable progression from past through to future. 'At present' evokes simultaneously the apparent immediacy of the moment and its ephemeral span.

Hartfield can be read metaphorically as symbolising those national values, revered by Burke, of tradition, stability, fixture and civility. In the terms set out by Michel de Certeau, Hartfield is a 'place' as opposed to a 'space'. A place, de Certeau suggests, is ruled by the law of the proper.[17] 'Place' implies stability, boundaries and order. By contrast, space is composed of intersections of mobile elements. While the former is viewed rather in the manner of a completed tableau, the latter exists largely as an experience of movement. In the novel, Hartfield is perceived by all the characters as a small world existing under the inviolable law of regularity and fixity. Geographically, socially and mentally it exists complete within the boundaries of its own self-sufficiency. Although Hartfield 'did really belong' to Highbury – the language again signals reluctance by its inhabitants to accept that reality – it is separated from the town by extensive lawns and shrubberies, another hint of Sleeping Beauty seclusion (p. 5).

Mr Woodhouse is the almost caricatured representation of all of Hartfield's time-resisting values. He hates the idea of matrimony because it is the origin of change. He is correct about this in that marriage alliances are the nexus of money and property transactions, of status and power relations, and of generational movement of past to future. The transformation of Miss Taylor into Mrs Weston not only introduces change into Hartfield, it also signifies the possibility of movement across divisions of rank, as formerly dependent governess becomes wife of property-owning Mr Weston. Not surprisingly then, perhaps, the marriage provides the catalyst which sets in motion, directly or indirectly, all the other changes and social reconfigurations in the narrative.

Emma, too, is set firmly against change. She is resolute in her determination not to marry. 'I cannot really change for the better', she tells Harriet with wonderfully unknowing irony (p. 90). For most of the story she is adamant as to the importance of maintaining a fixed social hierarchy, a wholly vertical ordering in which only the speech and visibility of the higher classes are deemed worthy of notice. Emma's language echoes that of conservatives in the public sphere of the day. 'One should be sorry to see greater pride or refinement in a teacher of a school' she asserts (p. 58). Her immediate negative assumption is that Robert Martin and his family are intent on climbing out of their lower-class invisibility (p. 27). As this suggests, she views any mixed social interaction as occasioning risk of irregularity, insubordination and transgression of the proper. Even Frank Churchill displeases her with his 'indifference to a confusion of rank, [that] bordered too much on inelegance of mind' (pp. 213–14). Emma maintains a social distance around herself no less than the physical separation of lawns and shrubbery. Her language suggests an almost visceral fear that contact with the socially unrecognised will contaminate the integrity of her sovereign self. Her 'horror [. . .] of falling in with the second rate and third rate of Highbury' is such that she 'seldom went near them' (p. 165). To fall from privileged eminence is to lose perceptibility in the mass of undistinguished others.

Hartfield, then, as a place, symbolises a regime of vertically regulated order, and absolute, unchanging values. Highbury, by contrast, can be understood horizontally as a space of possibility and change, brought about by chance meetings, empirical contiguity and unregulated social interaction. Harriet bumps into Robert

Martin and his sister when she is sheltering from the rain in Ford's shop. Jane Fairfax is seen by Mr John Knightley as she goes to the post-office to forestall any letter from Frank Churchill (p. 316). Highbury, a 'populous village', in the process of becoming a town (p. 5), can be seen as a synecdoche for a changing England. It is a space in which social boundaries are porous and social relations largely governed by reciprocity rather than patronage. In particular, the continual circulation of gossip in Highbury constitutes a space in which identity is understood as primarily social rather than private and in which truth is dispersed into an interactive multiplicity of viewpoints.

It is worth noting that Emma's hatred of Highbury gossip is not because it is in any way malicious, but because it flows horizontally violating her strict sense of vertical social divisions. It takes liberties in other words. Highbury gossip can be thought of in terms of what Rancière calls the garrulous muteness of previously inconsequential social life to which democratic realism gives voice. The text offers an intriguingly modern image of the nation as a larger version of an interactive community brought into being through a continuous, horizontal circulation of news, gossip and shared consciousness. 'The post-office is a wonderful establishment,' Jane Fairfax declares, 'The regularity and dispatch of it! [. . .] So seldom that a letter among the thousands that are constantly passing about the kingdom, is ever carried wrong' (p. 320). John Knightley, in agreeing, attributes the efficiency and capacity of the system to the fact that it serves and is paid for by 'the public', the new, anti-hierarchical force in post-revolutionary politics.

Another way of reading the contrast of values between Hartfield and Highbury is that of the Enlightenment opposition between idealism and materialism, continuing Austen's critique of the former mode of thought. Throughout *Emma*, recurrent distinctions are drawn between body or person, terms used synonymously, and mind. Mr Woodhouse is introduced as a valetudinarian, inactive in 'mind or body' (p. 5). Emma finds little elegance of 'person or of mind' in Highbury, while Mr Elton is deemed by its inhabitants to be perfection 'both in person and mind' (pp. 179, 187). Even more frequent than these dualistic references in the text is the recurrence of the word 'idea'. Many of the characters speak of having an idea but Emma does so most of all. She uses the term three times in her speculations with Mr Knightley as to what sort of person Frank Churchill will prove to be. 'I have no idea of him being a weak young man,' she asserts, adding, 'My idea of him is, that he can adapt his conversation to the taste of every body' (pp. 160, 161). Later in the story, she comically accuses Mrs Weston of taking up an 'idea' and running away with it and later she 'even wept over the idea' of leaving her father should she marry (pp. 244, 474). What this last example demonstrates is the emotive force of ideas, and yet what the many textual references also imply is that this mental speculation is often untested by material reality. The world of mind is largely unchecked by physical actuality. There is similarity here with Marianne Dashwood, in *Sense and Sensibility*, whose enthusiasm for her own 'systems of thought' are based upon 'ignorance of the world'.

As in *Sense and Sensibility*, Austen ironises the willingness to allow mind tyranny over matter, especially the imposition of subjective perceptions upon the lives of others. Mr Woodhouse is the most humorously treated example of this dominance of the mental over the actual. His 'general benevolence' remains just that, a largely abstract principle undirected by any real knowledge of others. Typically he 'protects' his guests from those very dishes they would most enjoy. Such vague well-meaning has little moderating force upon his life-long 'habits of gentle selfishness' (p. 6). Like other idealists he is 'never able to suppose that other people could feel differently from himself' (p. 6). Equally, like many idealists he is governed by a pervasive bodily fearfulness and dislike of the physical world. He shuns exposure to outside elements just as doggedly as he shuns any opinion he dislikes, rarely venturing away from the fireside and even then fearful of draughts. Indeed, a striking feature of the text, generally, is a preoccupation with the state of the weather. This is one of the several means by which Austen underlines the physical nature of existence in contrast to Emma's concern with ideas. Mr Woodhouse regards food, also, with deep suspicion, as harmful rather than nurturing, only able to recommend thin gruel. Apart from events organised 'on his own terms' he has a horror of change to routine, of any activity or event, seeing them only as openings for physical harm, illness and discomfort (p. 19). As far as possible, Mr Woodhouse disavows the fact of physical life.

Emma lacks her father's nervous rejection of the physical and the text is at pains to stress her bodily vigour. Indeed, Emma's vitality is represented as so integral with her lively imagination and feelings that notions of the mind–body separation as invoked by Emma and others are implicitly challenged. Austen's representation of her characters, especially her heroines, gives powerful dramatic expression to David Hartley's sense of self as embodied energies, the physical, the mental, the imaginative and the affective completely inseparable. So, too, Mr Knightley 'always moves with the alertness of mind' that suggests the indivisibility of physical and mental activity (p. 420). One reason why readers are convinced of the sexual charge between her characters is that, although she is the least explicit writer, she nevertheless conveys a full sense of them as embodied beings. Part of Austen's irony in *Emma* is that Emma is so sure of her own mind that she fails to notice what her bodily feelings might well be able to tell her.

Certainly, for most of the narrative Emma privileges the mental realm at the expense of the empirical. She has 'a mind delighted with its own ideas' and she readily imposes these upon reality, as Mr Knightley terms it, quoting William Cowper, 'Myself creating what I saw' (pp. 23, 373). Typically, with Mr Elton she is 'too eager and busy in her own previous conceptions and views to hear him impartially or see him with a clear vision' (p. 105). We could understand this as a case of the metaphorical form of prospect or 'vision' overriding the basis of physical sight from which the figurative meaning ultimately derives. The distribution of the perceptible is regulated by the mind, as Austen's persistent linking of the mental realm with verbs of seeing and hearing indicates. Emma's prospect is indeed governed by her willed sense of the distanced eminence she enjoys, an Olympic perspective, conferred by the privileged entitlement of Hartfield. This produces, in Emma, a belief in her own panoptic insight, the source of much of the text's irony. Emma assumes a patrician, god-like confidence in her knowledge of others and thus a habit of treating them as objects, subordinated to her greater scheme of things. This is the characteristic perspective of the idealist who imposes a mental conception on the particularity of the actual world. Adam Smith's warning, in *The Theory of Moral Sentiment*, that the idealist is 'so often enamoured with the supposed beauty of his own ideal plan' that he imagines people can be arranged in accordance with it as easily as pieces can be arranged on a chess board applies with great aptitude to Emma.[18]

Emma repeatedly asserts that her judgements are beyond error. 'There can be no doubt of your being a gentleman's daughter', she tells Harriet with sweeping confidence based upon nothing (p. 30). Similarly, she 'could not feel a doubt' about directing Harriet's feelings towards Mr Elton, and as for her ability to manipulate and predict Mr Elton's intentions, 'I cannot have a moment's doubt,' she proclaims, adding, 'I could not be so deceived' (pp. 43, 78). This sense of vertical overview of others objectifies those who are subjected to such Olympic speculation. They are indeed treated like chess pieces. Emma thinks of Harriet in terms of 'how useful' she will be; she was exactly 'the some*thing* which her home required' (p. 25, emphasis added). Jane Fairfax, equally, is of interest only for the use-value she has for Emma's imaginative plots and even Frank Churchill figures as much in Emma's romantic self-fictions as he does for her as a real person in his own right.

That Emma does have the redeeming capacity to enter into the perspectives of others is perhaps hinted at in her practical approach to poor families where she attends to their real physical needs. This contrasts positively with her father's inactive 'general benevolence' but even more so with Mrs Elton's Marie Antoinette posturing in wishing to ride to the strawberry-picking at Donwell on a donkey (p. 386). Mrs Elton's desire for a donkey as symbol of Arcadian simplicity provides a wonderfully comic image, yet it is typical of Austen's materialist psychology. Idealist assertions of the mental realm as the primary reality are undercut in her novels as objects persistently point to the way things are required to give substance to the immaterial. Things, in Austen's texts, demonstrate the necessary interdependence of the subjective and the objective, the idealist and the empirical. We know ourselves, even our interiority, through our interaction with things. The most explicit example of this in *Emma* is the sad little collection of '*Most precious treasures*', comprising a piece of plaster and a pencil stub, that Harriet stores away as a means of substantiating her romantic dreams of Mr Elton (p. 366).

In her fiction, Austen frequently foregrounds the metaphoric substantiation of immaterial values by means of those things closely associated with the physical necessities of life. This effects a transference from the empirical realm to the ideal, a shift which paradoxically disguises the physicality that the mental realm depends upon for existence. In this way, Austen's realism brings to notice a field of visibility – the materiality of human life – just as it is about to be rendered invisible in genteel discourse. As the nineteenth century progressed, only the embodied materiality of the poor, a presence betokening lack, the absence of interiority, was allowed perceptibility. In *Sense and Sensibility* references to fires and hearths afford substance to the textual opposition between cold-hearted civility and the warmth of traditional embodied sociability. In *Emma*, food is the main material thing by which immaterial values are mediated and concretised. As such, food participates in the characters' imaginative constitution of a self. While the text shows characters wittingly and unwittingly using food to convey abstract meanings, Austen's references are meticulously particularised: leg of pork, fricassee of sweetbread, scalloped oysters, asparagus and baked apples. Methods of cooking are also detailed as is the fact of butchering. For Mr Woodhouse, it is this materiality of food that provides him with means of expressing, by contrast, his sense of self as purely nervous sensibility. He elaborates exacting rules for cooking to render food less dangerous and is particular in sending away from the table anything he deems not up to his fanciful standards. Cooking is, of course, the most basic means by which we transform the physical into cultural values.

For Miss Bates, food constitutes one of the main currencies of traditional sociable reciprocity, a reciprocity firmly based in the physical exigencies of existence. When Emma unexpectedly gratifies her with a rare visit, Miss Bates's welcome flows metonymically, but always materially, from anxiety about wet shoes, to concern for Mr Woodhouse's health, to pressing invitations to take some 'sweet-cake from the beaufet' which Mrs Cole had earlier 'been so kind as to say she liked very much' (p. 166). When the Bateses receive a gift of pork from Hartfield their immediate response is to invite friends to share it. Miss Bates welcomes apples from Donwell so that they can be given to Jane who is without appetite. For Miss Bates, who has no wealth, food is a means of generosity, of expressing her care for others. As such, it secures her sense of self as a wholly social being.

Quite the opposite is the case with Mrs Elton. Food for her functions as individualistic self-promotion and status enhancement. She boasts to Emma of living in such a style as makes unexpected guests for dinner no inconvenience. 'I should be extremely displeased if Wright were to send up such a dinner as could make me regret having asked more', she declares (p. 306). She plans to impress Highbury with a 'very superior party' with waiters engaged 'to carry around refreshments at exactly the proper hour, and in the proper order' (p. 314).

References to giving, cooking and eating food form a continuous, discursive thread throughout the text, indicating the interdependence of the physical with the immaterial. Yet, the 'thing' that most dramatically appears in the story is the piano given to Jane Fairfax. This is certainly not merely a device required by the plot. The piano can be thought of as a 'gathering' to use Bruno Latour's terminology.[19] It constitutes a pivotal intersection of the various forces contending for national dominance in early nineteenth-century England.

In particular, the piano mediates the mixture of competition and emulation by which the middle class sought to impose themselves as part of the perceptible nation. It is Austen's ironic representation of this competitive emulation that drives the narrative of *Emma*, as Mrs Elton's assertive individualism challenges Emma's presumption of inborn right.

In *Men, Women and Pianos: A Social History*, Arthur Loesser associates the rapid growth in popular appeal of the piano, from its first introduction into England in the 1750s, with a growing obsession to achieve and maintain gentility. By the nineteenth century, he claims, this was the 'most anxious ambition, the very aim of life of most English middle-class people [. . .] an endless quest [. . .] [that] was relative and competitive'.[20] As middle-class wealth grew this aspiration for gentility was proclaimed by conspicuous display of 'all its paraphernalia and insignia. Among the latter, one of the most persistent was the keyboard instrument' (*Men, Women*, p. 188).

In *Piano Roles: Three Hundred Years of Life with the Piano*, James Parakilas confirms this centrality of the piano within the cultural shift taking place in post-revolutionary England, whereby power and status were in process of transferring from the old landed elite to a widening 'circle of the population thinking of itself as "the people"'.[21] Parakilas goes further, linking the role of the piano in this cultural revolution with the processes of change set in motion by the Industrial Revolution. It constituted a shift towards the mass production and consumerism that would breach the exclusivity of the cultural capital of landed wealth. The rapidly growing market for musical products fostered by the competitive cultural ambitions of the middle class 'involved new means of producing and distributing cultural goods – pianos, printed music, journals, systems of education and opinion – on a mass and international scale' (*Three Hundred Years*, p. 93). In his study, Loesser argues that the actual physical form of the piano rendered it adaptable to mass production. The piano, unlike other instruments, was 'the factory's natural prey' (*Men, Women*, p. 233). John Broadwood's son, James, seems to confirm this claim. In 1798, he wrote to a wholesaler anxious for his order to be filled, 'Would to God we could make them like muffins!' (quoted in *Three Hundred Years*, p. 41).

In addition to its situation as a nexus of cultural competition and widening access to taste through mass production processes, the piano also played a pro-active role in directly promoting and enlarging the public sphere. In doing so it was part of the forces that commercialised the public realm. The drive to make the piano an ever-cheaper product to meet a mass market required a commensurate increase in public promotion of the instrument. One of the first means of advertising the virtues of pianos was by putting on public concerts entirely of piano performances. This in turn fostered the production and mass sale of music for the piano, as well as an expanding job market for music teachers. Soon, leading journals began to carry regular reviews of new music, musical clubs were formed and specialist music publications acted, in effect, like mail-order catalogues allowing the public to keep up with all that was new and fashionable in the musical world. This range of activity, spreading horizontally across the public sphere, undoubtedly helped to bring into being an imagined national community of those aspiring to be recognised as bearers of taste and cultivated consumerist life-style. More generally, like the circulation of mail, the circulation of music helped generate and swell a self-identifying national community of 'the people'.

It is not surprising that both Loesser and Parakilas include sections on Jane Austen in their books, as a writer keenly aware of the cultural implications of the instrument. Certainly music features throughout *Emma*. One of Frank Churchill's first questions to Emma is whether Highbury is a musical society (p. 206). In contrast to Frank's enthusiasm, Emma fears that musical events will entail inattention to proper social divisions. Certainly, music is most emphasised by those characters wishing to underpin or enhance their social status. The newly wealthy Coles have purchased a grand pianoforte for display in the drawing room although the expensive instrument is only of use for the daughters' music lessons. Mrs Cole explains that Mr Cole is 'so particularly fond of music that he could not help indulging himself in the purchase' (p. 233). Mrs Cole is also careful to point out that although the piano sent to Jane is 'a very elegant looking instrument it is not a grand' (p. 232). As the price of pianos fell with increased production, competition in display was safeguarded by the ostentatious size and luxury wood and fittings of grand pianos only available to the wealthy.

Mrs Elton, rather like Mr Cole, protests that while her playing is mediocre, 'I am dotingly fond of music – passionately fond; – and my friends say I am not entirely devoid of taste' (p. 298). What is registered here is an elevation of subjective taste over physical performance. For young women, like Jane Fairfax, needing to earn a livelihood as governesses or to sustain claims to gentility as an asset in the marriage market, the ability to play well depended on long hours daily devoted to the physical drudgery of repetitive practice. For the well-to-do, affirmation of passionate appreciation was sufficient to confirm privileged status as superior interiority. Mrs Elton almost claims that music replaces physical needs to sustain her life. 'I do not think I can live without something of a musical society,' she declares, 'without music, life would be a blank for me' (p. 298). In addition to substantiating inner superiority, music provides Mrs Elton, as it did non-fictional middle-class women, with opportunities to gain visibility and influence. Mrs Elton proposes that she and Emma establish a musical club to hold regular weekly meetings (p. 299).

Mrs Elton's challenge to Emma's privileged position extends beyond the sphere of musical activities, however. She asserts the right of patronage. In so doing she threatens the fundamental vertical structure of class power. Emulation in this particular is highly competitive. Emma is loud in her protests against the offensiveness of Mrs Elton's patronising manner, largely because Emma's own patrician identity is given substance by exercising her power for benevolence.[22] Early on in their friendship, Harriet assures Emma that while she finds favour at Hartfield she has no fear of others looking down upon her birth. Emma replies complacently, 'You understand the force of influence pretty well, Harriet' (p. 30). Later, Emma comically boasts that her patronage has had a beneficial influence on Harriet in that she has 'perhaps given her a little more decision of character' (p. 44). She has, of course, completely undermined and confused whatever independence of mind and action Harriet might originally have possessed. When Harriet shows even the most deferential impulse to follow her own inclination towards Robert Martin, the threat of displeasure and penalty, always present in relations of patronage, is quickly revealed. 'It would have grieved me to lose your acquaintance, which must have been the consequence of your marrying Mr Martin [. . .] I could not have visited Mrs Robert Martin, of Abbey-Mill Farm' (p. 56). Harriet is aghast at her narrow escape from exile from favour and rendered more debilitatingly grateful than ever.

The case of Mrs Weston, by contrast, points to the desirability of independence over dependence, even for one so affectionately regarded by those she serves. 'She had lived long enough to know how fortunate she might well be thought [. . .] her [new] situation was altogether the subject of hours of gratitude to [her]' (p. 17). Mr Knightley is of the same opinion: 'I have a great regard for you and Emma,' he tells Mr Woodhouse, but, he asks rhetorically, 'when it comes to the question of dependence or independence!' (p. 9). Mr Woodhouse deplores the changes brought about by the marriage and another way of understanding these changes within the narrative structure would be as a movement away from vertical relations of superiority and subordination towards a less hierarchical social formation in which patronage and dependence are replaced by horizontal interdependence and reciprocal esteem.

It is Mr Knightley who points out the dangers involved for those who exercise influence. It fosters a complacent sense of their own self-sufficiency with a consequent blindness to the actual needs and rights of others. The flattery inherent in any relations of patronage enhances the patroniser's sense of power and omniscience, hence the egoistic dividend it constantly provides in magnifying the idea of self. Harriet is, in this sense, the 'very worst sort of companion' Emma could have, Mr Knightley complains, 'She is a flatterer in all her ways [. . .] How can Emma imagine she has anything to learn herself, while Harriet is presenting such delightful inferiority?' (p. 39). Emma does indeed boast, 'I cannot change for the better.'

The Woodhouses are 'first in consequence' in their community due to birthright.[23] They represent neither new money nor new blood, Emma takes pride in thinking. What infuriates Emma is that Mrs Elton utterly refuses to give place or recognition to the old hierarchy of rank upon which Emma relies. 'I am Lady Patroness, you know. It is my party', Mrs Elton informs Mr Knightley in regard to the strawberry-gathering at Donwell (p. 385). She graciously bestows her favour upon Mr Woodhouse, this 'dear old beau of mine', and Mrs Weston, 'I was rather astonished to find her so very lady-like! But she is really quite the gentlewoman' (pp. 326, 300). By thus sweeping everyone in Highbury into her condescending bestowal of recognition, she magnifies her own imagined idea of self as measured by the extent of her social dominion. Mrs Elton is one of those many characters in Austen's fiction whose representation seems strikingly to dramatise self as factitious; yet it is a performance driven by embodied needs and passions. Mrs Elton's discourse resembles a torrent of egoistic energy that sweeps all topics into the vortex of her sense of self-importance. Hartfield becomes only a copy of Maple Grove, the distance from Enscombe in Yorkshire to London only a means of comparison for the distance of Maple Grove to the capital. Her speech might be understood as a discursive caricature of the new, unstoppable, highly audible force of individualistic ambition.

The humiliation inflicted upon those who are in no position to resist patronage is most graphically demonstrated in Mrs Elton's officious assumption of the right to take control of Jane Fairfax's life, to promote her social visibility. Soon after her arrival in Highbury, she tells Emma grandly, 'my resolution is taken as to noticing Jane Fairfax [. . .] [I] shall introduce her wherever I can, shall have musical parties to draw out her talents' (p. 306). Although Emma would have been loath to recognise it, there are ironic parallels here with her own objectification of Harriet. Her resolution on first meeting Harriet is, '*She* would notice her; she would improve her' (p. 23). Mrs Elton is also like Emma in her sweeping assumption that Olympian elevation over others affords her a privileged perspective into their characters. 'I know what a modest creature you are', she informs Jane Fairfax (p. 325). She reassures Mr Knightley, 'Indeed I do you justice my good friend. Under that peculiar sort of dry, blunt manner, I know you have the warmest heart. As I tell Mr E., you are a thorough humourist' (p. 387).

Emma's trajectory from the idealist exclusivity of Hartfield towards a more integrated mode of social interaction requires a rejection of her sense of interiority as location of privileged knowledge, authorising the right to speak and decide for others. This process is narrated as a movement from the vertical hierarchies of place to the horizontal motility of space, from metaphor to metonymy, and from subjective idealism to social being. Emma is first impelled beyond the social exclusivity of Hartfield by an invitation from the Coles to admire the new pianoforte. After much hesitation she is forced to recognise that her former 'dignified seclusion' no longer compensates for the denial of social interchange, even if some of those contacts are vulgar. She agrees to dine with a large socially mixed party of Highbury folk at the Coles, although she still condones this to herself in terms of patronage: 'She must have delighted the Coles – worthy people, who deserved to be made happy' (p. 249). From this point her shift of orientation towards Highbury continues until her brother-in-law, John Knightley, can point out, 'There can be no doubt of your being much more engaged with company than you used to be [. . .] Your neighbourhood is increasing, and you mix more with it' (p. 337). Through this expansion beyond the boundaries of Hartfield, Emma slowly learns to move beyond her solipsistic complacency, exchanging a vertical perspective on others for a horizontal ability to enter into viewpoints that differ from her own and to accord them validity. Her extended recognition dramatises a redistribution of the perceptible.

This entails a radical transformation. When Mr John Knightley perceptively warns her of Elton's romantic interest in her, Emma laughs to herself at his mistake in terms which are much more applicable to herself: 'She walked on, amusing herself in the consideration of the blunders which often arise from a partial knowledge of circumstances, of mistakes which people of high pretensions to judgement are for ever falling into' (pp. 120–1). With such comical self-certainty, it takes considerable time and some painful experience before she is able to recognise the narrow partiality of her own construct of reality. She is reluctantly forced to concede that from Mr Elton's perspective a very different notion of truth might have seemed reasonable. 'Emma was obliged in common honesty to stop and admit that her own behaviour to him had been so complaisant and obliging [. . .] if *she* had so misinterpreted his feelings, she had little right to wonder that *he*, with self-interest to blind him, should have mistaken hers' (pp. 147–8). What Emma begins to move towards here is a shift into the perspective of others, as advocated by Adam Smith (*TMS*, p. 157). For Smith, it is this capacity for extended consciousness that promotes and sustains a just and humane community.

Throughout the story, Harriet is the recurrent victim of Emma's delusions of Olympian knowledge of others. The final catastrophe is when she again imposes her own perspective upon Harriet's mind and mistakenly gives approval to Harriet's inclinations for Mr Knightley. It is this final shock to her sense of self-security that drives home to Emma the harmful folly of presuming the right to know and direct the lives of others. 'With insufferable vanity had she believed herself in the secrets of everybody's feelings; with unpardonable arrogance proposed to arrange everybody's destiny [. . .] She was proved to have been universally mistaken' (p. 449).

For much of the novel, Miss Bates forms a striking contrast with Emma's patrician self-sufficiency. For Miss Bates, no-one is beyond or beneath the range of her sympathetic recognition. Her being is almost wholly social, a continuous metonymic flow from self to others. Her unstoppable discourse is sometimes likened to that of Mrs Elton but, in fact, it represents the opposite pole from egoistic self-assertion. Miss Bates's speech is largely responsible for the narrative constitution of the imagined community of Highbury; it teems with the presence of others. 'I do not care for myself', she declares at the beginning of one of those voluble outflows that moves without pause from Jane, to Mrs Weston, to Mrs Stokes, to Mr Woodhouse, to Mr Dixon and Colonel Campbell and so on (p. 348). If Mrs

Elton's speech represents the acquisitive centripetal energy of individualism, Miss Bates's discourse represents the centrifugal force of social being. Austen's representation of Miss Bates gives audibility to those who are indeed part of the national community but who are unheard and unseen within the privileged consensus of who constitutes England.

She goes further than this. Miss Bates becomes the agency by which Emma begins to radically adjust her vertical system of values towards a perception of egalitarian mutual esteem. Miss Bates, a woman without money, status, husband, beauty or youth becomes an active determinant upon the course of Emma's privileged life. On Box Hill, Emma thoughtlessly sacrifices Miss Bates's feelings for the sake of exhibiting her own wit. As Mr Knightley insists, just for 'the pride of the moment', Miss Bates is humiliated in front of her friends (p. 408). The truth of this accusation strikes home. Emma 'felt it at her heart. How could she have been so brutal, so cruel to Miss Bates!' (p. 409). The starkly physical language registers embodied shock as Emma takes in the inhumanity of her conduct. Her enclosure within an imaginary realm of self-complacency is shattered. Miss Bates had, up to then, no tangible presence for her. Social distinction, like Emma's, does not lead to shared consciousness of others as fellow beings; rather it renders others imperceptible, of no consequence. In Adam Smith's words Emma has to accept that she is 'but one of the multitude and in no respect better than any other in it' (*TMS*, p. 158). When the consequence of her brutality is brought home to her, Emma commits herself to a complete transformation of attitude: 'it should be the beginning, on her side, of a regular, *equal*, kindly intercourse' (p. 410, emphasis added).

Robert Martin is the other character whom Emma regards as existing beneath the level of the perceptible. Ironically, he, too, like Miss Bates, measures the transformation of Emma's viewpoint from vertical distance to horizontal respect. When Harriet first mentions Robert Martin, Emma's dismissal of him is unequivocal, 'A young farmer [. . .] is the very last sort of person to raise my curiosity,' she says haughtily, 'The yeomanry are precisely the order of people with whom I feel I can have nothing to do [. . .] a farmer can need none of my help, and is therefore in one sense as much above my notice as in every other he is below it' (p. 29). At this point in the story, Emma can only envisage social relations in terms of bestowing patronage. Her use of the already somewhat old-fashioned term 'yeomanry' also suggests the backward-looking perspective she is adhering to. It echoes the perspective of those nostalgic for a mythical 'old England'.

Emma's enforced further considerations of Robert Martin serve in the text to challenge conservative opinion as to what constitutes a gentleman and claims to gentility. Austen's representation engages actively with current debates in the public sphere as to who constitutes 'the people' of a modern nation. It was a conflict between two regimes of the perceptible, the one structured upon a traditional vertical order and the other on an emergent possibility of social inclusion. Robert Martin represents the growing, heterogeneous public realm of the literate and informed. Indeed, Emma's class prejudices are most strongly challenged by the articulacy of Robert Martin's letter proposing marriage to Harriet. Emma is compelled to recognise that it is a composition that 'would not have disgraced a gentleman', grammatically correct, using strong, unaffected language and expressing 'good sense, warm attachment, liberality, propriety, even delicacy of feeling' (p. 53). Faced with such unimpeachable material evidence of admirable human qualities, Emma uneasily admits surprise. She quickly reasserts her superiority, however, through the assumption of knowledge, 'Yes, I understand the sort of mind' (p. 53). Soon she is happy to ignore the physical substance of the letter. She reverts to her mental preconception, reconsigning Robert Martin to those who can be dismissed from visibility and audibility as 'the society of the illiterate and vulgar' (p. 56). The stark contradictions within Emma's judgements here are further foregrounded by the subsequent ill-natured and affected behaviour of Mr Elton, whom she has been holding up to Harriet as the gentlemanly model against whom Robert Martin must be found wanting.

Mr Knightley's consistent praise for Robert Martin also sustains the text's questioning of what is meant by 'gentleman' and 'gentility' within a changing social order. When Emma insists that Harriet 'knows what gentlemen are' and will not be satisfied with less, Mr Knightley retorts, 'Robert Martin's manners have sense, sincerity and good-humour to recommend them; and his mind has more true gentility than Harriet Smith could understand!' (p. 69). In contrast to Emma's snobbish rigidity in asserting she can have no curiosity about Robert Martin since she can be of no use to him, Mr Knightley communicates with him as a friend. What is more, he overthrows the relations of patronage by readily admitting his dependence upon Martin's good sense (p. 516). The complete transformation of Emma's view of social possibilities is confirmed in her acknowledgement that 'It would be a great pleasure to know Robert Martin' (p. 519). Knowledge of others, she recognises, at last, does not reside in the Olympic perspective conferred by privileged place, but arises out of the horizontal processes of non-hierarchical social interaction in a space of possibility.

It needs to be stated that while the narrative structure of *Emma* points to the possibility of a new inclusive representative regime of who constitutes the nation, it in no way contemplates a redistribution of wealth or property. Sandie Byrne rightly points out that despite Austen's depiction of a 'mobile and consumerist society [. . .] Robert Martin is not invited to the Donwell strawberry-picking [. . .] anymore than he is to the ball or the Box Hill expedition'.[24] Of course, the fact that he is a busy working farmer would deny him the leisure for the first and last of these events. What the novel seems to advocate is a shift of recognition from the rules of vertical exclusion to a more horizontal and egalitarian engagement with the perspectives of a wider social interaction. In advocating this new regime of perceptibility, Austen engages dialogically in the more progressive, inclusive discourse of 'the people' and 'the public' of the post-Revolutionary era. Like them, she welcomes the prospect of the nation as a less hierarchical community, a view of social interaction at odds with an idealist version of 'old England'. The several references in *Emma* to England and Englishness are striking. Yet while Austen joins in the criticism of rank and patronage, as expressed by liberal journals like the *Edinburgh Review*, she saves her harshest satire for the new force of competitive individualism, as exemplified by Mrs Elton. As against both exclusivity of birth and the aggressive dominance of self-interest, Austen holds out the possibility or prospect of horizontal social interaction as a basis of self and of England. What is more, the vehicle of this radical transformation is a young woman, Emma.

The novel is set in motion by a marriage and it concludes with one. Since marriage instigates change it is reasonable to ask what kind of values will be inaugurated in the union of Emma and Mr Knightley. Claudia Johnson argues persuasively that Mr Knightley represents a modern, business-like, untraditional hero; that he is 'in some respects a new man'.[25] Yet, some readers and critics have been uneasy about Emma's apparent capitulation into wifely domesticity at the conclusion of the story. Emma certainly expresses deep humiliation at her conduct and acknowledges the superiority of Knightley's judgement in regard to Robert Martin, yet her sense of the ridiculous cannot sustain prolonged moral penitence, 'there was no preventing a laugh' (p. 519). Similarly to Woolf, laughter, for Austen, is a radical force against presumption and power. Indeed, the strongest bond between Emma and Knightley resides in their egalitarian willingness to tease and challenge each other. 'Do you dare suppose me so great a blockhead,' Knightley cries with mock masculine outrage, 'What do you deserve?' Emma's reply, 'Oh! I always deserve the best treatment because I never put up with any other' does not suggest a wife willing to subordinate herself (p. 517). This point is underlined more seriously by the narrator's comment that Mrs John Knightley's 'extreme sweetness of temper must hurt his' (p. 100).

Emma's readiness to argue for her opinions and point of view ensures no such dominance of one perspective over the other's. After a typical conflict of views, Knightley says, 'let us be friends', a word denoting equality of respect (p. 106). The contrast with her sister's and John Knightley's mode of marriage also suggests that domestic privacy will not be the ideological ethos of Emma's and Knightley's partnership. The narrative is at pains to represent Knightley as more sociable and communicative than his brother, John, and while her brother-in-law's self-sufficient attachment to home at the expense of sociability is awarded respect by Emma, she is luke-warm in her approbation (p. 104). This suggests she and Knightley will inhabit a location that has more of the openness of a space than the vertical proprieties of a private, domestic place. The marriage, after all, locates change at the very heart of Hartfield.

Perhaps the national 'prospect' represented by the union of Emma and Knightley is figured imaginatively in the moment of shared vision (of both sight and thought) when Emma comes across Mr Knightley teaching Harriet about agricultural matters (surely a challenge to gender divisions) at the end of the lime avenue at Donwell overlooking Abbey-Mill Farm: 'It was a sweet view – sweet to the eye and the mind. English verdure, English culture, English comfort, seen under a sun bright, without being oppressive' (p. 391). It is 'a sweet view' of a horizontal prospect of the nation, bringing together Harriet of illegitimate birth, Robert Martin, tenant farmer, Knightley, landed-proprietor, and Emma of ancient stock. It is a scene in which oppression is absent, one uniting the needs of eye and mind, the physical equally with the mental, and associated with Emma's and Knightley's good-humoured tolerance of their differences of perspective.

It is, though, a mental prospect or idea of the nation only, without material evidence to substantiate it. It shimmers as a possibility, a vision. It is significant, perhaps, that almost the last word in the novel is awarded to Mrs Elton as voice of the new force of individualistic competitive consumption: 'Very little white satin, very few lace veils; a most pitiful business! Selina would stare when she heard of it' (p. 528).

Notes

1. Roger Sales, *Jane Austen and Representations of Regency England*, p. 17.
2. Edmund Burke, *Reflections on the Revolution in France*, p. 135.
3. Richard Bourke, *Empire and Revolution: The Political Life of Edmund Burke* offers a detailed account of Burke's influence upon conservative ideology.
4. *Edinburgh Review*, 1814, vol. 23, p. 2. Napoleon abdicated in April 1814 following the decisive invasion of Paris and capitulation of its leaders to the Coalition powers. He was exiled to Elba, from where he escaped in March 1815. In June 1815, he was conclusively defeated by the combined armies of Prussia and Britain, commanded by the Duke of Wellington.
5. Jane Austen, *Emma*, p. 460.
6. *Gentleman's Magazine*, 1814, vol. 84, p. 131.
7. Ibid., p. 30.
8. *Gentleman's Magazine*, 1808, vol. 78, p. 406.
9. Richard Price, *British Society 1680–1880: Dynamism, Containment and Change*, pp. 261, 262.
10. Jacques Rancière, 'Ten Theses on Politics', in *Dissensus: On Politics and Aesthetics*, pp. 1–2.
11. *Edinburgh Review*, 1814, vol. 22, p. 29.
12. *Monthly Review*, 1813, vol. 70, p. 60. In 1801, William Pitt had been forced to resign when he was unable to enact an emancipation bill due to the opposition of George III. The topic continued to arouse passionate public debate even though a bill was not passed until 1829.
13. *Monthly Review*, 1814, vol. 73, p. 291.
14. *Edinburgh Review*, 1814, vol. 22, pp. 416–34.
15. See, for example, *Gentleman's Magazine*, 1812, vol. 82, pp. 80, 85, 285, 479–80, 483.
16. *Gentleman's Magazine*, 1811, vol. 8, p. 502.
17. Michel de Certeau, *The Practice of Everyday Life*, p. 117.
18. Adam Smith, *Theory of Moral Sentiment*, p. 275.
19. Bruno Latour, 'Why has Critique Run out of Steam: From Matters of Fact to Matters of Concern', in Bill Brown, ed., *Things*, p. 158.
20. Arthur Loesser, *Men, Women and Pianos: A Social History*, p. 187.
21. James Parakilas et al., *Piano Roles: Three Hundred Years of Life with the Piano*, p. 13.
22. William Galperin, *The Historical Austen*, also notes the aspirational similarities between Emma and Mrs Elton, but he argues that while those of the latter typify a utopian nostalgia, Emma moves from an early longing for a possibilist world to an acceptance of the regulatory nostalgia of domestic ideology.

23. Janine Barchas, *Matters of Fact in Jane Austen: History, Location and Celebrity*, argues that Austen's recurrent use of names, like Emma Woodhouse, belonging to actual people from the ranks of the nobility, often of some notoriety, is deliberate; if this is the case, it would add another layer of irony to the representation of Emma's transition from the snobbery of rank to a more egalitarian sense of social being, pp. 3–4, 225.
24. Sandie Byrne, *Jane Austen's Possessions and Dispossessions: The Significance of Objects*, p. 117.
25. Claudia Johnson, *Equivocal Beings*, p. 201.

Chapter 4

The Waves: Blasphemy of Laughter and Criticism

The Waves (1931) is widely acknowledged as Woolf's most ambitious and achieved modernist work.[1] Woolf herself appears to underwrite the critical consensus as to its radical break with past conventions, most notably realism. In her diary entry, setting out her aims for the new novel, she writes, 'I mean to eliminate all waste, deadness, superfluity [. . .] this appalling narrative business of the realist: getting from lunch to dinner: it is false, unreal, merely conventional.'[2] The impression that, in *The Waves*, Woolf is relentlessly excluding the social and material in order to focus upon the subjective and spiritual realms of experience is strengthened by further comments in her diary as to the novel's genesis. Her remarks are undeniably couched in what seems the language of idealist interiority. She writes, on 28 September 1926, of experiencing, while at Rodmell, an introspective, melancholy mood that she recognises as the intimation of a new novel. The solitude of Rodmell, she says, allowed expansion of 'this odd immeasurable soul' so that 'one goes down into the well and nothing protects one from the assault of truth' (*Diary*, 3.112). A month later, she notes in her diary that the new work is to be a 'dramatisation of my mood at Rodmell. It is to be an endeavour at something mystic, spiritual; the thing that exists when we aren't there' (*Diary*, 3.114). And yet this 'thing' that exists in our absence is not otherworldly or immaterial. Adding some remarks 'on the mystical side of this solitude', she concludes, 'it is not oneself but something in the universe that one's left with' (*Diary*, 3.113).

The bypassing of self and focus upon the physical universe here is crucial. *The Waves* is, indeed, a supremely ambitious work. Stylistically and thematically, Woolf moves radically beyond both individualist psychological realism and actualist social realism. Her aim is to produce a comprehensive materialist vision of existence. It is a vision that bases understanding of human life upon the fact of self as embodied and thus in metonymic continuity with the vast scale and duration of the physical world. This worldly realism produces a new egalitarian regime of the perceptible. The language of *The Waves* ranges horizontally and inclusively from the motility of atoms, nerves and fibres to the movement of tides and solar system. Politically, this practice of worldly realism launches a comprehensive attack upon all the sacred tenets of idealist ideology. In *Mrs Dalloway*, Woolf indicts the collaboration of idealist modes of thought with the working of the social and political system 'at its most intense' (*Diary*, 2.248). In *The Waves*, she turns her attention to the complicity of idealist views of culture with structures of power and inequality. She attacks the culture system at its most intense. In *Mrs Dalloway*, the heterogeneity of life that Clarissa Dalloway celebrates in the space of London streets is threatened by an authoritarian desire for discipline and regularity. In *The Waves*, the imposition of a vision of authoritarian conformity looks to globalised technology as a means of conscripting universal space into its own regulated order.

Two events during the time Woolf was thinking about and writing *The Waves* would have intensified her concern with the cultural and political threat of idealism, reminding her, if that were necessary, of the perils of vision not challenged by fact. In 1927, following his death, a second edition of F. H. Bradley's *Ethical Studies* was published and in 1928, Clive Bell published *Civilization: An Essay*, with a dedication to 'Dearest Virginia'. In his preliminary address to Woolf, Bell recalls their early friendship in the pre-war days when 'we were mostly socialists' and before he had considerably modified those youthful ideas.[3] Certainly there is little of socialism or even of egalitarianism in the 1928 essay, but Bell's understanding of 'civilization' and 'culture', as expressed in that work, shares much common ground with Bradley's idealism. Both texts are imbued with what Woolf, in *Mrs Dalloway*, understands as 'the spirit of religion', the urge to venerate an immaterial ideal at the expense of bodily life. Both Bradley and Bell subscribe to a regime of the perceptible as a vertical order, regulating who and what counts as worthy of notice and what is other and undistinguished within the nation and beyond. In subjecting the values and institutions they revere to the blasphemy of laughter and criticism in *The Waves*, Woolf expands the scope of her critique of idealist structures of thought to encompass global and scientific forces well beyond the elitist mental worlds of those like Bell and Bradley.

Both Bell and Bradley elevate an intensely individualistic notion of self. For each, the only purpose of human existence is spiritual and intellectual self-realisation.[4] For Bell the aim is 'complete self-development and complete self-expression' (p. 98). Bradley writes, 'the end and the standard is self-realization'.[5] Drawing upon the tradition of Edmund Burke, Bradley sees self-fulfilment solely in terms of a conscious, intellectual and spiritual identification with the 'soul' of the nation as inhering in its culture, social order, laws and institutions. 'But the child is not merely the member of a family,' he declares, 'he is born a member of the English nation' (*Ethical Studies*, p. 169). This willed identification of self with an ideal of the nation entails acceptance of the duties that inhere in the station in life into which one is born. The religious reverence inculcated in the self's identification with the nation as a vision of the Good entails within it the logic of sacrifice. Bradley writes, the heart of the nation, 'rise[s] high and beat[s] in the breast of each one of her citizens, till her safety and her honour are dearer to each than life [. . .] and death seems a little thing to those that go for her to their common and nameless graves' (*Ethical Studies*, p. 184). This total merging of self with nation even resolves the apparent antithesis between despotism and individualism, Bradley claims. 'The truth of despotism is saved, because, unless the member realises the whole [nation] by and in himself, he fails to reach his own individuality' (*Ethical Studies*, p. 188).

Certainly Clive Bell cannot be accused of chauvinistic glorification of the state. 'Nationalism is a terrible enemy to civility', he claims (*Civilization*, p. 109). His focus upon civilisation rather than nation as the location of self-realisation seems to comprehend a more expansive view of human achievement. Yet this turns out not to be the case. Bell's definition of civilisation constitutes a more highly individualistic focus upon interiority at the expense of the material world even than Bradley's. It is also entirely Eurocentric. Like idealists generally, Bell sees education as the primary means of fostering the perfection of the inner life. Indeed, education is the gateway to inner nobility, but Bell's view of education invokes no sense of wider national life. 'Civilized people', he asserts, value knowledge 'as a means to exquisite spiritual states' of mind (*Civilization*, p. 92). 'Without education [. . .] [there is wanting] the key to the inner palace of pleasures' (*Civilization*, pp. 170–1). Given this exclusive focus upon interiority it is not surprising that his ideal of civilisation encompasses only the mental realm of those with access to an elite, public school, classical education. No aspect of the material world attaches to Bell's view of a civilised national community. 'Civilization', he writes, 'is the flavour given to the self-expression of an age or a society by a mental attitude; it is the colour given to social manifestations by a peculiar and prevailing point of view. Whence comes this colouring view of life [. . .]? From individuals of course' (*Civilization*, p. 165). A civilised society, therefore, depends upon the existence of a group of highly cultivated individual people of sufficient influence and number 'to affect larger groups and ultimately whole communities' (*Civilization*, p. 166).

A state 'may be held to have become highly civilized', Bell claims, 'when an appreciable part of the mass, though barbarous enough [. . .] has yet absorbed a tincture of the precious dye' (*Civilization*, p. 191). This absorption of mental values by the community at large does not imply any progress towards political, social or economic equality, however. The need to provide for material wants is wholly inimical to the development of highly civilised minds. The poor, 'so long as to be poor means to be unfree and uneducated, are concerned actively with civilization only in so far as by their labours they make it possible' (*Civilization*, p. 71). A civilised society, Bell maintains, requires a leisured class and 'a leisured class requires the existence of a class of slaves' or, more preferably 'willing servants [. . .] people content to make sacrifices for an ideal' (*Civilization*, p. 205). For that reason, he argues, democracy and civilisation are incompatible: 'There has never been a civilized democracy', he declares (*Civilization*, p. 220). Moreover, he suggests, sweetness and light have certainly 'radiated from the courts of tyrants and usurpers' (*Civilization*, p. 226). In the present age, the example of Mussolini and Lenin may well spread across the world, Bell says, 'And I do not know that civilization stands in the long run to lose by the change' (*Civilization*, p. 224).

Bell's gender politics are no more democratic than his class sympathies. In the perceptible cultured community as he constitutes it, women are as mute and invisible as workers. In the highly civilised society of fifth and fourth century Athens, Bell notes, the only roles available to women were that of wife and mother or of *hetaerae*. Among the latter, most were common prostitutes, but a privileged few were cultivated enough to become companions and mistresses of highly civilised Athenians (*Civilization*, pp. 234–5). Bell implies that for present day British women the options are even more limited; 'they must become either wives or old maids' (*Civilization*, p. 236). For the former, once she is mistress of a house and mother of children, it is difficult for her to 'keep her place in the first flight' (*Civilization*, p. 237). Spinsterhood leads to an even worse fate. 'The peculiar intelligence and sensibility of youth fade [. . .] her understanding shrinks [. . .] I sometimes wonder whether an old maid is fit for anything less than the kingdom of heaven' (*Civilization*, p. 238). The actual importance that Bell attaches to women's role in fostering a civilised nation is indicated in the mere eight pages he devotes to the subject, clearly as an afterthought at the end of his essay.

Even if Woolf did not read the second edition of Bradley's *Ethical Studies* when it was published in 1927, she would have been familiar with its ideas and teaching since these were widely discussed and dispersed throughout the intellectual and political domains. She most certainly read Clive Bell's *Civilization*, which Leonard Woolf dismissed as 'very superficial' (*Diary*, 3.184). *The Waves* constitutes a 'blasphemous' rebuttal, by means of criticism and ironic laughter, of the idealist glorification of self as cultured interiority and of a Burkean nation as revered tradition and guarantor of civilisation. Woolf overturns the vertical hierarchy of spirit over matter and thereby challenges the myths of individualism, interiority and spirituality that are sustained by it. *The Waves* insists upon the materiality not the spirituality of the self. No other novel can be so crammed full of descriptions of bodily sensation. Other novelists may well deal in more graphic detail with bodily excretions, tortured flesh and visceral experiences. Yet in most cases these details are significant in terms of the individual character to whom they happen and are more usually represented as part of extreme events and heightened moments within the narrative. In *The Waves*, the focus upon embodied matter is much more impersonal and is represented as the norm of life, not the exception; it is there for its own sake as part of the continuum of physical existence.

Whereas idealists, like Bell, impute value to human life only in so far as it attains 'exquisite states of mind', Bernard, in *The Waves*, recognises that we are all 'undifferentiated blobs of matter'.[6] Instead of a vertical social order, this wholly unelevated view of human existence contributes to the novel's emphasis upon the communality of the body, as Gillian Beer points out.[7] As in *Mrs Dalloway*, interiority is often experienced by the characters in *The Waves* not as private thought but as shared consciousness, as a metonymic movement through different perspectives. Poetry and culture, more generally, are shown, in *The Waves*, to depend upon the here and now of the common life of bio-social being. While education is valued by idealists as the primary means of transmitting civilised mental being, Woolf recognises it as a mechanism that conscripts the body into subjection. 'Civilisation' is depicted as a euphemistic abstraction that spins an idealised veil over the imposition of coercive material practices and structures. Woolf's own vision wholly lacks the nostalgia and religiosity that typify both Bradley's and Bell's imagining of ideal or civilised national communities. It is a perspective she shares with Leonard Woolf: a futuristic recognition of the development of technological, global capitalism, the ultimate system of abstract macro idealism, and one capable of conscripting global space into the hierarchical order of a place.

Finally, through the ambitious scale of her novel, Woolf challenges limited views, like Bell's, of women's potential within the world of culture and the public sphere. In defiance of canonical tradition, Woolf sets out to discover a new empirical poetics. Her aim is to articulate a celebratory vision of the immensity and power of the universe that contains human life. Yet it will be a vision stripped bare of idealist religiosity and consolation. Woolf explores this ambition for a new artistic distribution of the perceptible in a series of essays written while she was preoccupied with *The Waves*. In all of these essays she calls for a rejection of the vertical hierarchy of novelistic form that lavishes attention on psychological individuality and a shift, instead, towards a wider, horizontal vision of human existence, as a continuity with the physical universe. Clearly there is a risk here of simply displacing subjective idealism with the macro idealism of universalism. In her essays Woolf counters this danger by insisting that the moment of comprehensive vision can only arise in the here and now of lived experience, that vision and fact must co-exist.

In her essay 'The Cinema' (1926), for example, she writes that the estranging effect of cinema which allows us to behold events 'as they are when we are not there' produces a more comprehensive vision of existence, the ability 'to generalise, to endow one man with the attributes of a race'.[8] Yet this process of abstraction must be continually dissolved in the motility of actual existence in the here and now. 'We get intimations', she writes, 'only in the chaos of the streets, perhaps, when some momentary assembly of colour, sound, movement, suggests that here is a scene waiting a new art to be transfixed' (*Essays*, 4.595).

In 'Poetry, Fiction and the Future' (1927), Woolf again expresses the need to encompass the immediacy of actuality within a generalising vision. She praises Shakespeare's ability to move without a hitch 'from philosophy to a drunken brawl; from love songs to an argument; from simple merriment to profound speculation' (*Essays*, 4.431). She argues that the novel will evolve to comprehend both particularity and 'the wide, general ideas which civilization teaches'

(*Essays*, 4.434). This new form will focus very little upon individualising details of 'the houses, incomes, occupations of its characters [. . .] but [instead] it will give the relation of the mind to general ideas' (Essays, 4.435). Yet this philosophical vision derives from immersion in the material world. The 'democratic art of prose' is 'so humble that it can go anywhere; no place is too low, too sordid, or too mean [. . .] It can lick up with its long glutinous tongue the most minute fragments of fact and mass them into the most subtle labyrinths' (*Essays*, 4.436). It is from facts that the vision evolves.

In 'Women and Fiction' (1929) Woolf again argues that the new novel 'will cease to be the dumping ground for personal emotions' (*Essays*, 5.34–5). It will observe men and women 'as they cohere and clash in groups and classes and races'. Future women writers 'will look beyond the personal [. . .] to the wider questions [. . .] of our destiny and the meaning of life' (*Essays*, 5.34). In the extended version of this essay, given as a lecture at Girton and published as *A Room of One's Own* (1929), Woolf chooses to end with a ringing rejection of individualism and the limited perspective this ideology imposes upon any art that embraces it. 'I am talking', she says, 'of the common life which is the real life and not the little separate lives we live as individuals [. . .] we [shall] escape a little from the common sitting-room and see human beings not always in their relation to each other but in relation to reality; and the sky, too, and the trees.'[9]

There is no doubt that Woolf was personally preoccupied, during the period in which she was writing *The Waves*, with the nature of the physical universe and of the relationship of human life to that immensity. She recounts an intense experience that occurred one evening in February 1926, as she walked through Russell Square. She evokes a metonymic movement beyond the individuality of self out to the vastness of the physical world: 'I see the mountains in the sky: the great clouds; and the moon which is risen over Persia; I have a great and astonishing sense of something there, which is "it"' (*Diary*, 3.62). With this recognition of immensity comes also a sense 'of my own strangeness, walking on the earth [. . .] of the infinite oddity of the human position'. Two years later, she describes a similar experience that begins with a feeling of loneliness and terror in which she 'got then to a consciousness of what I call "reality" [. . .] something abstract; but residing in the downs or sky' (*Diary*, 3.196). It would seem that this intense experience of the infinitesimal compass of a single human life in the scale of the life of the universe is what urges her shift of focus from the individual to human kind generally.

She writes, 'How little one counts, I think: how little anyone counts; how fast and furious and masterly life is; and how all these thousands are swimming for dear life' (*Diary*, 3.201). A vision of transient human life as metonymically part of the continuity of universal life offers a compassionate transcendence that is rooted in materiality rather than idealism. 'It may be', she suggests, 'that though we change; one flying after another, so quick so quick, yet we are somehow successive, and continuous – we human beings' (*Diary*, 3.218).

Woolf recognises these experiences as in some sense metaphysical. This is the term also used by Peter Walsh, in *Mrs Dalloway*, to describe Clarissa's sense of self as extended out into the wider world. Yet Peter also concedes that Clarissa Dalloway is 'one of the most thoroughgoing sceptics he had ever met' (*Mrs Dalloway*, p. 66). The language Woolf uses to recount her intense sense of connection to the larger universe evokes that of another determinedly anti-religious poetic sceptic: Lucretius. His poem, *De Rerum Natura*, was long regarded as the most dangerously blasphemous work of the classical writers. It is indicative of the high claim Woolf is implicitly making, contra Bell, for the role of women within cultural life that *The Waves* is a palimpsest of *De Rerum Natura* and of Shelley's unfinished poem, *The Triumph of Life*. Her choice equally declares the antipathetic position to the 'great tradition' she is occupying. Shelley, like Lucretius, is notoriously at odds with established authority.

All three 'blasphemous' texts open with a powerful poetic invocation to a totally non-spiritual, natural creative force, the engendering light of the rising sun. Throughout *The Waves* there are echoes of imagery from *The Triumph of Life*, especially in the words of Rhoda. Yet the primary importance of Shelley for Woolf's ambition in *The Waves* is that he unites poetic vision to worldly politics. Indeed, as Harold Bloom points out, Shelley shares the same philosophical heritage as Woolf. 'Shelley', Bloom claims, 'is the most Humean poet in the language [. . .] and it is Hume, not Berkeley or Plato, whose view of reality informs *Prometheus Unbound* and poems that came after.'[10] In *The Triumph of Life* only the figures of Aristotle and Bacon among the great and famous of the world appear uncorrupted by false beliefs and illusions of power. Both are usually regarded as the originators of empirical materialism. The poem contrasts the grotesque triumphal procession of life with interludes of dream-like platonic vision but implies that both dystopic and idealist perspectives are illusionary. In *The Waves*, each of the six main characters describes the life in city streets as a procession. Woolf uses the discrepancy between these views of 'reality' to point to the subjective screen habitually imposed upon the empirical world by subjective mental values and attitudes. So Jinny declares, 'This is the triumphant procession; this is the army of victory' (p. 161). Rhoda, however, contemplates the scene with revulsion, 'This is Oxford Street. Here are hate, jealousy, hurry and indifference frothed into the wild semblance of life' (p. 132).

Not only does Lucretius open *De Rerum Natura* with an image of the sun as source of life, like Woolf, he associates this creative force with a female image rather than a masculine solar deity. Throughout the poem, Lucretius' language, like Woolf's, foregrounds power and movement. The rising sun, Lucretius writes, will 'envelop and flood the whole world with [. . .] light [. . .] and [its heat] beats its way, so to speak, through waves of air'.[11] Lucretius' poetic imagination, like Woolf's, is particularly responsive to vast skyscapes of 'great caverns' and immense clouds 'swimming through the air' (*DRN*, pp. 513, 291). There is, in the language of both, a sense of the plenitude of the physical universe. Woolf even seems to have transplanted the description Neville gives of boyish comradeship lying in the long grass watching cricket straight from *De Rerum Natura* where Lucretius enthuses on the simple delight arising 'when stretched forth in groups upon the soft grass beside a rill of water under the branches of a tall tree men merrily refresh themselves at no great cost, especially when the weather smiles' (*DRN*, p. 97).

Like Shelley (whose poem is also a palimpsest of *De Rerum Natura*) and like Woolf, Lucretius fuses celebration of physical life with political critique. His passionate aim in writing the work was his desire to free human beings from the fetters of false belief in otherworldly powers by expounding the Epicurean materialist philosophy of the universe. At present, Lucretius writes, human life lies 'foully grovelling upon the ground, crushed beneath the weight of Superstition' (*DRN*, pp. 7–9). The abject fear spawned by thought of non-existent powers and deities is cause of most of the greed, cruelty, ambitions and wars that curse human existence, Lucretius claims. He points specifically to idealism and its imposition of subjective mental visions upon the object world. 'We see in marvellous fashion', he writes, 'many things [. . .] which all try as it were to break the credit of our senses' (*DRN*, p. 313). They deceive us 'because of opinions of the mind which we bring to them ourselves' (*DRN*, p. 313). Lucretius' arguments against idealism, along with his atomic theory of matter, in which chance collisions 'heedless, without aim, without intention', produce the entire universe had renewed relevance for Woolf's generation in the wake of Einstein's atomic theory (*DRN*, p. 177). In 1918, for example, H. Woods published a defence of materialism with the Lucretian title *On the Nature of Things*.[12]

What most outraged religious authority through the ages was Lucretius' insistence upon the materiality of the soul. The mind, he says, 'which we often call the intelligence [. . .] is part of man, no less than hands and feet and eyes are parts of the whole living being' (*DRN*, p. 195). Lucretius declares that only by means of the conjoined physical existence of body and mind is sensation and feeling possible (*DRN*, p. 213). Since both are material, both are mortal (*DRN*, p. 221). Woolf, too, attacks any spiritualised view of human life and subjectivity. Throughout *The Waves*, there is repeated focus upon the material basis of sensation and feelings. Subjective emotions and responses, normally taken as indication and guarantee of the uniqueness of individual sensibility or soul, are located in the corporeal system. Bernard comments on the feeling of domestic contentment at breakfast time with his wife, 'Muscles, nerves, intestines, blood-vessels, all that makes the coil and spring of our being, the unconscious hum of the engine, as well as the dart and flicker of the tongue, functioned superbly' (pp. 217–18). Jinny describes the heightened sensations arising after the dinner to bid farewell to Percival in bodily terms: 'our senses have widened. Membranes, webs of nerve have [. . .] spread themselves' (p. 110). Similarly, in *A Room of One's Own*, Woolf writes, 'heart, body and brain [are] all mixed together and not contained in separate compartments' (p. 14). The soul situated 'half-way down the spine', kindles to a warm glow as a direct effect of good food and wine (p. 9).

De Rerum Natura combines scathing critique of the degradation of human existence in thrall to false beliefs with an expansive poetic celebration of the physical universe. Woolf's artistic ambition in *The Waves* is similarly two-fold. The narrative sections constitute a critical and ironic examination of the pretensions, inequalities and oppressions that result from veneration of false idealist beliefs. The interludes, by contrast, express a powerfully imagined evocation of the majestic sweep and immensity of physical life. Whereas Clive Bell locates a mythic ideal of civilisation in an elite subjective realm, Woolf sets out a wholly communal materialist vision of the universe. She focuses persistently upon the shared materiality of self and culture. Instead of the Burkean veneration of the nation as inherited traditions and institutions, Woolf calls attention to the processes whereby the self as a body is conscripted into the fetters of coercive belief systems. To be embodied, she shows, is always already to be the site of cultural practice. Idealism needs to be rejected as an ideology because it veils corporeal forms of subjugation behind an elevated metaphysical rhetoric of spiritual self-realisation and cultural glorification.

Woolf's anti-idealism, her insistence upon the materiality of body and mind, accounts for the unusual narrative method and the structure of *The Waves*. It is a stylistics that constitutes a radically horizontal regime of the perceptible, replacing vertical hierarchies. The use of the word 'said' rather than 'thought' to distinguish the personal accounts given by the different characters underlines the embodiedness of each. Thought is the register of subjectivity. To speak is a physical act, engaging tongue, lips, throat and breath, 'the dart and flicker of the tongue', as Bernard says. Speech is thus one of those liminal sites where there occurs a metonymic transaction across the porous boundaries of self and world, the biological and the cultural; it is the recurrent enactment of bio-psycho-social being. The structure of the novel is also metonymic, expressing the horizontal co-extension of physical and social existence. The descriptive interludes move from sea and sky, operating as metonymies for the larger whole of the physical universe, to the house, with its table of plates and cutlery, as metonymies of the wider social and cultural world. To find 'lodgement', an embodied place in the social world, is a recurrent motif in the novel. Yet the plates, set out ready for food, point to the corporeal basis of cultural life, while the windows of the house transact the movement backwards and forwards between the two interconnected realms. The garden where the children's first social experiences are laid down is another metonymic site of cultural and physical contiguity.

'What have you made of life?' Neville asks on behalf of all six characters (p. 176). It is the question or compelled urgency that drives the idealist goal of individualist self-realisation. The novel radically undermines the ideological myth of self-making as an endeavour of innate mental will. Self emerges, is realised, as embodied being. Bernard describes how at bath-time water squeezed from the sponge 'pours down the runnel of my spine. Bright arrows of sensation shoot on either side. I am covered with warm flesh' (p. 19). Later in the novel Bernard expresses a wish that children might be spared that inscription into fleshly being (p. 200). The biographical narratives of the six characters have a strikingly Lockean, anti-idealist opening. The first word of the first sentences initiates the grammar of separation as the subject registers the sensations of a world external to the self, '"I see a slab of pale yellow," said Susan.' Later in the novel, Bernard again documents the empirical process of self-realisation, 'I am not part of the street – no, I observe the street. One splits off, therefore' (p. 94). The production of a factitious self from fleshly being, ensures, as Elizabeth Hamilton pointed out at the beginning of the nineteenth century, a residual fear of dissolution.[13] As Louis says, 'But if I do not nail these impressions to the board and out of the many men in me make one [. . .] then I shall fall like snow and be wasted' (p. 141). Self-realisation as Louis suggests here, is an impulse driven more by fleshly vulnerability than by willed intellectual or spiritual seeking after perfection.

What is notably absent in the first section of the novel is the Freudian family. The self, as Woolf represents it, is not produced by individual psychology so much as by socio-physical forces. The children's early and formative traumas derive from the shock of those events in which the social collapses back into the physical: violent death, sexual love, putrefaction. Bernard describes the process of individuation wrought by these encounters with brutal aspects of physical being, 'The wax – the virginal wax that coats the spine melted in different patches for each of us. The growl of the boot-boy making love [. . .] the dead man in the gutter [. . .] the rat swarming with maggots [. . .] our white wax was streaked and stained differently by each of these [. . .] We suffered terribly as we became separate bodies' (p. 202). In make-believe play and story-telling, the cultural is shown as already at work transforming physical actuality into a socially produced realm. Although the children impose the exotic adventures of imperialism on the English garden, their preoccupation is still the trauma of emergence of self from flesh and the fear of dissolution back into matter: 'We are in a swamp now; in a malarial jungle. There is an elephant white with maggots, killed by an arrow shot dead in its eye [. . .] that is a hooded cobra [. . .] with a festering brown scar to be mauled by lions' (p. 16). It is perhaps significant that loss of secure identity boundaries – swamp, jungle, putrefaction, wounds, death – is transposed to a non-English geography, the otherness of a space to be colonised.

In the narrative sections that follow early childhood, the characters speak as if they are making autonomous individual choices and pursuing interior personal goals. Yet their words equally suggest that far from self-realisation they are being made by the unrelenting pressures that constitute the continuity of physical and cultural being. Later in life, Neville says, 'We have chosen now, or sometimes it seems the choice was made for us – a pair of tongs pinched us between the shoulders' (p. 178). By the end of the novel there is little sense of chronological progression in the six lives. Their stories are more a series of repetitions like the waves on the shore than a linear trajectory towards self-realisation. Even Susan's narrative, which most approximates to the conventional *Bildungsroman* of unhappy childhood leading to eventual marriage and motherhood, is denied any sense of individual fulfilment.

Readers of *The Waves* sometimes complain that it is difficult to distinguish between the different characters. That would seem to be the anti-individualistic aim for a new form of novel that Woolf calls for in her essays of the time. Frequently, characters in *The Waves* express a sense of extended or shared consciousness. Neville says, 'As he approaches I become not myself but Neville mixed with somebody' (p. 67). Bernard, the character who is most attracted to imaginative identification with others, speaks of the desire 'to embrace the whole world with the arms of understanding [. . .] Am I not, as I walk, trembling with strange oscillations and vibrations of sympathy, which, unmoored as I am from a private being, bid me embrace these engrossed flocks' (p. 93). In her diary of 1926, Woolf writes of what she terms the screen making habit: 'If we had not this device for shutting people off from our sympathies, we might, perhaps, dissolve utterly. Separateness would be impossible. But the screens are in the excess; not the sympathy' (*Diary*, 3.104). *The Waves*, then, can be read as an anti-*Bildungsroman*. It is Woolf's attempt to replace the self-centredness of the traditional realist novel with a worldly realist distribution of the perceptible foregrounding the material common life and culture of shared physical being and intersubjective consciousness. It is typical that Bernard's moment of extended sympathies is perceived by him as physical sensation, as oscillations and vibrations.

The Waves, thus, sets out an alternative sense of community to that of identification with the nation as spiritual ideal and location of abstract values demanding reverence. It constitutes a more radical recognition of the common life of shared fleshly being, in which the sympathies arising from the fellowship of physical existence are not totally screened off by self-preserving individualistic separateness. In the novel, all six characters experience moments when the boundaries of self give way to horizontal flows of consciousness. This shared commonality has its being in physical bodily events like eating. Neville describes how he loses 'all knowledge of particulars as I eat'. The occasion is one of the shared meals where they all meet up together. The experience causes even Louis to confess that the 'attempts to say, "I am this, I am that", which we make, coming together, like separated parts of one body and soul, are false' (p. 112). Bernard, as so often, sums up, 'We have come together, at a particular time, to this particular spot. We are drawn into this communion by some deep some common emotion' (p. 103).

Equally, though, the body forms the basis of social division and separation; distinctions are inflicted upon the flesh. Judith Butler draws attention to those reiterative practices, those habitual physical rituals and actions, which, through their constant repetition, inscribe a gendered identity upon the body.[14] Woolf, too, foregrounds the way routine bodily events determine the gendering of self. Bernard recounts the behavioural rituals of leave-taking that accompany departure for boarding school, differentiated into 'this hand-shaking ceremony with my father' and 'this gulping ceremony with my mother' (p. 22). The masculine suppression of tears is enforced early in life. Later in his narrative, Bernard refers to the daily male ritual of 'shave, shave, shave' and a visit to the barbers is one of the final 'ceremonies' enacted in the story (pp. 153, 233). Louis' reiterative hanging up his coat and placing his cane on entering his office constitutes a daily reinscription of masculine authority (p. 166). Susan recites as an incantation the habitual female practices of her daily life: 'I knead; I stretch; I pull, plunging my hands in the warm inwards of the dough' (p. 80). As she grows older she assures herself that 'my body has been used daily, rightly, like a tool by a good workman, all over' (p. 179). Jinny's womanly self is continuously produced by the bodily sensation of her 'silk legs rub[bing] smoothly together' while her feet are pinched in her fashionable shoes (p. 81). Later, the practice of applying powder and lipstick sustains her identity against physical changes inflicted by age (p. 162). Even Rhoda teaches her body to do 'a certain trick' (p. 185). The emergent embodied self, the novel suggests, is, from the beginning, a process of simultaneous material and cultural production. Susan's rooted, maternal, country life is as unnatural in that sense as Jinny's city existence.

The physical inscription of a gendered identity is consolidated by differential educational experiences. In the early section and continuing throughout the narrative the six characters form three pairs, sharing very similar qualities. Both Rhoda and Louis are fearful, solitary and poetic. Bernard and Susan conform most to the normal social expectations of marriage and family. Jinny and Neville are epicureans in taste and promiscuous in pursuit of sexual encounters. Yet by the time they reach adulthood the social status of the woman in each pair is utterly different from that of her male counterpart. Louis, Bernard and Neville are at the centre of public life, secure in commercial, intellectual and social approval and success. The women are marginalised from that public world. The novel suggests that education is the means by which women's exclusion is effected and it is an exclusion taught to the body as much as the mind.

For Clive Bell and for British idealists, education is seen as the main vehicle for progression towards the highest form of mental self-realisation. For Bell it offers the key to 'the inner palace of pleasures' (*Civilization*, p. 171). In *A Room of One's* Own, Woolf had already satirised the telling contrast between the splendour of dining in a male college and the scantiness of provision at the college for women. In *The Waves*, she represents a similar stark difference in the facilities of the school attended by Rhoda, Jinny and Susan. It could hardly be further from a 'palace of inner pleasures', offering no higher aspirations than that of embroidery and occupations as nurses or missionaries for the empire (pp. 24, 31). The meagre and ugly material conditions of the school preclude any entry into a more inspirational mental realm. Susan records her hatred of the 'wind-bitten shrubs' and 'the ugly, the encaustic tiles' (pp. 24, 31). The dining-room smells of meat, the corridors of carbolic and the schoolrooms of chalk (pp. 34, 48). Unsurprisingly, no attachment is formed to this impoverished mental and physical experience. Women need to find other spaces within the social world that will provide them with a sense of physically belonging. The only positions on offer are those designated by their female bodies. For Jinny, a sexual milieu of entertainment and parties creates a sense of being bodily at home. 'This is my world [. . .]' she says, 'I am a native here' (p. 82). In domesticity, Susan finds 'a dwelling-place made from time immemorial after an hereditary pattern' (p. 179). Rhoda, in denial of her bodily self, is condemned to a hopeless search for the security of embodied belonging: 'I wish above all things to have lodgement' (p. 107). In these three characters Woolf ironically depicts the place allotted women in Clive Bell's view of their roles within civilized society: mothers, *hetaerae*, old maids.

Bernard, Louis and Neville, by contrast, experience school physically as a world that is spacious, generous of provision and endowed with dignity. 'A noble Roman air hangs over these austere quadrangles'; there are a courtyard and statue, library and laboratories, and playing fields with towering elms (p. 23). A material world, in other words, that fosters an embodied sense of entering into possession of cultural heritage. 'I come like a lord to his halls appointed' is

Neville's initial response (p. 23). 'Above all, we have inherited traditions', Louis thinks gratefully and Bernard describes the ceremonies, like taking breakfast at the headmaster's table, by which the necessary routines sustaining physical life are transformed into elevated cultural rituals (pp. 45, 46). There are no distasteful smells of soap and meat here to register corporal being as mean and repugnant. The school lends itself to an idealist interpretation as embodiment of a spiritual community. All three men come to assume they will achieve entry into the great tradition as writers and play a full and ambitious part in national and international life.

In *A Room of One's Own*, Woolf turns from the exclusion of women to wonder whether 'it is worse perhaps to be locked in' and asks what the effect is of 'the safety and prosperity of the one sex [. . .] and [. . .] of the effect of tradition' (p. 19). *The Waves* is an exploration of the cultural, political and social costs, both for self and for others, of mental enclosure within privileged entitlement to revered traditions. For idealists, national culture, tradition and heritage constitute the expression of the nation's best soul. Inculcation of these values is therefore the means of achieving spiritual realisation of the best self for those members of the community who are most in harmony with the highest form of national life. For idealists it is pre-eminently education that fosters this process of identification between individual best self and the nation as ideal community. It is this sense of privileged unity between self and nation that allows the material realities of sacrifice, coercive authority, colonial enforcement and even despotism to be veiled by a rhetoric of reverence, sanctity and nobility.

In *The Waves*, the factual reality that underlies and upholds a privileged vision of national identity is represented as that of a hierarchical, divisive and ultimately brutal order. The public school education of the three male characters interpellates them into mutually reinforcing value systems of religion, nationalism, heroism and sacrifice.[15] Despite the 'spiritual' nature of these ideals, they are literally embodied in the material practices of school routine. Ideology is both naturalised and sanctified in bodily experience: the communal processions into chapel, the half-holiday on the playing fields in honour of the Duke's birthday, buckling on cricket pads and the physical adoration of sporting heroes like Percival. It is not individuality, certainly not elevated interiority, that is nurtured by this corporal regime but the conformity of homo-erotic tribalism. This finds expression in competitive nationalism as the boasting boys brag of a father who has scored a century at Lords or an uncle who is the best shot in England (pp. 36, 23).

The dark underside of this glorification of physical prowess is an ethics of brutality. The boasting boys 'make little boys sob in dark passages' and leave butterflies with their wings torn off (p. 36). In the late 1920s, fascism and Hitler were on the march in Germany and Mussolini was dominating Italian politics. 'The world is passing through an era of dictatorship' commented a writer in *The New Statesman* on 9 October 1927.[16] While Woolf was writing, Mussolini was conscripting boys in Italy into fascist youth organisations. In *The Waves*, the boasting boys are 'marching in troops with badges on their caps; they salute simultaneously passing the figure of their general' (p. 36). The analogy could not be clearer. In *A Room of One's Own*, Woolf equates all forms of adversarial competitiveness with the 'private-school stage of human existence where there are "sides", and it is necessary for one side to beat another side' (p. 80).

In *The Waves*, Woolf suggests that even national culture is impoverished by an idealist regime of the perceptible that devalues the embodied self and its continuity with the material world, elevating instead a dream of spiritual community. She overturns this vertical ordering, claiming that poetry demands a living, horizontal connection of the self to social and physical realms. It is through the voices of Rhoda and Louis that she explores the damaging effects of enclosure within an idealist vision and the consequent loss of connection to the common life of bio-social being. Both characters are in search of timeless verities not inhering in material existence. Rhoda dreams of 'a world immune from change' (p. 86). Louis sees himself as the companion of Plato (p. 76). In her essays, Woolf often speaks admiringly of poetry as the most universalising of literary forms but, she adds, the vision must be balanced by detailed observation of the actual. In the diary entry recording her aims for *The Waves*, she expresses her impatience with the particulars of routine life, the 'appalling narrative business of the realist' (*Diary*, 3.209). Poets, she continues, succeed by simplifying so that 'practically everything is left out'. So in *Mrs Dalloway*, the idealist dreams that 'all this fever of living were simplicity itself; and myriads of things merged in one thing' (p. 49). Woolf rejects this desire for idealist simplicity in *The Waves*, declaring, 'I want to put practically everything in' (*Diary*, 3.210).

Rhoda and Louis are the two characters in *The Waves* most closely associated with poetry. Both attempt to impose a subjective screen upon actuality, shutting out what they do not want to see. ‘So terrible was life’, says Rhoda, ‘that I held up shade after shade. Look at life through this, look at life through that’ (p. 170). The allusions in their speech to Shelley’s representation of Keats in *Adonais* suggest that both see themselves as wounded by contact with a hostile material world (pp. 78, 86). As in *Mrs Dalloway*, Woolf implies that the idealist impulse, despite its rhetoric of elevated spirituality, is frequently motivated by flight from physical reality perceived as distasteful, even repulsive, especially in the mass. Rhoda voices a visceral fear of and disgust for human life generally. ‘Oh, human beings, how I have hated you! [. . .]’ she cries, ‘I have been stained by you and corrupted. You smell so unpleasant, too, lining up outside doors to buy tickets’ (p. 169). She equally disavows her own ‘clumsy [. . .] ill-fitting body’ (p. 85).

This rejection of the corporeal prevents her from embracing material existence. Instead, Rhoda seeks to impose a subjective idealist vision of a perfect but inhuman world upon imperfect actuality. It would be a world without ‘compromise and right and wrong on human lips’ (p. 192). In total contrast to Woolf’s view that the mental screens are in excess not the sympathy, Rhoda’s would be a world without compassion, with no sense of continuity with the shared common, embodied life of physical existence. So fanatically does Rhoda pursue the dream of perfection, she fails to notice physical suffering, ‘the poor hold[ing] out matchboxes in wind-bitten fingers’ (p. 164). Ultimately, her Romantic visions of icy caverns and marble columns where the swallow dips her wing are beautiful but ethereal, bereft of life (p. 85). Bernard records, ‘The willow as she saw it grew on the verge of a grey desert where no bird sang’ (p. 210).

The allusion to Keats’s *La Belle Dame sans Merci* implies that words shrivel into silence in an uninhabited place. Despite her shrinking from the world, Rhoda senses that poetry requires a shared, living community that can only exist among embodied beings. It is not spirit alone that nurtures art, it needs equally the life of the body. After reading Shelley’s poem, ‘The Question’, Rhoda dreams of gathering a garland of unworldly flowers to present: ‘O! to whom? [. . .] to whom shall I give all that now flows through me, from my warm, my porous body?’ (p. 44). In addition to a living audience, poetic inspiration, Rhoda recognises, draws nourishment from a shared bodily life. Art is inherently democratic not exclusive, or otherworldly, or dwelling in palaces of the mind. ‘I am drawn here across London to a particular spot, to a particular place [. . .]’, Rhoda says, ‘to light my fire at the general blaze of you who live wholly, indivisibly and without caring' (p. 107). 'What can one make in loneliness?' she asks, and acknowledges that even the most heightened poetic pilgrimages 'start always in your presence, from this table, these lights, from Percival and Susan, here and now' (pp. 133, 114).

As David Hume had said much earlier, artistic inspiration is a horizontal not an individualistic force; it 'runs along the earth; is caught from one breast to another'.[17] Woolf echoes Hume in *A Room of One's Own*: 'masterpieces are not single and solitary births; they are the outcome of many years of thinking in common, of thinking by the body of the people, so that the experience of the mass is behind the single voice' (p. 49). Cultural vitality cannot be nurtured when it is locked within the subjective self or constitutes a purely mental vision whether individual or national; it requires also the democratic motility of ongoing embodied social life. Bernard describes the red carnation on the table at the farewell meal for Percival. The single flower has become 'a seven-sided flower, many-petalled [. . .] a whole flower to which every eye brings its own contribution' (p. 104).

Rhoda's voice articulates a powerful refutation of exclusionary class and gender prescriptions, like those of Clive Bell, for the preservation of an exquisite spiritual 'civilization' for the privileged few. Unable to accept the embodied womanly identities prescribed, Rhoda never succeeds in finding a sense of belonging and thus a living, as opposed to an imaginary, audience. She represents one fate of the woman artist in a 'civilization' that extols only an exclusive gender and class tradition. She is denied cultural heritage and is bereaved of recipients for her song. Conversely, national culture remains unnurtured by her woman's voice and perspective. Within an elite regime of the perceptible she is invisible and mute.

The critique of Louis' idealism is both harsher than that of Rhoda's and a more direct challenge to the political consensus. Louis' Australian origins and accent are the source of a sense of vulnerability and exclusion that renders him eager to identify with values and institutions that command reverence. The disciplined procession into chapel pleases him in its imposition of homogeneity upon the variety of boys in the school (p. 25). In the figure of the headmaster he secures for himself an imaginary sense of empowerment: 'my heart expands in his bulk, his authority' (p. 26). Whereas Rhoda's poetic vision screens out the material messiness of physical life, Louis' poetic aim, like that of the idealist in *Mrs Dalloway*, is to bring all the 'fever of life', the 'myriad things' into a formal unity, to impose a regime of the proper upon the unregulated (*Mrs Dalloway*, p. 49).

His desire is 'to make a steel ring of clear poetry that shall connect the gulls and the women with bad teeth, the church spire and the bobbing billycock hats' into one vision (p. 105). There is something more than a little worrying about the steeliness of Louis' image of poetry's function here. Louis recognises that the 'disorderly procession' of physical city life, the 'vapourish smell of beef and mutton', the commonplace conversations, waitresses with trays of apricot and custard constitutes 'the central rhythm [. . .] the common mainspring' of existence (pp. 75–6). Yet he remains always an outsider to this common life, lacking sympathetic, embodied extension into the being of those he watches and overhears. They remain for him an alien, physical animality, nothing but bodies, 'twitching with the multiplicity of their sensations' (p. 75).

Neville recognises that Louis' idealism renders him unable to share ordinary human hopes, anxieties and sorrows because he is 'too cold, too universal' (p. 39). He is unable to respond sensuously to the grass and trees of the playing field, admitting that they only 'hint at some other order, and better, which makes a reason everlastingly' (p. 30). His solemn conviction remains that 'the discrepancies and incoherences [. . .] must be resolved' (p. 167). 'I have tried', he says, revealingly, 'to draw from the living flesh the stone lodged at the centre' (p. 167). Bernard, in his final soliloquy, sees Louis as 'without those simple attachments by which one is connected with another' (p. 204). Louis himself admits that 'so imperfect are my senses that they never blot out [. . .] the serious charge that my reason adds and adds against us' (p. 182). Lacking the capacity for sensuous response to the materiality of embodied life, Louis is trapped in his own mental universe. He is, he concludes, 'happiest alone' (p. 183). Louis' reiterated 'I, I, I' reminds one of Woolf's comment in *A Room of One's Own* that the egoistic dominance of the letter 'I' in much male writing produces an aridity in which nothing will grow, and in which 'the fountain of creative energy' is blocked and shored up 'within narrow limits' (p. 76). Far from nourishing civilisation, the idealist tradition of the individual talent risks producing an unsympathetic cultural sterility.

There is, however, a greater cost and danger than that of loss of cultural vitality inhering in the compulsion, as represented in Louis, to press the multiplicity of life into a subjective vision of an orderly, disciplined ideal. His assertion, in response to the varied mass of city life, 'I will reduce you to order', articulates both a poetic and a political vision (p. 76). As has been recognised, Woolf modelled Louis, at least in part, on T. S. Eliot.[18] Eliot wrote his doctoral thesis on F. H. Bradley's philosophy. In *The Waves*, Louis' values are extremely close to those of Bradley. Through the character of Louis, Woolf explores the complicity of ideals of culture with forms of national and international capitalist domination. The linkage of poetry and world capitalism may seem unlikely. It comprehends, however, Woolf's radical insight into idealism as a system of thought frequently driven by a desire to impose control and conformity upon what is perceived as unregulated and different to the self. It is a desire, that, as she says in *Mrs Dalloway*, is prepared to smite roughly out of the way 'the dissentient or dissatisfied' (*Mrs Dalloway*, p. 85). The privileged educational heritage offered to the three male characters in *The Waves* does not constitute a generous, egalitarian ideal of national community, as shared human fellowship. Rather, as Woolf represents it, it entails the subscription of self into the repressive cultural hegemony of a brutal nationalistic masculinity. It is a heritage adapted for those it so trains to impose national and colonial rule.

Clive Bell was not the only one within the Bloomsbury circle to write on civilisation in 1928. In that same year, Leonard Woolf published *Imperialism and Civilization*. The title indicates Leonard Woolf's very different perspective from that of Bell's backward-looking classicism. Leonard Woolf's is a perspective devoid of reverence and idealism. Indeed, he recognises the way the rhetoric of cultural and intellectual superiority is used to justify the imposition of Western imperial rule. The fact behind this vision, he insists, is a rapacious and ruthless exploitation of the colonised world.[19] Woolf points specifically towards the influence of British idealism when he argues that national self-interest is elevated into a form of religion in which the state becomes a glorified object of worship.

The revered conception of national culture not only serves to cover aggressive colonial expansionism with a veil of glory. The imposition of Western culture upon colonised peoples inculcates a sense of grateful inferiority in any so interpellated. As Jane Marcus points out, in a pioneering realist reading of *The Waves*, it is a novel primarily 'concerned with race, class, colonialism'.[20] The novel additionally asserts that national culture, identified as civilisation per se, is the prime means of perpetuating these various forms of subordination. Challenges to Western cultural domination were certainly being voiced by colonised peoples themselves during the time that Woolf was writing *The Waves*.[21] This was especially true of India and Leonard Woolf points to Ghandi as demonstration of 'the renaissance of Asiatic civilization in its conflict with the imperialist civilization of Europe' (*Imperialism*, p. 58). Woolf challenges the Eurocentrism of idealists like Bradley, here, reminding them that Asia, too, has its traditions of civilisation.

The contrast between growing resistance to cultural imperialism in countries like India and the attitude adopted by white supremacist colonialists in Australia is stark. During the late 1920s, Australian politics and media were characterised by a passionate and vociferous insistence upon total identification with British culture and traditions. An article in *The New Statesman*, on 17 September 1927, comments, 'The vindication of British blood which repeats itself in numberless perorations is no mere frill of patriotic oratory: the people is intensely, almost alarmingly British.'[22] It seems likely that in the character of Louis, Woolf ironically represents Australian desire for British hegemonic identity. Her purpose is also serious. Leonard Woolf refers to Australian white supremacists in the context of his discussion of South Africa and the southern states of America. All three are cultures typified by a repressive determination to exclude peoples regarded as other and hence potentially contaminating of the purity of 'blood' sustained and made evident in traditions of cultural ideals. A subjective but pervasive myth of white, Western identity is held in reverence even as it functions brutally to coerce and discipline a recalcitrant racial diversity.

For Leonard Woolf, civilisation, far from being identified with cultural superiority, is inseparably linked to financial, industrial and technological expansion and dominance. In *The Waves*, Virginia Woolf, too, draws attention to those systems of transport, commerce and communication that form the infrastructure of empire. Often these references are linked to ideas of control and power. Early on in the narrative, Bernard approaches London by train and he compares the capital with that of the classical world. 'Not even Rome herself looks more majestic', he says. Yet the London he sees is not characterised by classical architecture but by industry and technology, 'by gasometers, by factory chimneys' (p. 91). The image Bernard uses to describe the impact of the hurtling train into the city is, disturbingly, that of invasion and violence, military and sexual. It is 'like a missile [. . .] about to explode in the flanks of the city like a shell' (p. 91). Shells are part of new, deadly forms of industrially mass-produced weaponry underwriting Western global supremacy.

Travelling in the novel is a recurrent experience of all the characters, as they cross and recross national and international space, in a way that inevitably shrinks its imagined dimensions. The text further suggests the way technology diminishes the scale of the world, bringing it within a systematised order. As Bernard answers the telephone, unregulated space becomes place, namely the British Empire. Technology, simply by the invisibility of its means, enhances the sense of intellectual mastery so that, 'my mind adjusted itself to assimilate the message – it might be [. . .] to assume command of the British Empire [. . .] [and] had created, by the time I had put back the receiver, a richer, stronger, more complicated world in which I was called upon to act my part' (p. 218). Undoubtedly there is irony in the presentation of Bernard, here, since he is the least commanding and coherent character. The same is not the case with Louis who also looks to technology as a means of imposing his personal control impersonally across the vastness of global geography. 'I am half in love with the typewriter and the telephone,' he says 'with letters and cables and brief but courteous commands on the telephone to Paris, Berlin, New York' (p. 138).

Louis aspires to follow in the footsteps of statesmen like William Pitt, First Earl of Chatham, who oversaw British colonial expansion and is credited with the birth of the Empire. Percival represents the heroic romance of an ideal of empire as venerated in public school traditions.[23] Louis points to the future form of global rule: financial, technological and cultural domination. 'I roll the dark before me,' he claims, 'spreading commerce where there was chaos in the far parts of the world' (p. 139). Louis' language, here, not only makes the racist identification of darkness with chaos, his boast of the universalism of commerce is indistinguishable from current neo-liberal rhetoric. Louis' response to chaos, both at home and abroad is 'I will reduce you to order' (p. 76). The order that he seeks to impose, like that of British idealists such as Bradley, is hierarchical and male, an order in which each fulfils the duties of his station. Workmen should earn 'two pound ten a week at the command of an august master' while the corridors of power resound to 'the heavy male tread of responsible feet' (pp. 139, 140).

Woolf brings the blasphemy of mockery to bear on Louis' pride in Western sanitary ware, as he boasts of toilets, swimming baths and gymnasiums exported to those unhygienic, dark places of the world (p. 183). Yet there is serious critique too. International trade in Western industrially-produced goods inevitably brings, along with those material things, the value systems, ways of life, structures and institutions inhering in their forms. A study of the introduction of toiletry goods to Zimbabwe, for example, revealed how this consumer innovation instituted new demands and norms into the society that 'once established, acquired a life and a legitimacy of their own'.[24]

In effect, global heterogeneity is traded, quite literally, for financial, commercial and cultural homogeneity.[25] The space of a multiply varied world becomes a homogenised place. As Louis explains, those superior mental attributes of the will, 'assiduity and decision', have imposed system upon physical geography. It is their force that has 'scored those lines on the map [. . .] by which the different parts of the world are laced together' (p. 139). Louis astutely recognises, as the thorough-going idealist that he is, that dominion works most efficiently when the order of the perceptible is a naturalised consensus; one world in which patterns of consumption and the vertical values of status and life style they sustain are accepted as inevitable. 'The weight of the world is on our shoulder,' Louis asserts, 'its vision is through our eyes' (p. 140).

In *The Waves*, Woolf articulates a vision of reality that challenges the dominant regime of the perceptible as propagated by idealists like Louis. She reverses the vertical hierarchy that elevates Western subjective individualism and abstract universalism. Her counter vision is that of worldly realism: the horizontal, inclusive continuum of embodied selves, social and physical worlds. The structure of the novel formalises Woolf's Lucretius-scale ambition to present a wholly materialist account of the universe that is two-fold in expressing both critique and celebration.[26] The narrative sections of *The Waves* follow Lucretius in showing that coercive idealist modes of thought are responsible for much of the cruelty, domination and exclusion that human beings suffer and inflict upon bodily life in the name of glorified cultural and national myths. The deities of Woolf's modern world are the venerated abstractions of nation, culture, civilisation, religion, commerce and technology that coerce the world into a regulated place by means of the subordination of bodies.

While Woolf subjects these venerated forms of authority to mockery and to criticism she moves, in the interludes between the narrative, to a poetic celebration of the immensity and motility of global space. The language of the interludes is frequently described as lyrical. It is even suggested that Woolf's writing in these sections can be thought of in terms of the unconscious, or of the semiotic drive set out in Julia Kristeva's theory.[27] Yet, in the main, the language of the interludes is emphatically empirical.[28] It is in the mode of the children's first responses to the world: 'The stalks are covered with harsh, short hairs,' said Jinny, 'and drops of water have stuck to them' (p. 5). This could be understood as Woolf's intent. Just as children come fresh and indiscriminately to experiences, so she evokes a new regime of the perceptible in which the physical world is as much regarded as the mental. 'I want to put everything in', she declares of *The Waves*. And indeed, the novel stretches the field of the perceptible from the life of intestines to the unbounded distances of skyscapes and oceans.

The writing directly challenges the idealist contention (and more recent anti-realist ones) that knowledge of the world beyond the self is unattainable. This is not to suggest that Woolf naively assumes the transparency of language or the total objectivity of knowledge. As Bernard says, words 'hide with thickness instead of letting the light through' (p. 239). Despite the rejection of idealism, Woolf is very clear that to describe the world without a self, although desirable, is actually impossible. Within the interludes, the constitutive and interpretive function of language is foregrounded by means of frequent deployment of the comparative phrase 'as if'. This draws attention to the subjective element brought to all acts of observation and their cognitive assimilation. Strikingly, the comparisons are made between some aspect of the larger physical universe and a homely domestic object, somewhat in the way a child might express it. In the first interlude, for example, 'the sea was slightly creased as if a cloth had wrinkles in it', the dark horizon gradually lightens 'as if the sediment of an old wine bottle had sunk' and the unrisen sun burns below the horizon 'like the smokey fire that roars from a bonfire' (p. 3).

This linguistic pattern of comparison effects a repeated syntactic continuum between the two material worlds that constitute the universe: that of culture, in the widest sense, and that of the physical realm. It invokes, moreover, a temporal continuum between the here and now of ordinary life and the widest sweep of existence. In addition, the phrase 'as if' provokes a sense of the active sensation of observing and semantically ordering what is being observed. This linguistic tracking of the physical act of perception is further emphasised by the use of very precise notation as if for the purpose of scientific empiricism. 'The sun had now sunk lower in the sky. The islands of cloud had gained in density and drew themselves across the sun so that the rocks went suddenly black' (p. 151). The impression produced is of meticulous attentiveness to the scene and things in themselves as perception changes continually in the fading light. The aim is to convey the physical world without the screen of subjective self.

This does not imply the attainment of objectivity devoid of any human perspective. The prose of the interludes frequently uses deictic formulations such as 'now'. Deictics are a recurrent stylistic feature of Woolf's writing, as they are also of Jane Austen's. In *The*

Waves such features are particularly striking. By definition, deictics are always particular, and function to anchor discourse in an immediate temporal and spatial context. In *The Phantom Table: Woolf, Fry, Russell and the Epistemology of Modernism*, Ann Banfield suggests that Woolf's use of 'here/now' deictics within past tense discourse 'is crucial in creating perspectives whose language is subjective without being psychological'.[29] Woolf's experimental use of language in the interludes thus suggests a way of perceiving and representing reality that acknowledges the subjective, constructed nature of all denotation. Yet because of the immediacy and intensity of the 'here and now' focus, the objects observed impinge themselves, rather than the observing subject imposing the screen of self upon the external world, as idealists tend to do. One problem with abstraction and universals is that they lack the sharpness of what is experienced by the senses. Woolf's artistic achievement in the interludes is to convey a celebratory vision of universal life that is intensely realised even while it is temporally and spatially unbounded. This unlimited spaciousness provides a stark contrast to the regulated inscription of the globe by empire and capitalism.

It is perhaps somewhat easier to evoke a poetic, empirical vision of the physical universe than it is to see individual life in similar celebratory terms. Human existence as a physical fact lacks immensity, duration and power. 'Our flame, the will-o'-wisp that dances in a few eyes, is soon to be blown out, and all will fade' Bernard observes in his closing monologue (p. 229). It is the apparent 'formless imbecility' of life, as Neville terms it, that drives an emergent being to magnify the idea of self by imposing its desires for grandeur, power and identity upon the actuality of the world. Yet these interpretive screens function to separate the self from a grander view of human life that is common, non-individualistic and continuous with the whole of physical reality. In her autobiographical writing, Woolf suggests that a sudden shock that disrupts the flow of quotidian existence often produces a momentary loss of social self and thus allows an almost impersonal awareness of human life in its relationship to the universe.[30]

In *The Waves*, Bernard experiences two such moments. The first is produced by a sudden perceptual estrangement at the sight of two figures turned away so that they lack individuality. 'There are figures without features robed in beauty' (p. 226). 'Thus in a moment,' he says, 'in a drawing room, our life adjusts itself to the majestic march of day across the sky' (p. 227). The death of Percival produces another such moment. Alienated from the process of living going on all around him, Bernard is able 'to see things without attachment, from the outside, and to realize their beauty in itself [. . .] pretence and make-believe and unreality are gone, and lightness has come with a kind of transparency, making oneself invisible' (p. 220). Woolf's language is precise here. This is not a moment of inwardness, of subjective vision of an ideal truth. It is a sharp sense of materiality, of things in their own being freed from the neediness of self. Bernard quickly recognises the danger of trying to immortalise this moment, to imbue it with veneration and thereby impose transcendent meaning. 'So the sincerity of the moment passed;' he notes, 'so it became symbolical; and that I could not stand. Let us commit any blasphemy of laughter and criticism rather than exude this lily-sweet glue; and cover him with phrases' (p. 221).

The blasphemy of laughter and criticism is, I suggest, a good way of describing Woolf's worldly realism in its antagonism to idealist structures of thought, and to the spirit of religion and reverence that idealism seeks to impose.[31] Bernard's response to religious ritual, with its trumpets, ceremonies and coats of arms, and to Louis' desire to 'roof us all in [. . .] confine us, make us one, with his red ink' (p. 235), is to seek out some curious gargoyle, some battered nose or absurd tombstone. Like Septimus, in *Mrs Dalloway*, Bernard turns to things and their incongruities for the sanity of laughter. The dissolution of the idealist urge for authority, fixity and conformity, held in place by the lily-sweet glue of veneration, is enacted earlier in the novel when the headmaster's sonorous benediction, bidding the boys acquit themselves like men, is disrupted by the random, incongruous importunity of a bee (p. 46). Laughter and the challenge of the empirical world of things are the two forces that idealist absolutism, in all its forms, finds most difficult to withstand. The continuous, dynamic process both of the origin of vision and its dissolution in the motility of life are, for Woolf, equally the means of art and of human knowledge. The ludic impulse that is inevitably inscribed in the very fact of a bio-psycho-social self is also the ground of the vision, of the utopian possibility of change. There is always an alternative viewpoint.

At the end of the novel, Bernard is reluctantly hauled back into embodied being by the reiterative process of pulling his coat on over his arms. As he steps out into the darkened streets it is as if 'the canopy of civilization is burnt out' (p. 247). A canopy is traditionally the emblazoned cloth held over a sovereign or priest, emblematic of their majesty and power and protecting them from the physical world. For idealists, 'civilization' functions as a canopy imbuing a sense of power and authority and protecting those inside its enclosure from a larger reality. It is, in Rhoda's words, 'so vast a bubble that the sun might set and rise in it and we might [. . .] escape from the here and now' (p. 187). Bernard's escape from that bubble or canopy allows for a momentary utopian vision, but it is a vision grounded in the physical cycles of the world and perceived in terms of a common life: 'There is a sense of the break of day [. . .] some sort of renewal [. . .] Another general awakening' (p. 229).

Notes

1. Mark Hussey, *The Singing of the Real World: The Philosophy of Virginia Woolf's Fiction*, is one of the few critics to argue that *The Waves* is an aesthetic failure, pp. 82–95.
2. *Diary of Virginia Woolf*, 3.209.
3. Clive Bell, *Civilization: An Essay*, pp. v, vi.
4. Bell's emphasis on states of mind almost certainly comes from the ethical teaching of G. E. Moore as much as from Bradley. Although Moore was an empiricist in terms of epistemology and attacked idealist rejection of knowledge arrived at by the senses, his ethics were centred upon the mental life. Michael Whitworth, *Virginia Woolf*, quotes Keynes's comment that for Moore 'Nothing mattered except states of mind' p. 132. Moore's philosophy is hard to pin down and by 1922 he had come to dismiss his own essay 'The Refutation of Idealism' as confused (see G. E. Moore, *Philosophical Studies*, 1922, p. viii).
5. F. H. Bradley, *Ethical Studies*, p. 125.
6. Virginia Woolf, *The Waves*, p. 205.
7. Gillian Beer, *Virginia Woolf: The Common Ground*, p. 50.
8. *The Essays of Virginia Woolf*, 4.349. For comparison of Virginia Woolf's concern with the technology of modernity to that of Walter Benjamin, see Pamela L. Caughie, ed., *Virginia Woolf in the Age of Mechanical Reproduction*.
9. Virginia Woolf, *A Room of One's Own*, p. 86.
10. Harold Bloom, ed., *Romanticism and Consciousness: Essays in Criticism*, p. 381; for a more recent exploration of Shelley's complex relationship to Hume, scepticism and materialism, see Tim Milnes, *The Truth about Romanticism: Pragmatism and Idealism in Keats, Shelley, Coleridge*, pp. 105–44.
11. *De Rerum Natura*, p. 107. Further references to this work will be given in the text as *DRN*. Woolf recorded reading Lucretius in September 1918 (*Diary*, 1.192); there are a number of translations of Lucretius in Woolf's library, now in Washington State University Library.
12. H. Woods, *On the Nature of Things*.
13. Elizabeth Hamilton, *A Series of Popular Essays*, 1.272.

14. Judith Butler, *Bodies that Matter*, pp. 9–10.
15. Michael Whitworth, *Virginia Woolf*, discusses the way '*The Waves* addresses the presence of militarism above all in education' and he links this interestingly to the anti-militarism tradition within the suffrage movement, pp. 157–67.
16. 'A Study in Dictatorship', *The New Statesman*, 8 October, 1927, p. 807.
17. David Hume, *Essays, Moral, Political and Literary*, p. 114.
18. Gillian Beer, 'Introduction', *The Waves*, p. xxxiii.
19. Leonard Woolf, *Imperialism and Civilization*, pp. 10–11.
20. Jane Marcus, 'Britannia Rules *The Waves*', in Karen Lawrence, ed., *Decolonizing Tradition: New Views of Twentieth-Century 'British' Literary Canons*, pp. 136–62; Linden Peach, *Virginia Woolf*, documents the novel's responsiveness to the Indian independence struggle that was much in the news during the late 1920s, pp. 155–67.
21. See, for example, Ikbal Ali Shah, 'The Revolt of Asia', *The New Statesman*, 2 April 1927.
22. 'Australian Nationalism', *The New Statesman*, 17 September 1927, p. 707.
23. Linden Peach reads *The Waves* as Woolf's exploration of what the end of Empire will mean for British upper-class masculinity; the death of Percival, he claims, can be understood as 'analogous to the demise of the British in India' (p. 163). This is a persuasive reading but what also needs to be stressed is Woolf's recognition of the continuity of economic, technological and cultural imperialism. In this sense Louis' global imperialist idealism replaces Percival's more unthinking conformity to earlier British traditions of empire.
24. Elizabeth Shove, *Comfort, Cleanliness and Convenience: The Social Organization of Normality*, p. 89.
25. For a neo-liberalist account that celebrates the triumphant global spread of Western corporate technology and finance, see Thomas Friedman's bestseller, *The World is Flat: A Brief History of the Twenty-First Century*; I am indebted to David Harvey's discussion of Friedman's thesis in *Cosmopolitanism and the Geographies of Freedom*, pp. 51–9.
26. For a fascinating account of the scale of Lucretius' own achievement, see Stephen Greenblatt, *The Swerve: How the Renaissance Began.*
27. See Makiko Minnow-Pinkney, *Virginia Woolf and the Problem of the Subject: Feminine Writing in the Major Novels*, pp. 152–86; Garrett Stewart, 'Catching the Stylistic D/rift: Sound Defects in Woolf's *The Waves*', *English Literary History*, 1987, vol. 54, p. 128.
28. In his 1924 *Daedalus or the Future of Science*, J. B. S. Haldane attacks the narrow classical education as extolled by Clive Bell, commenting 'if we want poets to interpret the physical science as Milton and Shelley did [. . .] we must see that our possible poets are instructed [. . .] science is vastly more stimulating to the imagination than are the classics' (pp. 28–9).

29. Ann Banfield, *The Phantom Table: Woolf, Fry, Russell and the Epistemology of Modernism*, p. 317.
30. *Moments of Being*, pp. 84–5.
31. Gillian Beer, *Virginia Woolf: The Common Ground*, comments briefly on the 'humour of *The Waves*' (p. 67); this is a pervasive feature of Woolf's writing that is consistently overlooked by critics.

Part III

Guns and Plumbing

Chapter 5

Persuasion: Fellow Creatures

Austen frequently condenses into the opening of her novels intimations of the themes and ideological debates that will structure the entire narrative. Nowhere is this condensation of narrative concerns achieved with more effective economy than in the first paragraph of *Persuasion* (1816) where the final phrase 'ELLIOT OF KELLYNCH-HALL' circles back, mirror-like, to repeat the opening words.[1] This narcissistic formation comically figures Sir Walter's essentialist pride in the accidents of appearance and title while the subsequent four repetitions of 'there' within the single sentence point to the solipsistic fixation of Sir Walter's imagined idea of self as in every sense entitled. The circularity of the paragraph structure mimics Sir Walter's denial of time and change within his own mental world, expressed by him as contempt for those unable to resist the material depredations of empirical temporality. By contrast, the actual physical vulnerability of all creaturely life and the processes of change to which it is necessarily subject are relentlessly foregrounded by the many accidents and illnesses that recur throughout the narrative. Mrs Clay's hypocritical assumption of elitist hauteur when she declares that only those not obliged to work hold the blessings of 'health and good appearance to the upmost' is more literally true than she perhaps realises (p. 23).

The recognition of life as physically embodied derives from Enlightenment thinkers like David Hume, David Hartley and Elizabeth Hamilton, a perception that challenges the Cartesian mind–body hierarchy. It is this materialist perception of human nature that informs Austen's radical representation of self and consciousness as a biological, emotional, rational and social dynamic. In so doing, she inaugurates a redistribution of the perceptible. In the representation of Sir Walter she turns into caricature the idealist verisimilitude which, Jacques Rancière claims, 'asserts a naturalised affinity between characters, situations and forms of expression'.[2]

Sir Walter's class essentialism constructs an absolute congruence between self, rank, physical body, speech and action. In opposition to this myth of congruent identity, the novel asserts a heterogeneous, biological and communal recognition of human existence. Rancière claims that a new inclusive regime of writing institutes a form of realism embraced by modernist writers. Undoubtedly, Austen's innovative realism, especially in *Persuasion*, looks directly forward to Virginia Woolf's equally materialist perception and representation of the horizontal continuities of consciousness and world.

It is not only the idealism of the classic self that Austen rejects. She is also highly critical of the solipsistic enclosure of any self-contained social world. The looking-glass constitution of Sir Walter's class-bound mentality, within the first paragraph, is repeated in other mental worlds represented in the text that are cut off from and unchallenged by larger empirical realities. The shallow surface implication of the mirror image, moreover, suggests the emptiness, the lack of substance, beneath the pride of title, rank and estate. Kellynch-hall rests upon debt; the metaphoricity of 'place' as inherited order, in this final completed Austen novel, has been hollowed out. The idealist claims of enduring honour, reverence and dignity, associated by Edmund Burke with a landowning, patrician order, no longer endure.

Given the ridicule directed at Sir Walter in the story, it is not surprising that many critics have read the novel as expressing a radical change in Austen's social views. David Monaghan, for example, argues that *Persuasion* deals with Austen's painful realisation that the social order upheld by her previous novels is 'finally falling apart'.[3] Roger Sales even suggests that '*Persuasion* [. . .] casts doubt on the benefits to be derived from male lines of descent'.[4] Mary Poovey also believes that Austen intends the moral bankruptcy of Sir Walter to be read as condemnatory of the entire patriarchal landed class and Tony Tanner emphasises what he sees as the fragmentation of community and language in the social world that Austen represents.[5] This sense of radical change in Austen's perception of the social order is not a consensual view of the politics of *Persuasion*, however. Alistair Duckworth warns that 'one should be careful not to overemphasise the modernity of *Persuasion*'.[6] Austen is not rejecting the ethical values of a conservative social morality, he argues, but rather displacing those values from the estate onto the character of her heroine. David Spring substantiates this non-radical view of the novel in a reading that emphasises the many social continuities between the traditional country gentry class, as represented by the Musgrove family, and the naval officers that some critics have claimed to be a new progressive order.[7] John Wiltshire agrees with Spring's reading of *Persuasion* as expressing continuity of Austen's social values rather than any break, suggesting that 'radical' readings are motivated by a critical need to 'vindicate or explain Jane Austen's status as a canonical or classic author' by attributing to her an interest in social theory which is unwarranted by the texts.[8]

One recurrent weakness within this debate as to Austen's conservatism or radicalism is a lack of precision in discussing the fluid social and political allegiances and divisions of Austen's world: for instance, the interpenetration of city finance with landed wealth as represented in *Sense and Sensibility*, or the intermix of emulation and rivalry in Mrs Elton's approach to Emma Woodhouse. The deployment of terms like 'gentry', 'middle class', or 'landowners' in discussions of Austen's novels are at times too static and homogeneous in implication to comprehend the complex dynamics of the social world that the fiction represents. This world is not that of idealised rural seclusion as favoured in 'heritage' interpretations of her novels. Neither is it constituted of a stark binary opposition between patrician values and middle-class ambition. As Robert Clark and Gerry Dutton show, Jane Austen's father was not simply a rural rector. Much of the family income was tied up in his farm and hence dependent on the fluctuating price of corn and sheep, prices that were at the centre of some of the most contested politics of the era. Consequently, 'Jane Austen's mentality was formed in a household very much [. . .] engaged with the shaping forces of the British economy.'[9] Nicholas Roe claims Austen's novels 'typically focus on sections of English society that inhabit the vulnerable cusp or borderline between different groups and classes, so that we are always aware of the extraordinary mobility of English society.'[10] Moreover, this social mobility is inseparable from and shaped by transformations in material forces: agricultural innovations, the explosion of consumerism, improved transport, technology and industrial expansion.

My argument throughout this study is that Austen's novels persistently enact the inevitability of change and dramatise this process in the narrative experience of her female protagonists, encompassing a transition from stability to mobility, from social homogeneity to social heterogeneity. Undoubtedly, this transition grows increasingly marked in the later novels but it does not entail any radical break in Austen's social perspective. Land, for Edmund Burke, represents permanence, it embodies the eternal order of the nation.[11] Alistair Duckworth aligns Austen with Burke in her representation of the estate as 'symbolic of an entire inherited culture' (*The Improvement*, p. 55). The properly run estate, Duckworth claims, functions in the novels as 'an objective paradigm of order', a source of stability (*The Improvement*, p. 184). For John Wiltshire, *Persuasion* 'is a study in the moral atmosphere of place' (*Jane Austen*, p. 161). Traditional, inherited place does undoubtedly operate in the metaphorical mode throughout Austen's fiction, embodying idealist values of settled order, hierarchy, exclusion and privilege, but 'place' in this metaphorical sense is criticised in the writing as associated with fixity, disavowal of change and fear of embodied realities.

In *Emma*, Hartfield represents, in the person of Emma as well as Mr Woodhouse, a determined adherence to a traditional vertical social order, a resistance to the new. *Persuasion* not only offers the mocking caricature of Sir Walter Elliot's absurd pretension that he literally embodies an order immune to change, it also represents the heroine's life before she leaves Kellynch as arrested in time due to her refusal of the risky change that marriage to Wentworth would have entailed. Emma moves socially from the paradigmatic values of Hartfield to engage fully with the metonymic structure of Highbury with its horizontal, non-hierarchical, reciprocal relationships based upon the interactive social perspectives of a shared world.

Anne Elliot is initially resistant and negative as to her move to Bath. Despite this reluctance, however, and even before the reunion with Wentworth, she becomes immersed there in more heterogeneous social networks, more energetic and egalitarian modes of social interaction and a cultural environment much closer than the 'sameness' and 'elegance' of Kellynch-hall to the prerequisites of 'good company' as she lists them to Mr Elliot: 'clever, well-informed people, who have a great deal of conversation' (pp. 9, 162). According to Paul Langford it is wrong to understand places like Bath nostalgically in terms of an embalmed world of Regency aristocratic glamour. The success of Bath 'was based upon its appeal to the broad mass of the propertied public [. . .] Aristocratic patronage, commercial exploitation, and the new social aspirations of bourgeois England were closely bound up in the new trends.'[12] In *Sanditon*, the heroine is immediately precipitated out of the stasis of her parents' time-resisting rural seclusion into a new society actively embracing rapid change.

To insist upon this recurrent narrative transition from stability to mobility and from hierarchical homogeneity to horizontal heterogeneity is not to claim for Austen a radical, let alone revolutionary, class politics. Indeed, her greatest hostility is directed towards emerging ideologies of individualism. There is no wholesale rejection of traditional values in her fiction. In particular, earlier forms of sociability, even when ironised, are represented warmly, as in the case of Mrs Jennings in *Sense and Sensibility*, Mr Weston in *Emma* and the Musgrove family in *Persuasion*. Austen recognises that this tradition of sociability can be insensitive in its non-admission of private space for the self, but her most hostile critique is of those characters, like Lucy Steele, Mrs Elton and Mr Elliot, who typify the cold-hearted, self-interest of the new force of competitive individualism.

What is radical, both artistically and politically, is the rigorous materialism of Austen's representation of her world and her pervasive critique of idealist modes of thought that inform elitist visions of social order and of self. It is this worldly realist perception that brings about a revision of the perceptible in her writing. In opposition to the ideology of both subjective and competitive individualism, Austen, through the mobility of her heroines, seeks a transition from earlier traditions of sociability towards a modern identity for the self as embodied and social. Self, as represented within Austen's worldly realism, exists as a dynamic part of a continuous, changing social, cultural and material universe. Jacques Rancière claims that around the end of the eighteenth century a classical, vertical, hierarchical order of representation gave way to a new regime of the perceptible that brought into the field of visibility an egalitarian recognition of equality between people, things and biological matter (*Politics of Literature*, p. 26). This new regime of representation foregrounds process, horizontal continuities and inclusive multiplicity. Within British literature, Austen is undoubtedly a practitioner of a radical new mode of representation that has many points in common with Rancière's designation. Her writing brings into visibility the micro horizontal intersections of material, social and psychological forces that comprise macro processes of change.

David Spring is literally correct in pointing out that the naval officers in *Persuasion* are similar, in terms of social class, to other more traditional characters in the story. Yet Austen's representation of the navy undoubtedly does suggest new possibilities of social relations. In *Persuasion*, the navy, like Highbury in *Emma*, acts as a synecdoche for a more inclusive, mutually caring community, ordered horizontally rather than vertically. Moreover, it represents the largeness of actual geographical space as opposed to the enclosed mental provincialism of Kellynch and Uppercross. Mrs Croft enthusiastically lists her travels to Cork, Lisbon, Gibraltar and the West Indies and the officers refer to a whole variety of geographic postings around the world. The naval characters also represent the horizontal flow of temporal continuity; they both perpetuate and transform the traditional values of sociability. Like Sir John Middleton in *Sense and Sensibility*, the elder Musgroves at the Great House maintain the tradition of open hospitality expected of and enjoyed by the rural squirearchy over generations. The Musgroves 'were visited by every body, and had more dinner parties, and more callers, more visitors by invitation and by chance, than any other family. They were more completely popular' (p. 51). When the younger Musgroves and Anne visit Lyme they encounter similar sociability in the 'kindly hospitable' invitation they receive to dine with Captain and Mrs Harville. Anne contrasts this genuine pleasure in receiving guests as an act of friendship with the 'usual style of give-and-take invitations and dinners of formality and display' (p. 105).

Anne is thinking here of the stilted fashionable form of entertainment preferred by those like her father and elder sister whose invitations are motivated competitively by the desire to impose their entitlement to privilege and admiration on their carefully selected guests. The parties at the Great House lack any such urge to impress or aggrandise, yet there is a significant difference between Mr and Mrs Musgrove's sociability and that of the Harvilles. As its name implies, the Great House has the amplitude to accommodate large numbers of people without any inconvenience to its owners. By contrast, Anne has a moment of astonishment when she enters the Harvilles' house to find 'rooms so small as none but those who invite from the heart could think capable of accommodating so many' (p. 106). This represents a temporal transition beyond the traditional sociability that goes with a generous sense of the dues of inherited position. The sociability practised by the Harvilles is untied from rank: it is informal, reciprocal and egalitarian.

As this suggests, the representation of naval characters in *Persuasion* continues the critique, made in *Emma*, of traditional deference to gentility and birth. In contrast to vertical hierarchy, the navy stands for greater social movement and inclusiveness. The brilliant career of Nelson from relatively humble origins to national hero meant that, in the popular imagination, at least, the navy was perceived as less influenced by patronage and rank than other professions. Sir Walter voices deep offence at the way the navy brings into social visibility those who should remain beneath notice. The navy is 'the means of bringing persons of obscure birth into undue distinction, and raising men to honours which their fathers and grandfathers never dreamt of', he complains (p. 21). A writer to *Gentleman's Magazine* makes a similar point, deploring the way naval and military officers take precedence over gentlemen. 'How should we like to see', the writer asks, 'the son of a tailor, a stonemason [. . .] rank before a man [who] [. . .] partakes of the blood of the noblest families?'[13] Sir Walter insists, again just like the correspondent to *Gentleman's Magazine*, that the term 'gentleman' belongs exclusively to 'a man of property'. Without that inherited connection to land and birth a person can be dismissed as a 'nobody', denied even the visibility of physical existence (p. 26). With her deferential prejudice for rank, Lady Russell makes a similarly dismissive judgement of Captain Wentworth, commenting with unwitting irony that he is 'a young man, who had nothing but himself to recommend him', lacking alliances and connections (p. 29).

Anne's narrative progress integrates her into the world of horizontal, social mobility. In contrast to the frozen immobility of her father's and sister's world, Anne embraces reciprocal friendships with the Harvilles, living in reduced circumstances due to Captain Harville's injury, with Charles Hayter, heir to insignificant property and living upon a curate's stipend, and with Mrs Smith, an impoverished widow renting what Sir Walter describes as 'paltry rooms' in an unfashionable part of Bath (p. 171). Anne's egalitarian sympathies are demonstrated when she refuses the company of Dowager Viscountess Dalrymple and her daughter to keep a promised visit to Mrs Smith. In contention with Captain Harville as to the merits of women's or men's affections, Anne exclaims passionately, 'God forbid that I should undervalue the warm and faithful feelings of any of my fellow-creatures' (p. 256). The whole sentiment is striking in the inclusivity of respect Anne asserts here. But the term, 'fellow-creatures' is especially egalitarian in its evocation of a commonality based upon shared creaturely being in a novel that insists on the physical vulnerability of all bodily life.

Far from extolling the virtues of tradition and stability, in *Persuasion* Austen goes so far as to insist upon the necessity of change for mental and physical well-being. The experience of the naval characters in the text demonstrates that the health of embodied creatures depends upon activity and varied social interaction. Hence the greater restrictions placed upon women are damaging to their physical and mental resilience. Anne fails to recover her vitality after the loss of Wentworth because 'no aid had been given in change of place [. . .] or in any novelty or enlargement of society' (p. 30) and when she moves to Uppercross, her 'spirits improved by change of place and subject' (p. 50). Later in the story, Wentworth offers sympathy for the suffering of spirit she must have experienced at Lyme, but she disagrees, 'So much novelty and beauty! I have travelled so little, that every fresh place would be interesting to me' (p. 200). Even her sister Mary's querulous spirits are raised when she experiences change from the routines of the small family circle of Uppercross.

It is Mrs Croft, however, who makes the novel's point most explicitly: 'The only time that I ever really suffered in body or mind, the only time that I ever fancied myself unwell, or had any ideas of danger, was the winter I passed by myself at Deal' (pp. 76–7). By contrast, Wentworth is able to mitigate the suffering he experiences when Anne rejects him by throwing himself into activity and exertion: 'It was a great object with me, at that time, to be at sea, – a very great object. I wanted to be doing something' (p. 70). The implication of all this must be that any small social world, like that of rank, closed off from the horizontal dynamics of change and social heterogeneity, will be stagnant and unhealthy, both physically and mentally.

Austen's representation of the husband and wife relations of Admiral and Mrs Croft offers a radically alternative ideal of marriage to the conservative ideology of separate spheres, and even more so of any hierarchical ordering of the sexes. Not only does Mrs Croft share her husband's dangerous sea-going life, Anne also recognises that Mrs Croft's active interventions into the Admiral's steering of their carriage offers 'no bad representation of the general guidance of their affairs' (p. 99). I have suggested that, in both *Sense and Sensibility* and *Emma*, Austen disassociates the concluding unions from any support for domestic ideology with its emphasis upon privacy, individualism and consumerism. The marriage of the Crofts is equally at odds with the prevailing idealisation of the home as site for displays of taste, wealth and thus individualised identity. Mrs Croft declares she was just as happy in her early, small, draughty home in North Yarmouth as in her present occupancy of the grandeur of Kellynch. Her sociability is enacted as much in the public sphere of Bath as in the domestic interior. Anne sees her constantly with the Admiral greeting friends as they walk about Bath, forming into little knots for eager conversation with 'Mrs Croft looking as intelligent and keen as any of the officers around her' (p. 183). The fact that Anne views this behaviour as 'a most attractive picture of happiness' not only underwrites the warmth of Austen's representation of the Croft marriage but must also suggest that it is the progressive ideal Anne will expect of her own married life.

Critical readings that dissent from a feminist interpretation of Mrs Croft's presence in the text tend to focus upon Wentworth's opposition to his sister as to women's presence on board ship. His assertion that they have no place at sea due to the fact that they cannot be accommodated with the degree of comfort that as women is their due, suggests he harbours a stereotypical view of women's 'femininity' as demanding protection from physical rigours and hardship (p. 74). This would account for his readiness to condemn Anne's refusal of him as 'weakness and timidity', attributes typically associated with the frailty of a womanly mind and body, indeed, even demanded of women in many conduct books at the time.[14] Wentworth's quarrel with his sister, however, takes place before he has learned to look more searchingly into his own values and behaviour and to recognise the errors in his thinking. The text ironically subjects Wentworth to what can be seen as a stereotypical feminine narrative, a staple of conduct literature, in which wilful, over-confidence in self by a young woman leads to error, a humbling sense of contrition and reformed behaviour.

This ironic plot structure of *Persuasion* is part of a wider examination in the story of what had commonly been deemed opposing masculine and feminine virtues. As with the essentialist myth of a totalised congruent identity deriving from rank, so, too, gender essentialism insists upon the necessary affinity of a womanly or manly identity with forms of feeling, speech and action. In contesting these stereotypes, the novel focuses interrogatively upon qualities like steadfastness, courage, tenderness and compassion. These words recur throughout the text in ways that suggest these emotions are not fixed attributes of gender identity but rather exist in a constant state of flux in both sexes irrespective of imposed boundaries. With his critical perception of Anne's 'weakness' in mind, Wentworth calls for 'fortitude and strength of mind [. . .] decision and firmness' when he speaks with Louisa Musgrove as to her sister's attachment to Charles Hayter (p. 94). Anne seeks to encourage Captain Benwick 'to fortify' his mind against a persistence of tenderness that borders on self-indulgence (p. 109). Unlike Wentworth, Anne is self-ironically aware that her own feelings throw her precepts into question. Wentworth learns that in the case of Louisa, strength of mind and firmness may be flattering terms for stubbornness but he takes longer to bring these accusations against himself in relation to his treatment of Anne.

Steadfastness, tenderness, fortitude and strength of affection are the terms of the debate Anne engages in with Captain Harville that concludes with her assertion of the equality of feeling in all human creatures. This assertion answers Harville's claim that women's sentiments, like their bodies, are more feeble than those of men (p. 253). Anne had earlier voiced her dissent from this stereotypical viewpoint when Admiral Croft speaks somewhat disparagingly of Captain Benwick's 'soft sort of manner'. In disagreeing with the Admiral, Anne is intent 'to oppose the too-common idea of spirit and gentleness being incompatible with each other' (p. 187). The text as a whole underwrites Anne's position demonstrating that men's and women's feelings and emotions, as fellow creatures, are interchangeable and that gender identity is by no means a bounded and destined opposition. This bold claim for masculine tenderness and female strength, challenging dominant gender ideology, is equally asserted in the text by the compassion and caring shown by the naval personnel to each other in times of trouble.

Again overturning essentialist expectations, it is Anne who is able to react with 'strength and zeal' at the moment of Louisa's accident, while Wentworth is wholly incapacitated, turning desperately to Anne for leadership (p. 119). Later, in Bath when he fears Anne is attached to Mr Elliot he suffers all the imposed passivity and impotency that is more normally the lot of women. 'But to be waiting so long in inaction, and waiting only for evil, had been dreadful' he tells her (pp. 264–5). Until he is sure of Anne's true feelings, Wentworth's behaviour is indecisive, fearful and agitated, all that is opposite of firmness and resolve. His language when he finally declares himself is emotional and exclamatory: 'You pierce my soul. I am half agony, half hope' (pp. 257–8). From a traditional representational point of view, one would term this feminine discourse and Austen uses the term 'he cried' rather than 'he said' again indicative of over-wrought emotionalism (p. 268).

The reconciliation of Anne and Wentworth at Bath repeats the same reversal of stereotypical attributes of courage and fear exhibited by them both at Lyme. In Bath, as in Lyme, Anne is represented as taking control with firmness and courage, rather similar to Mrs Croft's firm guidance of her husband's driving. In the expectation of meeting Wentworth at the benefit concert in the presence of her family she resolves, 'as to the power of addressing him she felt all over courage' (p. 195). When he appears in the entrance to the concert hall, 'she instantly spoke' and by taking the initiative she gives him courage to stop and talk with her, a reversal of normal gender rules of behaviour (p. 197). In the final episodes representing their reunion, it is Anne who is awarded the attributes that have been so variously investigated in the narrative. Anne 'grew steadfast and fearless in the thankfulness of her enjoyment' (p. 266). It is Anne who dryly points out that Wentworth has been largely the cause of his own unhappiness: 'I should have thought', said Anne, 'that my manner to yourself might have spared you much or all of this' (p. 266). While Anne insists 'I must believe that I was right', Wentworth not only has to acknowledge the weakness of his long-harboured resentment, he also has to accept the loss of his individualistic belief in his own masculine self-sufficiency.

It is not only through her representation of the navy that Austen challenges the traditional vertical regime of the perceptible with new, more fluid, horizontal ways of seeing social relations and human nature. In Chapter 3, Mr Shepherd, Sir Walter's agent, recommends Admiral Croft as a suitable tenant for Kellynch-hall, reporting that the Admiral would be glad of the hunting rights to the estate. The Admiral, however, seems an indifferent sportsman, having said that 'he sometimes took out a gun, but never killed' (p. 24). In his Introduction to the Oxford edition of the novel, Claude Rawson comments that this sentence has 'an odd eruptive force' disturbing the insipid surface of the lawyer's recital. The word 'kill', especially, 'announces a small sudden violence'.[15] The negative force of Austen's language in this context of guns and shooting is echoed later in Chapter 6 in the comment that 'the Mr Musgroves have their own game to guard, and to destroy' (p. 46). Again the unexpected violence of the word 'destroy' is striking within the calm, quotidian details of life at Uppercross. There is, in fact, a metonymic chain of references to guns and shooting running through the text, many, but by no means all, relating to Charles Musgrove's overriding 'zeal' for the sport (p. 47).

Austen's worldly realism is nowhere more evident than in her awareness of 'things' as foci of identity formations, discursive ideological networks, residual and emergent social relations and forces of production and consumerism. Things in her novels are 'gatherings' in Bruno Latour's sense of material objects as substantially imbued with the dynamic heterogeneity of historical processes.[16] In Jacques Rancière's terms, Austen subtly allows mute things to talk. In *Persuasion* guns point metonymically to transitions within consumerism, technological innovation and masculine identity. Use of guns was also a shaping force within the dynamics of class tensions and solidarities during Austen's lifetime. Additionally, discourses around issues of violence to animals engage with notions of sensibility and what constitutes human nature.

The production of guns was a highly skilled, prestigious craft. In the eighteenth century the main purchasers of quality guns were aristocrats whose propensity for duelling ensured they demanded weapons of the highest possible technical excellence. As duelling became increasingly discountenanced, the consumerist enthusiasm for fine guns shifted into a new passion for shooting as sport. Masculinity was no longer tied up with notions of honour, but with more rugged images of prowess on the sporting field. The invention of 'flying shooting', that is aiming at birds on the wing, demanded the technical innovation of fast firing mechanisms. The era during which Austen was writing brought to the fore a constellation of brilliant gunsmiths whose weapons have been likened to Rolls-Royces in their desirability, mechanical brilliance and cost.[17] William Lesley Richards opened his gun production enterprise in 1812, Thomas Boss also began in 1812 and James Purdey in 1814.

The competitive innovation among such elite gunmakers was intense and led to rapid improvement in gun technology, including the quicker firing mechanism of the two barrelled gun. In *Persuasion*, Charles Musgrove, as a connoisseur of fine guns, has an appointment with a gunmaker in Bath who has 'promised me the sight of a capital gun he is just going to send off [. . .] By his description, a good deal like the second-sized double-barrel of mine' (p. 261). It may seem surprising that Austen is so obviously well-informed about current improvements to gun manufacture, but, like Woolf, she is acutely aware of the ramifying material implications of technological innovation, whether of fireplaces, pianos or guns. According to historian, R. K. Webb, a true sporting enthusiast, such as Charles is certainly represented to be, 'devoted an enormous proportion of his income to keep up the apparatus of sport'.[18] The novel certainly suggests, negatively, that Charles's pursuit of this 'manly' outdoor activity involves excessive expenditure of his time and energies regardless of financial extravagance (p. 47).

The technological improvements to guns, brought about by consumer demand like that of Charles Musgrove, made possible a new pattern of leisure for land-owning men, the rituals of shooting as sport. In turn, this popular activity became central to a class-specific constitution of masculinity. Guns and shooting, therefore, interlink with the text's interrogation of gender essentialism that attributes fearlessness to men and timidity to women. In contrast to Charles's obsession with guns (he only visits Bath because the shooting season is over and he has nothing to do), others of the younger generation of men decline opportunities to shoot. Charles is critical and disappointed that although his cousin, Charles Hayter, has been preferred to a living 'in the centre of some of the best preserves in the kingdom [. . .] he will [not] value it as he ought [. . .] Charles is too cool about sporting. That's the worst of him' (p. 236). Captain Benwick also turns down Charles's invitation to shoot at Uppercross, saying that 'he never shot' (p. 141). This indifference to manly sport clearly causes unease, and Charles's misgivings about Captain Benwick are put to rest only when he joins in a morning of rat-hunting. 'He played his part so well', Charles says, 'that I have liked him the better ever since' (p. 237). Charles calls Benwick a 'brave fellow' for the way he acquits himself killing rats. Bravery, for men like Charles Musgrove, is essentially associated with the ability and willingness to kill. By contrast, Anne Elliot insists that spirit and tenderness are compatible.

The new passion for shooting also had a significant determining effect upon class relations during the first three decades of the nineteenth century, as well as upon the physical shape of the countryside. Although game preservation went back to the eighteenth century, it only became rigorous and widespread in the early nineteenth century. F. M. L. Thompson notes that the spread of root-crop husbandry and the cultivation of grain crops 'provided a farming environment increasingly palatable to the pheasant and partridge'.[19] The enclosure and consolidation of estates was in part motivated by a desire to make preservation more feasible and policeable. In *Persuasion*, Charles Musgrove refers admiringly to game preserves 'surrounded by three great proprietors, each more careful and jealous than the other' (p. 236). Charles speaks here as a future landed proprietor himself with his own game to 'guard and destroy'. F. M. L. Thompson claims that preservation rights were a means of consolidating political relations between landowners and the higher gentry, those comprising the magistrate class, by means of invitations to shoot on their land (*English Landed Society*, p. 140). Charles Musgrove is certainly generous with his invitations to Captains Wentworth and Benwick to join him in sporting activity.

The more serious impact of game preservation and especially of the laws that protected those rights, however, was to exacerbate class tensions between landowners and the unlanded classes, even those with a claim to be classed among the gentry. According to Paul Langford, 'the game laws, condemned even by Blackstone, offended many of middling status, not least the tenant farmers who found themselves potential law-breakers on their own farms'.[20] Historian Richard Price sees the game laws as a 'flash-point for social relations'.[21] The game laws, confirming hunting rights for those owning land, went back to 1671, but during the eighteenth and into the nineteenth century the penalties and the rigorous pursuit of transgression became ever more draconian. Known as the Black Acts, the game laws made poaching a transportable offence, thereby prohibiting the rural poor from supplementing their scanty diets with the odd rabbit or hare. This exacerbation of hardship became even more contentious during periods of acute distress in rural areas, as after the failed harvest of 1815. Tenant farmers, like the Reverend Austen, were legally prevented from protecting their crops from the depredations of game birds and rabbits. As the laws were made progressively more severe, even to be caught carrying a gun after dark became a capital offence. The right and willingness to kill were rigorously maintained class entitlements. The game laws were not reformed until 1830 but during Austen's time there was vociferous debate on the subject both in Parliament and the media.

In his detailed account of the Black Acts in *Whigs and Hunters*, E. P. Thompson cites a prosecution in 1814 when an Essex labourer, William Potter, was executed under the game laws for cutting down the orchard of a neighbouring miller.[22] The savage sentencing caused 'surprise' even to the magistrate involved. It may, perhaps, have been in response to this extreme penalty that a correspondent to *Gentleman's Magazine*, in 1815, informed readers that legal punishments for robbery of fruit in an orchard include 'fines, imprisonment, whipping and the pillory' but, contrary to general opinion, 'orchard trespass [is] *not* covered by the severity of the Game Laws'.[23] A property owner, the writer continues, is therefore not justified in shooting and killing anyone seen at night trespassing in his garden orchard to steal fruit. These details provide an informative context for the complaint made in *Persuasion* by Mr Shepherd against Mr Wentworth, the curate at Monkford, who refused to prosecute a 'farmer's man [caught] breaking into his orchard – wall torn down – apples stolen' (p. 25). Mr Shepherd finds this leniency in applying the law very odd, but it would seem that subtly throughout the text Austen disassociates a significant section of the younger generation from the legal, class and gender ideology inhering in the material substance and practice of guns and killing.[24] By this means, Austen looks progressively to a future society ordered by more compassionate values and fellow-feeling.

She was not alone in this. Growing public opposition to the game laws was not only due to concern over exacerbation of class conflict in the post-revolutionary era. Criticism of harsh legal punishments was part of a much wider shift in public sentiment towards a more humanitarian concern for all forms of creaturely life. This movement gave rise to any number of poetic effusions lamenting the loss of a favourite cat and even the inadvertent death of worms and flies.

Nevertheless, the humanitarian movement for greater compassion and respect for all physical creatures had influential and eloquent support in public figures like William Wilberforce and William Cowper, one of Austen's favoured poets. Cowper wrote movingly about hares he had saved from the hunt and kept as pets. In *Animal Rights, Political and Social Change in Britain since 1800*, Hilda Kean suggests that by the nineteenth century 'the way in which people treated animals became a distinguishing feature of being humane'.[25] Heated and polarised debates within Parliament during attempts to enact legislation for animal welfare kept the topic very much alive within the public sphere during the early decades of the nineteenth century, resulting in the establishment of the Society for the Prevention of Cruelty to Animals in 1824.[26] Within this context of heightened awareness, the violence of Austen's verbs 'kill' and 'destroy', rather than the more obvious and neutral 'shoot', seems very likely to be judgemental.

Evangelical critics of animal cruelty, like Wilberforce, drew analogies with the cruelties inflicted upon human sufferers of the slave trade.[27] This comparison points to a radical shift under way in the conception of human life. Instead of the vertical privileging of human beings as different in kind from other living creatures on account of the possession of divine souls and rational minds, horizontal continuities were increasingly recognised across human and animal life. This constitutes a movement towards empirical ways of understanding human nature as opposed to religious idealism. It was not, however, a rejection of divinity but rather a continuation of David Hartley's religiously inflected materialism in which physical life is understood as integral to God's benign moral order.

It is within this mode of thinking that a writer to *Gentleman's Magazine*, in 1814, makes the argument for humane treatment of animals in terms of both empirical observation and of shared creaturely life. 'Creature' was, indeed, the preferred term within this new humane discourse. Notably, too, the reviewer's claims rest upon a dynamic sense of the indivisibility of physical and mental being:

> Conscious, however, of being endowed with perpetual sensibility and thought, and not less so that the ordinary movements of our bodies are no other than the immediate result of our mental perceptions and volitions, it becomes morally impossible for us, when we observe in the motions of other creatures phenomena precisely similar to those which are exhibited in the voluntary movements of our own limbs, not to ascribe to those creatures [. . .] the possession of a nature at least equally sentient and self-directive with that of man.[28]

In a similar vein, the *Monthly Review*, in 1815, carried an account of Joseph Alphonse's *An Essay on the Spirit of the Education of the Human Race* which again demonstrated a belief in the shared nature of all living things. As well as encompassing the whole 'human race', the book includes a chapter on the education of domestic animals. The reviewer writes approvingly that Alphonse successfully shows how animals' minds and intellects, like those of humans, are greatly invigorated when they 'endeavour to understand hints rather than blows'.[29]

While certainly understood within a religious framework, recognition of continuities between human and animal nature and consciousness, based upon empirical observation, is, nevertheless, implicitly anti-idealist. The vertical regime of mind over matter is replaced by a more horizontal recognition of the body–mind continuum and of the continuities of physical life shared by all creatures. A similar inclusive view of reality underpins Austen's critique of the human propensity to construct closed mental realms at the expense of broader worldly perspectives. Throughout her fiction, over-reliance on their own subjective constructions leads characters into folly, confusion and error as they mistake what they desire for what is. In *Persuasion*, it is not only Sir Walter Elliot who inhabits a solipsistic looking-glass world of self-delusion, although he is undoubtedly the most extreme case. As Anne moves from Kellynch to Uppercross and then from Uppercross back to Lady Russell's home at Kellynch she is, each time, quickly 'sensible of some mental change'; each small world is largely the product of the inhabitants' own minds (p. 134). 'Every little social commonwealth', Anne realises, has 'its own matters of discourse' (p. 46). In language reminiscent of Adam Smith in *The Theory of Moral Sentiments*, Anne recognises that experience of different mental worlds offers a valuable sense of 'our own nothingness' (p. 45).[30] This lack of self-centredness facilitates the capacity to move horizontally across the different perspectives of fellow creatures to become what Smith calls the impartial observer. It is this fluidity of consciousness that underpins a communal attainment of justice, equality and compassion. Throughout the narrative, Anne, like Elinor in *Sense and Sensibility* and Emma more painfully, demonstrates this capacity to share the consciousness of others, recognising it to be 'highly incumbent on her to clothe her imagination, her memory, and all her ideas' in the world she currently inhabits (p. 46).

Anne says sombrely, 'What wild imaginations one forms, where dear self is concerned! How sure to be mistaken!' (p. 218). This is the anti-idealist teaching of all of Austen's novels. In particular, belief in their own rationality frequently blinds characters to the actual desires driving their behaviour. It is unclear whether Austen herself had indicated the choice of *Persuasion* as the title for the novel but it is certainly appropriate. Some of the finest comic scenes are those where characters earnestly seek to persuade others of the absolute rightness of their mental perspectives. Thus Mary seeks Anne's help in persuading Charles that she really is in ill-health, the various Musgroves also turn to Anne with their views on Mary's handling of her children and her servants, while Mary is equally certain of the errors committed by the Musgroves. Self-persuasion is also treated comically as when Mary convinces herself that her nerves are too fraught for her to stay at home with her sick child or when Henrietta Musgrove rehearses to Anne the good reasons why Dr Shirley should give up his parish duties to enjoy well-deserved retirement. This would, of course, leave a vacancy for Charles Haytor (pp. 61, 110). Apart from Anne, none of these persons is able to enter into the subjective perspectives of the others or recognise their own mixed motivations. Lady Russell complains of the noise made by the children at Uppercross, but the cacophony of traffic as they enter Bath raises her spirits (p. 146). 'How quick come the reasons for approving what we like!' comments the narrator earlier of Lady Russell's arguments in favour of Bath (p. 17).

David Hume initiated this scandalous dethronement of rationality when he declared that reason is always the slave of the passions. A similar willingness to displace reason as the defining attribute of humanness and morality informs Austen's radical revision of both emergent ideologies of self: the competitive, acquisitive self and the self of interior sensibility. Instead of interiority, Austen gives perceptibility to physical energies and feelings. The retrospective view of the 'age of reason', read through Jeremy Bentham's utilitarianism and its nineteenth-century proselytisers (and by current, selective neo-liberal emphasis on Adam Smith's *Wealth of Nations*), tends to identify competitive self-interest entirely with rationality. The only course of action for wholly reasonable individuals, according to utilitarian and neo-liberal thinking, is that which preserves and enhances the well-being of self.

Austen might seem to subscribe to this view of self-interest as directed solely by rational choice. In *Sense and Sensibility*, for example, those characters like Fanny Dashwood, whose behaviour and motivation are entirely selfish, are almost invariably described as cold-hearted, dominated by sense rather than sensibility. But the opposition between sense and sensibility in Austen is very far from being an opposition between selfishness and benevolence. Characters exhibiting either an excess of self-interest or of sensibility are equally represented by Austen as driven by what Elizabeth Hamilton termed the compulsion to enlarge the factitious idea of self.[31] This can take the form of competitive greed, as with Fanny Dashwood, the desire to possess as much of the world as possible. Alternatively, the self can be empowered and enlarged by imposing its subjective desires upon the external world, as is the case with Marianne Dashwood, Emma and Sir Walter.

In most of her novels, Austen's representation of characters dominated by competitive self-interest is striking in the physical sense she conveys, especially in their speech, of rapacious embodied energies, very different from rational calculation. Fanny Dashwood, Lucy Steele, Mrs Norris and Mrs Elton seem wholly compelled by the hungry passions of self. With Mr Elliot in *Persuasion*, however, Austen appears to move into new psychological and social territory. If earlier representations reveal the passions driving rational self-interest, in Mr Elliot Austen explores the more dangerous force of systematised rationality. There is absolutely no indication of outlandish energy or excess in the representation of his urbane demeanour that gains the approval even of Sir Walter. Indeed the only fault that Anne Elliot can find in him is an absence of strong feeling. His manner is polished, easy, agreeable: 'There could be no doubt of his being a sensible man [. . .] His tone, his expressions, his choice of subject, his knowing where to stop, – it was all the operation of a sensible, discerning mind' (p. 155).

Nothing in Mr Elliot's speech or behaviour hints that his only guiding principle is total selfishness. It is Mrs Smith who reveals the chilling and comprehensive nature of his self-interest. Mr Elliot, she says, 'is a man without heart or conscience; a designing, wary, cold-blooded being, who thinks only of himself; who, for his own interest or ease, would be guilty of any cruelty, or any treachery [. . .] he has no feeling for others [. . .] he is totally beyond the reach of any sentiment of justice or compassion' (p. 215). This must be one of the most damning verdicts against a character in all of Austen's novels. It is, of course, the judgement made by another character with just cause for resentment. Nevertheless Anne Elliot underwrites this view of Mr Elliot, concluding, 'It was a dreadful picture of ingratitude and inhumanity' (p. 227).

The problem for many readers of *Persuasion* is that this 'dreadful picture' is not conveyed with the dramatic immediacy and vivacity that almost everywhere typifies Austen's representation of character.

The device of Mrs Smith's detailed revelations seems clumsy, a means of resolving the narrative rather than an integrated element of the fictional dynamics. One cause of this problem may be the difficulty of the task Austen set herself in her innovative perception of what we may now call the 'banality of evil'. Mr Elliot, like many calculating and callous people, is only unnatural in his lack of singularity. Lady Russell warms to him because he never defies public opinion and is never run away with by spirits (p. 159). Anne condemns him on the same grounds: 'There was never any burst of feeling, any warmth of indignation or delight' (p. 175). Such a character presents a difficult challenge for representation. Mr Elliot is pleasantly unexceptionable to everyone with whom he wishes to be on politely sociable terms: 'he pleased them all' (p. 175).

There is no suggestion in the text that he knows himself in any different aspect from that of outward civility or that he is driven by hidden passions. It is perhaps the normality of Mr Elliot in his ruthless pursuit of self-interest that is Austen's point. By the early nineteenth century, self-interest was being hailed not only as a rational virtue in individuals, it was also being extolled as the morally beneficent driving force of national prosperity. Competitive individualism was becoming a totalising system of belief ordering perceptions of reality. It is this consensual normalisation of selfishness that the representation of Mr Elliot points to and is made chillingly explicit in Mrs Smith's explanation, 'I must own I saw nothing reprehensible in what Mr Elliot was doing. "To do what is best for himself," passed as a duty' (p. 218). When a specific vice becomes reconceptualised throughout society as unexceptionable behaviour, even as a duty, it becomes difficult to satirise.

To suggest that, in addition to attacking competitive individualism, Austen also undermines the ideal of subjective individualism is, perhaps, more contentious. This is especially so in the case of Anne Elliot. She is often seen as the most subjective of Austen's heroines and as marking a shift in Austen's psychological representation away from ironic treatment of romantic sensibility to endorsement of it. The heroine's emotional identification with seasonal change, the 'tender and underisive' treatment of her love for Wentworth, and the extensive use of free indirect discourse throughout the narrative, it is argued, all indicate increased influence of romantic subjectivity upon Austen's artistic practice.[32] Not all critics agree with this assessment. William Galperin claims that while 'the final ending of *Persuasion* nicely justifies the novel's designation as the most subjective of Austen's texts' and while 'the focus on Anne's interiority at the novel's close necessarily accords with the ideology of individualism', the narrator's perspective subtly disassociates itself from that of the heroine.[33] John Wiltshire also recognises an increased emphasis on interiority in *Persuasion*, but rejects a romantic Austen. He argues that the novel 'depicts Anne Elliot attempting to live the life of the Christian stoic. She feels deeply, but she seeks means, through the exertion of "reason", to combat her feelings' (*Jane Austen and the Body*, p. 175).

Wiltshire sees the transparency with which Austen presents invasions of feeling in *Persuasion* as an artistic achievement, allowing her to represent the heroine's struggle for rational control over emotion, in other words, as a reassertion of the mind–body hierarchy. There is an important distinction to be made here. In *Sense and Sensibility*, Marianne learns to submit her subjective views of the world to the external evidence of empirical reality. This is very different from disciplining self to submit to a religious or spiritual moral system such as Christian stoicism. To read *Persuasion* as either an endorsement of romantic sensibility, the ideology of individualism, as Galperin terms it, or, alternatively, to read it as advocacy of an abstract principle of self-discipline would necessarily imply a radical rejection by Austen of her earlier critique of the cult of subjective individualism. Both stoic rationalism and romantic subjectivity look inward, stressing an ideal of interiority. In so doing, they augment an idea of self dominant in the classical regime of representation structured vertically by the mind–matter hierarchy. It is a regime that demotes from notice embodied social being and diminishes the self's interaction with the world it inhabits.

Austen's worldly realism, by contrast, represents self as a dynamic continuum of social, emotional, rational and physical energies. Deriving from the empirical psychology of Hume and Hartley, this new perception of the self is brought into fullest visibility in *Persuasion*, especially in the representation of Anne Elliot. It is this extended view of self, challenging the separation of reason from feeling and mind from matter that propels Austen's most innovatory writing practice. In *Persuasion*, even more than in earlier novels, she emphasises the entangled inseparability of emotional, social and intellectual responses. This emphasis is marked throughout the text by recourse to near oxymorons as when Anne leaves Kellynch-hall 'in a sort of desolate tranquillity' or when Lady Russell listens to news of Wentworth's probable attachment to Louisa 'in angry pleasure, in pleased contempt' (pp. 38, 135). Moreover, the artistic transparency with which Anne's feelings and responses are depicted functions ironically to undercut stoic moral pretensions rather than illustrate them. Anne's reasoning is at fault at least as often as her feelings, and usually it is near impossible to disentangle the rational from the emotional. Until very near the end of the story Anne, like so many Austen heroines, is the victim of her own mistaken self-persuasion. Like Emma, her mind is sometimes more faulty than her embodied feelings.

The language used to describe Anne's relinquishment of Wentworth – the decision that propels the whole narrative – foregrounds the treacherous slipperiness with which rational, social and emotional feelings intertwine. The double epistemological uncertainty of the verbs 'persuade' and 'believe' subtly suggests that when 'she was persuaded to believe the engagement a wrong thing' this is very far from a rational acceptance by Anne of any material or moral grounds for that judgement (p. 30). This ambivalence is reinforced by the shaky implications of the verb 'imagined' to depict Anne's self-persuasion that she is consulting Wentworth's own good in ending the affair. And the repetition of 'belief' as the term for her thought that she puts Wentworth before her self inserts a further implicit questioning of the status of that 'belief' which forms 'her chief consolation'. The near impossibility of teasing out the impulses of emotional and social pressures from those of rational thought in this passage is compounded by the irresolvable uncertainty of where narrative discourse flows into free indirect discourse.

Throughout most of the narrative, the representation of Anne's responses dramatises a similar confused interflow of reasoning with emotion, emotion depicted as wholly embodied. In many cases, as with the initial refusal of Wentworth, the attempt at rationalising seems driven by the need for consolation or avoidance of pain rather than a stoic acceptance of truth. Indeed, Anne's and Wentworth's conflicting feelings need to be related to the novel's investigation of emotions like timidity, prudence, fearfulness and their opposites. Thus, after meeting Wentworth again for the first time after their separation, Anne 'began to reason with herself, and try to be feeling less' (p. 64). She represents to herself the absurdity of 'resuming the agitation' after an interval of eight years. Yet almost instantly she falls into wondering what his feelings had been on seeing her again, jumping to the enticing thought that his being there does not suggest he wishes to avoid her. The next moment she is 'hating herself for the folly which asked the question' implying as it does a wishfulness on her part that would leave her open to further hurt (p. 65).

Much later, when she is in Bath and expecting another imminent reunion with Wentworth she is still attempting to scold herself back to reason. Nevertheless, she gives way to 'a great inclination' to look out into the street to see if it rained, arguing with herself, 'Why was she to suspect herself of another motive? [. . .] one half of her should not be always so much wiser that the other half, or always suspecting the other of being worse than it was' (p. 190). This passage comically belies any possibility of wholly rational self-knowledge. The idealist identification of moral rectitude with the struggle for rational understanding and discipline of baser desires was to become the driving force of plot structure in much subsequent Victorian psychological realism. In contrast, what *Persuasion* does so brilliantly is dramatise the dynamic, self-persuasive, tangled powers of imagination, emotion and reason in simultaneously masking and pursuing desire. The congruence of classical verisimilitude is wholly undone.

In addition to challenging any privileging of abstract reason, Austen's writing foregrounds the dominance of the physical and social worlds in the constitution of self. It is not a stoic attempt at self-control that the representation of Anne suggests, in the early part of the novel, but physical depression. Anne has lost 'bloom' and the word precisely evokes the glow and flourishing that derive from the vitality of the whole embodied being. Anne is first described in the text as 'nobody' and the literalness of this epithet, lacking bodily existence, is driven home by her unacknowledged physical presence in the early episodes of the novel. Her very first comment comes as a small shock to the reader, so unnoticed has her presence been in the text. She speaks only three sentences in the first three chapters, her words having 'no weight' with her family. She is indeed a non-entity, effectually rendered invisible and mute. The telling contrast is with Mrs Croft, who 'had a squareness, uprightness, and vigour of form, which gave importance to her person' (p. 52). Here, again, Austen's language insists upon a sense of the indivisibility of physical, psychological and social identity.

Embodied identity cannot be derived from subjective introspection. A sense of bodily presence and social worth are constituted only in and by the regard of others, as Adam Smith had taught. Anne, it is made clear, has lacked the recognition from others that produces, in a fundamental sense, self-possession. Although a skilled piano player, 'she had never, since the age of fourteen, never since the loss of her dear mother, known the happiness of being listened to' (p. 50). Similarly, her attention to the needs of others brings no sense of self-worth through their expressions of recognition and gratitude.

Her sister declares that 'nobody will want her' during their removal to Bath and her other sister, Mary, confirms this negative judgement of Anne's uselessness: 'Dear me! What can *you* possibly have to do?' (pp. 36, 41). Anne's narrative trajectory, therefore, not only challenges gender hierarchy, it also enacts the injurious bodily and mental effects of social invisibility as enforced by vertical, discriminatory regimes of the perceptible.

Anne's acquirement of visible embodied self-possession is mediated by physical interaction and eye contact with others. The transition from nobody to somebody is traced as acknowledgement of her embodied visibility. When Wentworth arrives at Uppercross Cottage, Anne only half meets his eye (p. 64). Thereafter they avoid direct engagement with each other. This physical and social alienation is breached by the intimacy of touch. Wentworth releases Anne from her nephew by unfastening the 'sturdy little hands [. . .] from around her neck' (p. 86). The sturdiness of the child's hands draws attention to the act of physical touching involved. Shortly after this, Wentworth again comes to Anne's aid in a directly physical act when he lifts her into his sister's carriage. Once more Austen's language foregrounds Anne's awareness of bodily contact: 'Yes, – he had done it [. . .] his will and his hands had done it' (p. 98).

Apart from touch, the most powerful form of direct interaction with others is that of eye contact. Intersubjective perspective constitutes the shared world. Those denied notice are denied community. There is justified criticism of women's subjection to the male gaze and a similar objection could be brought against Austen's depiction of Anne Elliot as the subject of male admiration. This seems an unduly negative reading in the context of Austen's concern with the embodied self which is produced only through the recognition and approval of others. The description of Anne's appearance as admired by Mr Elliot focuses upon her renewed physical vitality, her 'bloom', 'freshness' and 'animation', rather than upon any stereotypical feminine attributes. The text makes clear that Anne knows she is admired and recognises this with pleasure, not with the inhibited modesty prescribed for young women. Moreover, the incident provides Anne with a double affirmation of her visible, embodied presence. She is alive to Wentworth's recognition of the admiration she is receiving, resulting in a moment of conscious eye contact between them, 'a glance of brightness' on Wentworth's part (p. 112). This phrase superbly evokes the continuity of physical and emotional energies. Anne's sense of self-worth continues to find reassurance in the affirmation she receives from Mr Elliot's notice at Lyme. When Lady

Russell, too, compliments her on her improved looks, she connects this 'with the silent admiration of her cousin [. . .] hoping she was to be blessed with a second spring of youth and beauty' (p. 134). Anne is amused at her own susceptibility to Mr Elliot's approving gaze, but her growing acceptance of her bodily person as respected and admired by others is marked by her easy willingness to believe herself the object of Captain Benwick's affections, a striking reversal of her earlier invisibility (p. 145).

Alongside embodied self-possession, Anne acquires the recognition and approval of others necessary for full perceptibility as a social being. The negative 'What can *you* possibly have to do?' of the early chapters is ironically transformed across the narrative to a general appreciative recognition of her strength and support in all contingencies. At Lyme, when Louisa lies unconscious, her brother Charles turns instinctively to Anne, crying, 'what is to be done next?' and shortly afterwards Wentworth is declaring, 'none so proper, so capable as Anne!' (pp. 120, 123). By the time she comes to leave the Musgroves, her departure was 'an event they all dreaded. "What would they do without her?"' (p. 132). In the final part of the story, Anne is so far from being a nobody that she is 'claimed as part of the family', part of a perceptible community (p. 239).

Austen's representation of Anne Elliot's achievement of visible, embodied self-possession, therefore, is not informed by the ideologies of either stoic or religious disciplinary conceptions of self and neither is it derived from romantic privileging of subjectivity. Rather it is informed by Austen's worldly, materialist understanding of the inseparability of physical, social and mental being, a perception she derives from eighteenth-century psychology. Roy Porter suggests that David Hume's early episode of self-monitored sickness convinced him that 'thinking could not divorce itself from sensation, and sensation was rooted in the senses, in the body'.[34] In *David Hartley on Human Nature*, Richard Allen argues that for Hartley, ideas 'are not simply the responses of the disembodied mind [. . .] rather they are the meanings an embodied, active, and speaking being develops through interaction with its social and physical environment'.[35] 'The continuing processes of sensation, perception, feeling, action, and thought, understood both physically and subjective, *are* the mind' for Hartley, Allen claims (p. 189). This could stand as a description of Austen's representation of consciousness as inherently physical as well as mental.

In *Persuasion*, Austen drives home her radical sense of the physicality of human life by the startling recurrence of accidents, illnesses and mortality suffered by so many characters. Creaturely being, the text implicitly claims, subsists in the fleshly life common to all. Mental well-being is shown to be dependent upon healthy physical activity. The innovative originality of Austen's worldly realism derives from the regime of visibility she brings to the physical basis of human subjectivity and social relations, and to the cultural force of the world of things. Typically, the Elliot family's pursuit of status is depicted by means of Mary's obsession with who takes precedence in walking into rooms; social privilege has to be literally performed in physical space by the physical body. For Sir Walter, bodily appearance is visible manifestation of inherent social superiority, carried in the aristocracy of blood. Moreover, Austen's language in *Persuasion* utilises strikingly physical and concrete phrases to evoke the embodied aspect of responses and emotions. Anne thinks of the rooms and groves of Kellynch as 'beginning to own other eyes and other limbs' and on leaving Uppercross she looks back at 'some breathings of friendship and reconciliation' with Wentworth (pp. 51, 133).

For materialists, like Hartley, all subsequent emotions and desires derive from the earliest physical experiences of pleasure and pain in infancy. Whereas idealist notions of sensibility are commonly associated with spiritual sensitivity and mental refinement, Austen's language insistently locates emotion in bodily sensation. It is, indeed, rare to find accounts of inner response that are not described physically. Her writing, thus, brings interiority into the realm of the perceptible, relocated from individualised privacy to a shared creaturely world. When Wentworth assists Anne into the Crofts' carriage, she experiences 'emotions so compounded of pleasure and pain, that she knew not which prevailed' (p. 98). Mrs Croft's declaration in favour of short engagements sends a 'nervous thrill all over her' (p. 251). Rather than refined sensibility, Austen's writing foregrounds the physical violence involved in processes of feeling. Anne's experience on seeing Wentworth again in Bath is 'overpowering, blinding, bewildering [. . .] It was agitation, pain, pleasure, a something between delight and misery' (p. 191). The word 'agitation' occurs again and again in the text to express the inseparability of the physical and the emotional. The bodily intensity of inner feeling is registered in powerful physical language, as in 'a gnawing solicitude never appeased', 'breath too much oppressed' and eyes that 'devoured' the words of Wentworth's confessional letter (pp. 247, 256, 257).

The perception of emotional and mental life, as embedded in and deriving from the physical world, forms the basis of Austen's strikingly innovative depiction of consciousness in *Persuasion*. Austen expands the field of the perceptible, representing consciousness not as a hidden personal possession, denoting individual moral worth, but as much fuller and more astonishing than such traditional idealist conceptions. Consciousness, in *Persuasion*, is simultaneous comprehension of and response to a single moment alive with multiple forces: social interaction, physical location, cultural implications and a flux of bodily and emotional sensations. When Captain Wentworth presents himself for the first time at Uppercross Cottage, the electric rush of Anne's heightened awareness is caught in the rapidity of Austen's syntax and use of hyphens and repetitions. In the same instant, Anne hears Wentworth's voice, judges the propriety of what he says to those present, all within the confusing physical swirl of a room full of persons and voices (p. 64).

This radical new recognition of the speed and fullness with which consciousness comprehends a moment of psycho-social and physical reality is even more intensely realised in the representation of the meeting between Anne and Wentworth as they attend a concert. Anne simultaneously registers the noises in the room, 'the almost ceaseless slam of the door, and ceaseless buzz of persons walking through', is acutely tuned in to every word Wentworth utters, flooded with a rush of intense, confused emotions and aware of bodily sensation, of 'beginning to breathe very quick' (p. 199). Such dynamic worldly realism pushes open the boundaries of how we perceive the motility of self in its continuities with the flux of socio-physical reality. Within Austen's fiction, human existence is that of embodied, sentient creatures sharing consciousness of the common socio-physical world. Her writing, therefore, constitutes a total rejection of the idealist hierarchy elevating mind over material being and inaugurates a new egalitarian representative order in which everything can be visible and audible. This democratic shift in the perceptible brings into being a writing practice that looks directly towards Virginia Woolf's artistic materialism.

Notes

1. Jane Austen, *Persuasion*, p. 3.
2. Jacques Rancière, *The Politics of Literature*, p. 153.
3. David Monaghan, *Jane Austen, Structure and Social Vision*, p. 162.
4. Roger Sales, *Jane Austen and Representations of Regency England*, p. 172.
5. Mary Poovey, *The Proper Lady and the Woman Writer: Ideology as Style in the Works of Mary Wollstonecraft, Mary Shelley and Jane Austen*, pp. 224, 234; Tony Tanner, *Jane Austen*, p. 216.

6. Alistair Duckworth, *The Improvement of the Estate: A Study of Jane Austen's Novels*, p. 183.
7. David Spring, 'Interpretations of Jane Austen's Social World: Literary Critics and Historians', in Janet Todd, ed., *Jane Austen: New Perspectives, Women and Literature*, pp. 53–72.
8. John Wiltshire, *Jane Austen and the Body*, p. 159.
9. Robert Clark and Gerry Dutton, 'Agriculture', in Janet Todd, ed., *Jane Austen in Context*, pp. 191, 192.
10. Nicholas Roe, 'Politics', in Janet Todd, ed., *Jane Austen in Context*, p. 361.
11. For a discussion of Burke, landowning and Austen, see Chris Jones, 'Landownership', in Janet Todd, ed., *Jane Austen in Context*, pp. 269–77.
12. Paul Langford, *A Polite and Commercial People: England 1727–1783*, p. 105.
13. *Gentleman's Magazine*, 1810, vol. 80, p. 14.
14. Hannah More, in *Strictures on the Modern System of Female Education*, insists that the greater 'delicacy of their sex' necessitates a more restricted upbringing for girls than for boys, 1.6.
15. Claude Rawson, 'Introduction' *Persuasion*, p. xix.
16. Bruno Latour, 'Why has Critique Run Out of Steam: From Matters of Fact to Matters of Concern', in Bill Brown, ed., *Things*, p. 170.
17. For information on early field gun production in Britain I am indebted to Douglas Tate, 'British Gunmakers', *The Field*, 3 April 2012.
18. R. K. Webb, *Modern England: From the Eighteenth Century to the Present*, pp. 371–2.
19. F. M. L. Thompson, *English Landed Society in the Nineteenth Century*, p. 137.
20. Paul Langford, *A Polite and Commercial people: England 1727–1783*, p. 301.
21. Richard Price, *British Society 1680–1880*, p. 319.
22. E. P. Thompson, *Whigs and Hunters: The Origin of the Black Act*, p. 255.
23. *Gentleman's Magazine*, 1815, vol. 85, p. 398.
24. Wentworth, who does go shooting with Charles Musgrove, is the striking exception among the younger generation. Possibly Austen was reluctant to jeopardise or even politicise the manly status of her hero, given the contentious nature of debates around masculinity, game laws and animal welfare at the time.
25. Hilda Kean, *Animal Rights, Political and Social Change in Britain since 1800*, p. 24.
26. Kathryn Shevelow, *For the Love of Animals: The Rise of the Animal Protection Movement*, provides a very detailed account of the long struggle in and out of Parliament to gain protective legislation for animals.
27. *For the Love of Animals*, pp. 228–30.

28. *Gentleman's Magazine*, 1814, vol. 84, p. 109.
29. *Monthly Review*, 1815, vol. 76, pp. 500–1.
30. Adam Smith, in *The Theory of Moral Sentiments*, argues for a recognition that 'we are but one of the multitude, in no respect better than any other in it', p. 158.
31. Elizabeth Hamilton, *Series of Popular Lectures*, 1.272.
32. Claude Rawson, 'Introduction' to *Persuasion*, p. vii.
33. William Galperin, *The Historical Austen*, p. 235.
34. Roy Porter, *Flesh in the Age of Reason*, p. 327.
35. Richard C. Allen, *David Hartley on Human Nature*, p. 144.

Chapter 6

The Years: Moment of Transition

There seems a pleasing comic irony in setting the conclusion of *The Years* (1937), a novel charting the disintegration of the bourgeois family, in the office of an estate agent. This location accords with Woolf's own anti-individualist ambition for the future of the novel, that it will 'escape a little from the common sitting room'.[1] As I have suggested, from *Sense and Sensibility* through to *Persuasion*, Jane Austen propels her female protagonists out from the patriarchal place into ever wider, more socially heterogeneous spaces. A similar process can be traced in Woolf's fiction. In *To the Lighthouse* and *Mrs Dalloway*, a culminating meal or party in the private home is the location for the dropping away of individualism, division and differences in an experience of shared commonality, a moment of common life. In *The Waves*, this experience of shared being occurs in the public space of a restaurant among those who have no family ties. The culminating party in *The Years* is located in a commercial office whose sole function depends upon social mobility. The occasion produces no moment of shared communality among the heterogeneous guests. This is perhaps unsurprising since in *The Years*, Woolf explores the challenges as well as the desirability of the common life, underpinned by shared creaturely necessity.

That the greater part of the 'Present Day' section of *The Years* takes place amidst sales notices for desirable domestic properties would have been taken by Woolf's first readers as indicative of the novel's topicality. During the whole of the 1930s, housing was an issue rarely out of the news. 'We are all housing reformers now', declared the *New Statesman* in 1935. Also in 1935, the Archbishop of York spoke out on the subject of housing conditions, as did the Prince of Wales in 1933 and H. G. Wells, Rose Macaulay and Hugh Walpole in a letter to the *New Statesman* that same year.[2]

Maynard Keynes put forward a proposal to set up a National Housing Corporation also in 1933.[3] Parliament, newspapers and multiple public bodies conducted an energetic and endless debate on issues of housing throughout the decade. By common consent the most urgent problem was that of the appalling conditions and over-crowding of working-class housing. Almost as contentious was the ribbon development of new, identical dwellings for the property-aspiring middle class along arterial roads, but also in areas of slum clearance within urban centres and inner suburbs.

The language of Woolf's novel at times parodies the language of estate agents. Martin, the most money-minded of the Pargiter children, designates Digby's home in Browne Street 'a house of character' and Abercorn Terrace as a 'convenient family mansion'.[4] But Woolf is not just having fun or being merely topical. The house as a physical thing forms the location of transitional exchange between human existence as creaturely beings subject to bodily necessity – need for shelter from the elements, even if only a cave, as Sara points out – and as socio-cultural creators (p. 170). 'I was going to have thanked this house,' says Nicholas towards the end of the story, 'which has sheltered the lovers, the creators, the men and women of good will' (p. 383). This duality of bodily–cultural being is, indeed, a major theme of *The Waves*, an insistence underwriting Woolf's attack upon idealism in that text. The need of shelter by all embodied creatures points to the basis of common life in shared physical vulnerability.

Yet the house that arises out of this commonality is also pre-eminently the site of individualistic privacy and possessiveness, as Martin's comments above indicate. Woolf's materialist imagination understands the house not only as a point of exchange between the biological and the social but also as a nexus or gathering of complex structural forces and processes. The house demarcates the division of public from private, it provides the physical geography of gender and class inequalities and hence the DNA of self-identity. 'Better than any other symbol,' John Burnett writes in *A Social History of Housing 1815–1970*, 'the house conferred and announced status.'[5] The house, Burnett goes on to suggest, is the stage on which the social codes of middle-class respectability and domesticity are repeatedly performed and reinforced. Thus at the beginning of *The Years*, Woolf depicts Milly imitating a grown-up voice as she reproves Martin for his language and Rose for her dirty dress, thereby reimposing across the generations the division of the proper from the improper (p. 10).

But if the house has a conservative function in perpetuating the embodied conduct and demeanour whose reiteration preserve gender and class divisions, it has a proactive role in generating the consumer demand that drives capitalist expansion and hence social change. Woolf has an acute grasp of the ramifying political and social implications of technology as substantiated in things. In *Mrs Dalloway*, cars function as a complex metonymy of new disciplinary systems of mass control and conformity. In *The Waves*, Woolf recognises the way communication technology and consumer capitalism further modern economic imperialism. In *The Years*, she foregrounds the house as agent of change. The 1930s saw a massive increase in house building and thus constituted a moment of transition in which invisible consumables, like gas, electricity and water, underwent vast expansion with radical consequences for the relations of the public and private realms, of the state to its citizens, of class relations and even of self-identity.

In *The Years*, Eleanor, aboard a bus, notes, as the district of shops turns into one of housing, 'there were big houses and little houses; public houses and private houses [. . .] Underneath were pipes, wires, drains' (p. 90). Beneath the surface difference of big and little, private and public distributions of property and wealth, in other words, there is testimony to common human needs. The demand for domestic supplies of gas, electricity and water inevitably involved state intervention in the previously privatised housing sphere. It also brought into being a new expanded public realm in that local authorities increasingly replaced private providers. As early as 1903, the Metropolitan Water Board was formed in response to public indignation at the inability of the nine private companies to provide adequate supplies of water to the capital. The 'water famines', as they were called, brought to public attention the contradictory nature of water supply: water is a physical necessity of all living creatures, a basic requirement for common life, yet it is also a commodity. In 1926, the Electrical Supply Act set up the Central Generating Board and the National Grid. In 1933, the *New Statesman* wrote approvingly that in its annual report for 1932, the Central Electricity Board had announced that the 'grid' was now nearly complete. This meant that 'Britain's experiment in the new method of socialisation, by means of public corporations, is fully established.'[6]

This 'socialisation' shaped a new understanding of local and national communities. Despite differences of wealth and divisions of class, people increasingly became sharers of common utilities that were coming to be seen as absolutely necessary to physical well-being. Embodied life was the interface with infrastructure. The common life seemed about to be joined up, given substance, in pipes and wires. Yet, like all social processes, this was a transition characterised by contradictions. Basic bodily needs for hygiene and food became drivers of a vast new realm of capital enterprise. Suppliers of electrical goods, in particular, were quick to seize upon the potential of such a huge market, especially in relation to women as consumers. At the beginning of the novel, the Pargiter women struggle to get a primitive kettle to boil; at the end, Eleanor admits she could not do without hot water and electricity (p. 297).

The Electrical Association for Women was founded in 1924 by the manufacturers, who also published a journal entitled *Electrical Age for Women*. In 1930, the upmarket furniture store, Heals, exhibited an all-electric 'Bachelor Girls' flat.[7] Electrical devices freed middle-class homes from the need for live-in servants but paradoxically this actually expanded the domestic responsibilities of middle-class wives as they began to undertake the work of cooking, laundry and cleaning for themselves. At the other end of the social scale, Labour councils were putting cable into working-class districts and offering credit schemes to assist with house wiring and installing penny slot meters to enable working-class consumers to buy electricity and gas. What was being inaugurated alongside the inception of public provision was a fundamental convergence of life styles, self-image and aspiration between the middle and working classes. This could be seen as a cultural movement towards recognition of the common life as brought about by public provision for shared needs.

On the other hand, the 1930s also marks the moment when domestic property became a central feature within national wealth flow and increasingly a primary financial asset dividing those who could buy property from those who had to rent. Because of the high demand for houses and despite, or perhaps because of, the Depression, borrowing became the widespread means of acquisition. Building Societies increased rapidly in number during the years between the wars, offering credit at relatively low interest and with a much-expanded time for repayment. Banks also began to offer mortgages for property purchase. Property development and investment became a new means of speculative wealth creation and expansion, offering the promise of much greater rewards than traditional sources of middle-class income. In *The Years*, Abel Pargiter accumulates more wealth from investment than his brother, Digby, gains from his prestigious public career. In London, especially, the flow of capital and wealth was increasingly channelled through property.

When Eleanor tells her sister-in-law, Celia, that the estate agent is advising her to cut up the family home into flats and just previously the house in Browne Street has been snapped up by a 'party from China [. . .] [who] had business in the city' (pp. 185, 132), Woolf is indicating the centrality of property to developing forms of speculative capitalism that present-day inhabitants of London would very easily recognise.

The image of the house, recurrent throughout the text and foregrounded in the final setting of the 'Present Day' section, points metonymically to many interrelated and changing worlds: physical, private, public, domestic, gender and class. The word 'world' is, indeed, much repeated in the narrative. In 1914, Kitty on the sleeper train, heading north, feels she is 'passing from one world to another; this was the moment of transition' (p. 244). The very first paragraph of the novel offers a sweeping horizontal perspective of the overlapping and interlinked worlds that constitute human existence. Narrative viewpoint is never still, like the weather, it is 'perpetually changing' (p. 3). It flows across the continuum of the natural world of sky and clouds to farmers in the countryside apprehensive for their crops, to the city streets where shoppers shelter under umbrellas. These four worlds – human and physical, countryside and city – are held, within the narrative perspective, in a relationship wrought by their interdependence upon weather. This brilliantly condensed style marks a moving on from *The Waves* in which the life of the universe is separated out structurally from the human. In its universal relevance to all of human existence, the weather, in the opening of *The Years*, even provides a shared topic of conversational exchange across the class divide between shop assistants and lady shoppers.

Within these four larger general worlds, invoked in the first paragraph, other more specific worlds co-exist. Despite the egalitarian continuity of narrative perspective, however, these are worlds constituted by social divisions. The separation between them is mapped onto actual physical geography. London streets are zoned into East and West ends, with the West end being the domain of lady shoppers, forming 'interminable processions' to department stores like Whiteley's. The East end is the male domain where 'business men' parade the pavements 'like caravans perpetually marching' (p. 3). The depiction of gendered worlds continues in the following pages with Colonel Pargiter dining in his Piccadilly club with old friends who, like himself, have spent lives in the male public sphere as soldiers, civil servants, colonial administrators. The world of London opens out, in this sense, to men's access to the wider intercontinental spaces of India, Africa and Egypt. Meanwhile, in the far smaller female realm of the private house, women preside over tea-tables or, like Mira, wait upon the arrival of the men on whom they depend. The ingrained frugality this economic inequality produces is indicated in the care taken by elderly spinsters to measure out the exact number of teaspoons of tea. The harsh contrast in scale marks out the severe limits of the world of women at the end of the nineteenth century compared to expansive male horizons.

Relations of both inequality and interdependence also typify two other distinct worlds present in the opening paragraph: the world of middle-class respectability, money and status and the world of the working-class poor. These hierarchically separate domains are substantiated in vertical physical space. The servant girl brings the silver teapot up to the drawing room from the basement that she inhabits. Colonel Pargiter looks down upon the teeming traffic in the streets from the panoptic elevation of his club window. While the affluent streets of London's East and West ends throb with the noise and bustle of shoppers, business men and traffic, in effect, of the flow of money, the streets where the poorer inhabitants of the city live are more accustomed to the cries of street sellers and musicians. Shops like the Army and Navy Store, however, constitute a site of interaction between middle and working classes that indicates the presence also of a new social world jostling with an older traditional world. The space within shops is more horizontal, less hierarchical in so far as shop assistants cannot be confined to the basement. Moreover, shop work provided women with an alternative to domestic service which, despite the exacting discipline imposed on the shop floor, offered female employees more independence and better wages than that of the live-in servant. In depicting the less deferential interaction between shoppers and assistants, Woolf marks a moment of transition in female employment and autonomy. This new, more egalitarian consumer culture contrasts pointedly to the traditional world of aristocracy and royalty still decked out in 'frock coats' and 'bustles' (p. 3).

Separating out for the purpose of critical commentary, the many distinct worlds Woolf indicates within the condensation of a single paragraph tends, unfortunately, to render the writing static. In fact, the swift motility of narrative viewpoint functions to enhance the dominant sense of energy and movement. These are worlds in constant flux, subject, like the sky, to ceaseless change. The effect of Woolf's worldly realism is to constitute physical existence as kaleidoscopic, comprehensive and wholly non-hierarchic. It is an egalitarian regime of the perceptible in which everything is worthy of representation. Single sentences slide from pigeons to ladies in many-coloured frocks and from the Princess to servant girls in cap and apron. What is conveyed is a horizontal sweep of myriad forms of life. The continuous interaction of one domain with another, the physical with the social, is reinforced by the image of the 'mixed light of lamps and setting sun [. . .] reflected equally in the placid waters of the Round Pond and the Serpentine' (p. 4). The concluding sentence of the paragraph expands to encompass human life within the impersonal immensity of universal space and time: 'Slowly wheeling, like the rays of a searchlight, the days, the weeks, the years passed one another across the sky' (p. 4). The poetic condensation of sentences like this, integrated within the text, are perhaps more successful in evoking the continuum of human life with the vast processes of existence than are the separate non-narrative interludes in *The Waves*.

Reading the novels of Turgenev was a critical factor influencing the powerful sense Woolf has of the novelist's need to represent the most comprehensive sweep of life. In 1933, while busy with *The Years*, Woolf was also writing her essay on his fiction in which she claims him to be one of the few novelists able to combine the truth of both fact and vision. Hermione Lee rightly observes that Woolf's reading of Turgenev's novels strongly influenced the writing of *The Years*.[8] In her *Diary*, 16 August 1933, Woolf notes that 'T, wrote and rewrote. To clear the truth of the unessential.' In the paragraph immediately above this she groans of *The Pargiters*, 'Oh Lord how am I ever going to pull all that into shape! What a tremendous struggle it'll be!'[9] In her essay on Turgenev, she returns to the notion of artistic struggle. The novelist achieves his extraordinary complex simplicity only by means of 'a long struggle of elimination', she argues.[10] Critics have perhaps tended to read *The Years* too much influenced by Woolf's own despairing comments on her struggle to eliminate and rather less in the light of the insights into what she wanted to achieve by that struggle and that she gained from Turgenev and also from Chekhov. Undoubtedly, the 'extraordinary complex simplicity' of the first paragraph of *The Years* is indebted to her reading of Turgenev and of Chekhov but she gains more from them than formal mastery. She gains a sense of form wrought by the needs of a vision of actual life in its substantive fullness.

In her essay on Turgenev she imagines him 'to be gazing out over the houses far away at some wider view' (*Essays*, 6.9). She notes approvingly that although his characters are utterly convincing they do not exert an individualistic domination over the story, 'because they are not the whole of life, but only part of the whole' (*Essays*, 6.13). This aspect of Turgenev's art chimes with Woolf's own artistic and political aim to create an anti-individualistic form of the novel in which human life is recognised metonymically as part of the much greater whole of the physical universe. Woolf, too, wants to look beyond the houses. In addition to the experiences of the characters in Turgenev's fiction, she points out, 'many other things seem to be going on at the same time. We hear the hum of life in the fields; a horse champs his bit; a butterfly circles and settles. And [. . .] we notice, without seeming to notice, life going on' (*Essays*, 6.13). This comment articulates the new egalitarian regime of the perceptible that Woolf seeks, an inclusive aesthetic, as recognised by Jacques Rancière, in which everything is worthy of notice. It constitutes the comprehensive, horizontal perspective of worldly realism which, as in the opening of *The Years*, sustains a sense of life, in all its myriad forms and sounds, 'going on'.

There was a production of Turgenev's play, *A Month in the Country*, at the Westminster Theatre in London in October 1936. The appreciative reviewer, in the *New Statesman*, noted that, as always with Turgenev, the invisible protagonist is Time. 'The play', the reviewer comments, 'foreshadows Chekhov.'[11] Also in 1936, there was a much applauded production of Chekhov's *The Sea-Gull*, starring Edith Evans, Peggy Ashcroft and John Gielgud. The Old Vic put on *The Three Sisters* in 1935. *The Cherry Orchard* was performed in 1933, to critical acclaim. Desmond MacCarthy wrote a long, intelligent review in the *New Statesman*.[12] It seems very likely that Woolf would have gone to these productions and she certainly went to see *The Three Sisters* in 1926 (Lee, *Virginia Woolf*, p. 505). Writing of Chekhov's short stories, Woolf argues that although he is clearly appalled by suffering and injustice, subtly analytical of human relations, and concerned with the health of the soul, none of these aspects seems adequately to convey his effect. Compared to English writers, she says, in his work 'nothing is solved, we feel; nothing is rightly held together' (*Essays*, 4.185). Yet, 'as we read these little stories about nothing at all, the horizon widens; the soul gains an astonishing sense of freedom' (*Essays*, 4.185). In contrast to this it is 'the teapot that rules in England; time is limited; space is crowded' (*Essays*, 4.187). As in Turgenev, Woolf recognises in Chekhov a much fuller and more expansive perception of reality than that conveyed in English fiction. The Russian novelists pursue a worldly realist form of writing that refuses to privilege the individual, positioning human life within a wide scope of time and space.

Alex Zwerdling quotes Woolf's lament after reading the first reviews of *The Years*: 'No one has yet seen the point – *my* point.' Given the failure of most recent critics to appreciate the novel, Zwerdling concludes, 'her fears were well grounded'.[13] The majority of critics who regard the novel unfavourably locate the problem in Woolf's failure to artistically assimilate what they take as a realist concern with factuality. In his Introduction to *The Pargiters*, Mitchell A. Leaska sees a 'deadly conflict' between fact and feeling.[14] As Anna Snaith points out, in *Virginia Woolf, Public and Private Negotiations*, many of those critics who stress the flawed nature of the text come to it through an examination of the radical process of cutting and omissions that Woolf imposed upon her original material.[15] Snaith suggests instead there should be more focus upon what Woolf adds to the narrative during the revisions. She points to the way Woolf's research on women's education develops and changes through the six years of writing, concluding, 'Just because Woolf leaves out the essays and direct references does not mean their influence is dissolved or erased' (*Public*, p. 101). The priority for Woolf, in the final version of the novel, Snaith argues, 'is not accuracy but rather the recognition of history as discourse itself' (*Public*, p. 111).

History, as a temporal process of change, is undoubtedly a determining presence in Woolf's fiction, as it is in Turgenev's and Chekhov's. Yet, her priority, like theirs, is with the transformation of material forces, literally the nuts and bolts, shaping embodied existence. Part of the problem for many recent critics is the negative identification of 'facts' with realism. There is almost a sense of embarrassment that Woolf should follow such an iconic modernist text, as *The Waves*, with an apparent retreat to traditionalism. For modernist critics, Woolf must either be deemed to have failed because she is tempted into a conventional representation of the real world or she must be rescued for modernism by recognition that realism is not her aim at all. The most ready means to hand for such exculpation is to understand her texts as meta-fictions about discourse, and history 'as discourse itself'. Linden Peach, for example, begins his chapter on *The Years* with an apologetic recognition that 'it displays at times the verisimilitude associated with traditional, social realist fiction'.[16] He then redeems the text by reading it dialogically as staging a discursive debate that facilitates release from three conflicting and falsifying discourses of the family dominating the inter-war years. In addition, he claims, the novel is yet more complicated, driven by awareness 'of the precarious, partial and changing nature of the social and cultural archive' (*Woolf*, p. 180). Yes, but, one wants to ask, what about the changing nature of the material world in which women necessarily live out their embodied lives? And how can we judge discourses to be false if there is no access to 'facts' beyond yet more discourse and archives?

Readings like those of Peach and Snaith offer valuable insights into Woolf's concerns as she wrote the novels responding to her own times. Historicised studies, such as Snaith's and Peach's, have provided a much richer and more nuanced understanding of the politics of Woolf's fiction. It is certainly the case, moreover, that Woolf was acutely aware of the often repressive power of discursive codes, especially those perpetuating an idealist regime of the perceptible. It is, however, not solely the intertextuality of discourse that Woolf seeks to represent. In line with her appreciation of Turgenev's art she wants to convey the textuality of material existence. In her essay on Turgenev's novels, she offers, as an example of his 'truth to facts', his description of a pair of gloves picked up by a character. They were 'white chamois-leather gloves, recently washed, every finger of which had stretched at the tip and looked like a finger-biscuit' (*Essays*, 6.11). What such writing brings home to our perception is the imprint of the processes of existence upon the very fabric of otherwise mute things. The physical is not always voiceless, as the worn gloves are not inarticulate. Woolf's writing is typified by a democratic stylistics that comprehends the life of what she memorably calls 'all breathing beings', but equally the worlds of plants, sky, inanimate objects and molecular existence, finding for what is mute, a voice.

In a literal sense, a house is an inanimate object, yet in *The Years*, it is shown to exert an active force upon human life. The house can be seen as a gathering point out of which radiate, rather in the manner of Eleanor's doodle on blotting paper, metonymic relations to past, present and emerging ideologies, consumer demand, material production, financial systems and structures of inequality. The specific houses inhabited by the first generation of Pargiters in the *The Years* can also be thought of in terms of de Certeau's distinction between a place as location of the static, hierarchic order of the proper, on the one hand, and of space as the arena of movement and possibility on the other.[17] Just as Austen represents both Hartfield in *Emma* and Kellynch-hall in *Persuasion* as places hostile to time and change, so too Woolf represents the family houses in Abercorn

Terrace, Browne Street and Oxford as places perpetuating a stultifying patriarchal order, resistant to time and change. Masculine privilege is materialised in house geography. While Eleanor, Milly and Delia occupy the drawing room, their presence there is largely ordered by a male itinerary: their day is organised around the return of brothers and father. In contrast, Abel Pargiter has the privilege of a study and Martin the exclusive use of the schoolroom. Rose shrinks at the doorway when she wants to speak with him, while he threatens her like an intruder. House geography also orders the vertical hierarchy of class. The servants of all three houses are inhabitants of the basements, often damp and lacking light. It is only as Crosby is leaving the house after all her years in service that Eleanor notices 'how dark, how low it was' (p. 195).

Patriarchal authority is perpetually reiterated in daily routines and ceremonies inscribed in the domestic objects of the house, a regulatory recurrence which defies the possibility of change. Martin hastily gets out of his father's designated chair when Abel Pargiter is heard entering the house, but it is Martin not the girls who has been sitting in it. Only sons can occupy the place of the father. Similarly, Abel is handed tea in the cup that had belonged to his father, a ritual of continuity that he upholds even though he dislikes tea. In the Lodge at Oxford, the painting of 'the old gentleman who had ruled the college over a hundred years ago' imposes itself when the lamps are lit. To Kitty, the portrait looks singularly like Dr Malone, her father, and current Master of the College. The authority that seems to be immune to change largely depends upon the material power of money and its unequal distribution. When Martin has done well at school his father rewards him with sixpence. Immediately prior to this, he has responded to Milly's trip to Whiteley's by commenting sharply, 'Spending money, eh?' (p. 12). Mrs Pargiter, on her death-bed, is still troubled by the need to account for any spending, 'The expense, Delia, the expense – that's what worries me' (p. 21). In Browne Street, Eugénie may be less subdued by domestic codes but she, too, is subject to the pervasive disapproval of her spending by Digby, her husband, and, as he sees it, her lack of responsibility. His daughters hear him interrogating Eugénie as to whether she has locked the house securely, and his voice sounds 'peremptory [. . .] querulous and cross' (p. 128).

As this suggests, speech is also organised hierarchically within the home; audibility is not democratic. Men interrogate women and children, holding them accountable. Women's sphere of speech is domestic, the regulation of servants and children. Eugénie never interrupts when Abel and Digby discuss politics (p. 111). Servants are rendered almost mute, unable to do more than speak when they are spoken to. Kitty wonders irritably of the butler, Hiscock, 'Why can't you talk like a human being?', failing to recognise that he is denied the full visibility and audibility of one (p. 66). Any movement over the allotted speech boundaries is met with rebuke or ridicule. When a woman guest at a dinner party in Oxford offers unsolicited knowledge, she is mocked by 'the great Dr Andrews' whereupon 'with a wave of the hand dictated by centuries of tradition, Mrs Larpent drew back her foot, as if she had encroached upon one of the chalk marks which decorate academic lintels' (pp. 50–1).

The rigidity of domestic order ensures that the house is experienced more as a place of repressive decorum than the ideal of home perpetuated within middle-class domestic ideology. Martin thinks back with dislike on the house 'where all those people had lived boxed up together, telling lies' (pp. 200–1). Men escape the claustrophobia and limitations of the domestic house into the more expansive, if more individualistic and competitive, public world of school, university, clubs, professions and business. The house marks out the boundary of public and private and, by extension, the invisible chalk marks that divide what is circumscribed and proper from what is excluded from the perceptible as improper and dangerously unbounded. As the text makes clear, this is a division that bears primarily upon girls and women. Men, like Colonel Pargiter and later his son Martin, have licence for improper relations outside the home.

In the early part of the narrative, women frequently look out of and throw open windows, as if in need of greater space. Windows offer glimpses of the world beyond the house but visibility is frowned upon as improper for respectable girls. Delia relieves her sense of tedium by looking down at the street, calling to Milly to join her when a young man gets out of a cab. 'Don't be caught looking', Eleanor says warningly (p. 17). Shortly afterwards, Crosby comes in to draw the 'thick sculptured folds' of the curtains, whereupon the 'world outside seemed thickly and entirely cut off' (p. 18). Kitty is also oppressed by her sealed-off, stuffy room, drawing back the curtains and throwing open the window, even while remembering her mother scolding her , 'Anybody might see in' (p. 54). Edward Pargiter identifies Kitty with Antigone who was immured alive for trespassing beyond the bounds of what is deemed proper for women. Kitty, as an adult, goes to the opera,

Siegfried, in which the heroine Brünnhilde is imprisoned in a deep sleep and encircled by a ring of fire. Her awakening and release depend upon acceptance of marriage to Siegfried and renunciation of her improper powers.

The Years enacts the moment of transition or dissensus as women begin to rebel against and escape from the imprisoning codes of domestic respectability. This entails a rejection of the house as physical building. Not all the Pargiter women are equally successful in escaping from a house-bound life. Delia and Kitty, who had most chafed against the limitations of family and dreamt of romantic escape to the improper worlds of Irish republicanism and working-class freedom from propriety, ironically settle for the mirror images of their dreams, as Kitty marries the aristocratic Lord Lasswade and Delia a staunch defender of Unionism and traditional order. Milly does not even want to escape, hoping to and succeeding in perpetuating the family home in her own married life. Eleanor is the only one of the sisters to find a wider life of movement and change that satisfies her. As a child, Rose transgressed most radically against proper limits, slipping through the locked door into the street to suffer a horrific encounter with male sexual violence. As an adult, she returns to the spaces of danger and possibility represented by the streets to fight in the public domain for women's right to equality. For this further transgression, she is incarcerated and subjected to the legalised violence of force feeding.

In Eugénie's house in Browne Street, the windows are thrown wide open, while in the garden the daughters of the house, Maggie and Sara, are encouraged by their mother to dance around an enormous bonfire of leaping flames as Eugénie shouts 'Make it blaze! Make it blaze!' (p. 110). Unsurprisingly, Sara is the least conforming of the second generation of women whilst Maggie's marriage to a Frenchman with a foreign name causes consternation to the more conservative in the family. Of the men of that generation, only Morris perpetuates the patriarchal order of the house-owning family. But the choices taken up by the other two are even more individualistic. Edward remains in his elite Oxford college and Martin has a plush bachelor apartment in a fashionable part of London. By contrast, Rose, Maggie, Sara and Eleanor have only sufficient financial means to live in small rooms or flats in the poorer city streets. In that sense, they have moved well beyond the proper place, geographically and financially, of middle-class respectability and out into spaces of possibility as well as threat. This, too, was Woolf's artistic aim for women writers, to move out of the private drawing room into a wider sense of the world.

This anti-individualism is central to Woolf's attack upon an idealist regime of the perceptible that elevates the realm of the mind at the expense of the embodied self as part of the whole material world. Woolf recognises that for women, strictly bound in by rules of the proper, this expanded sense of self is more difficult to acknowledge. The contrast between men's greater freedom of bodily life and women's circumscribed identity is illustrated comically as Martin admires a young girl at Kitty's dinner party, dressed demurely in virginal white and pearls, whilst he thinks 'only an hour ago I was lying stark naked in my bath' (pp. 225–6). There is less insistence upon the physical body in *The Years* than in *The Waves*. Nevertheless, characters are represented as beings whose experience, even of culture, is as much physical as mental. As Edward reads *Antigone* and sips wine, 'A soft glow spread over his spine at the nape of his neck' (p. 46). When Martin looks up at the dome of St Paul's Cathedral, 'All the weights in his body seemed to shift' (p. 205). Peggy experiences a disturbing conflict of emotion as a thrill runs 'down her thigh' (p. 295). When Peggy mentions sanitary towels, a previously taboo subject, Eleanor feels that 'A knife seemed to slice her skin, leaving a ripple of unpleasant sensation' (p. 303). Sara, in some ways the most interrogative character in the novel, directly challenges the idealist claim: '"And he says," she murmured, "that the world is nothing but [. . .] thought" [. . .] Well [. . .] she would let herself *be* thought [. . .] She stretched herself out. Where did thought begin?' (p. 118). Sara's attempt to be pure thought convinces her that it is an impossible endeavour; what she experiences when she tries is an imaginative sense of her body.

In *Persuasion*, Austen draws attention to the embodied nature of human life by the recurrent physical accidents and illnesses experienced by the characters. Similarly, in *The Years*, there are frequent references to bodily deformity, mutilation and injury. Like 'all breathing kind' human beings are vulnerable to physical necessities and harm (p. 43). The story opens with anxiety about damage to crops from the wet weather and shoppers putting up umbrellas as shelter against the rain. Shortly afterwards a sudden squall sends children scudding home. In addition, Eleanor's housing project is troubled by a roof that lets in the rain, while her sister-in-law, Celia, has to warn of a shortage of water for washing due to the hot, dry summer. Crosby, unable to afford transport, struggles against snow and mist: 'She looked so hunched and small that it seemed doubtful if she could make her way across the wide open space shrouded in white mist' (p. 273). The most threatening need for physical shelter in the story, however, is not as protection from the weather but from enemy bombers. The physical fear experienced by all those in Maggie's and Renny's cellar, sitting in breathless silence as a 'violent crack of sound' explodes right above them would resonate keenly with Woolf's first readers (p. 262). By the mid-1930s, war seemed increasingly inevitable and news of German rearmament proliferated in the press; so, too, did public apprehension about the imminent danger of air raids and the need to provide what came to be called 'shelters'. The effect of the unemotional pages of the government's handbook on air raids and anti-gas precautions, the *New Statesman* observed in 1935, 'is to turn what had hitherto been an horrific fantasy into a close and appalling reality'.[18]

The Years draws attention to the need of embodied creatures to find shelter from the blast of both bombs and weather. Yet the sheltering enclosure of middle-class privacy shuts out the possibilities of fuller existence. The text equally points to the opposite anti-individualist need for reconnection with the larger common life of the world. As the fear of the German air raid subsides, Nicholas speculates that human beings need to live more 'naturally', that the whole being wishes to expand, whereas now 'we live, screwed up into one hard little, tight little – knot' (p. 267). Delia, cooped up in Abercorn Terrace, notes 'a wildness in the spring evening, even here'. Dropping the blind on the scene, she exclaims desperately, 'Oh my God!' (p. 17). Eleanor feels a similar urge to escape the confined world of the Law Courts. Once outside, 'She felt herself expand. It was still daylight here; a rush, a stir, a turmoil of variegated life came racing towards her. It was as if something had broken loose – in her, in the world [. . .] Above was the dazzle of a watery but gleaming sky' (p. 99). When Sara tries to confine her being solely to thought, what she experiences is a sense of her bodily self extending into the physical being of a tree (p. 118). In Kensington Gardens, Martin asks himself that recurrent question in Woolf's texts, 'What would the world be [. . .] without an "I" in it?' (p. 218). As if in answer, 'the sun dappling the leaves gave everything a curious look of insubstantiality as if it were broken into separate points of light. He too, himself, seemed dispersed.'

In such passages, Woolf aims to reperceive human life as part of the molecular flow of shared material existence, the very opposite scale to that of the tea-pot regime she associates with English writing. At times, in *The Years*, the perceptibility of normally silent and invisible forces of vitality strikes into the awareness of the characters in the story. Equally there is recognition by the third-person narrator.

As Colonel Pargiter makes his way towards the street where his mistress, Mira, lives, he fails to notice that 'there was a sparkle, an animation everywhere' (p. 6). As Martin talks with Maggie in the park, everything is 'full of the stir, the potency, the fecundity of spring' (p. 221). A similar sense of tangible, physical vitality opens the 1914 section of the novel: 'Even the air seemed to have a burr in it [. . .] it vibrated, it rippled [. . .] The air over London seemed a rough sea of sound through which circles travelled' (p. 202). As this suggests, Woolf radically expands the regime of the perceptible so that the muteness of the common life of the physical world within which we live becomes audible as a voice. Kitty, alone on the Yorkshire moors, looks over the billowing land, 'uncultivated, uninhabited, existing by itself, for itself [. . .] A deep murmur sang in her ears – the land itself, singing to itself, a chorus' (p. 251).

Eleanor has a similar experience after the air raid: 'A broad fan of light, like the sail of a windmill, was sweeping slowly across the sky. It seemed to take what she was feeling and to express it broadly and simply, as if another voice were speaking in another language' (p. 271). Further on in the story, Eleanor looks out from her window high over roof tops, squares and gardens to a blue line of hills in the distance and the view seems to her 'like another voice speaking, to fill up the pause' (p. 296). These auditory experiences are attributed to characters, yet in a novel that foregrounds the pauses, the incomplete, fractured and interrupted nature of human intercourse, the writing seems to intimate the possibility of more inclusive communication across the chalk marks that divide individual and social existence from the common life of the universe. This may well be a metaphysical proposition but it is not a dream of transcendence. It is the physical world to which Woolf seeks to give voice, not the spiritual.

Indeed, equally with the natural realm, the text foregrounds the social world of city streets. Throughout Woolf's fiction, streets are represented as spaces of complex, interactive energies. Like the shared physical world, the common life of the streets, in *The Years*, contains both threat and possibility. Rose's childhood experience evokes an extreme sense of violent sexual otherness. The man's sucking mouth and mewing noises seem to come from a non-human form of life. The poorer working-class streets in which characters live or visit are frequently represented as sites of squalid drunkenness and casual violence. Maggie and Sara can hear the 'sound of brawling in the street outside; a scuffling and trampling as if the police were hauling someone along the street against his will' (p. 169). Later, they hear the 'hammer, hammer, hammer' of the drunk husband banging on his door (p. 171). The area, 'sordid' and 'dirty', is scrawled with a swastika, indicative of a more endemic will to brutality (pp. 280, 279). Eleanor, driving through such a neighbourhood, thinks, 'here was the vice, the obscenity, the reality of London' (p. 101).

At other points, the narrative voice draws attention to what is excluded from the clean and proper realm of the respectable and prosperous. The wind scatters along the pavement the disgusting detritus of bodily life: 'twists of hair, papers already blood smeared, yellow smeared' (p. 131). The effect is of revulsion from, rather than any embracing of, the common life of physical being. Perhaps the greatest unease in the text is registered by the undefined menace of women whom poverty seems to have rendered more animal than human. Such is the woman looking out on the street where Eleanor has her houses: 'Her eyes, rapacious, greedy, like the eyes of a bird of prey, were also sulky and sleepy, as if they had nothing to feed their hunger upon' (p. 86). The same word 'rapacious' is used of other women, 'raking' the street with a 'dissatisfied stare' (p. 102).

Yet this sense of threat and otherness is far from being the whole of the life of the streets represented in *The Years*. Even Maggie, admitting that 'the night is full of roaring and cursing; of violence and unrest', allows 'but also of beauty and joy' (p. 170). Pre-eminently, the streets express movement, noise and vitality: the 'turmoil of variegated life' that races towards Eleanor as she emerges from the Law Courts, or the crowds of travellers, workers and shoppers who swirl around the entrance of Charing Cross Station (pp. 99, 100). The images of caravans and processions like 'tribes migrating in search of water, driven by enemies to seek new pasturage' suggest the perpetual movement of peoples across the spaces of geography and time in search of new possibilities of life (p. 115). Europe in the 1930s was witnessing mass displacements in those countries threatened by Nazi expansionism. The shopping and business streets of London are filled by the noise of traffic, but in the poorer districts the 'swarm of sound' comprises not only 'the rush of traffic [but also] the shouts of the hawkers, the single cries and the general cries' (p. 146). Throughout the text, street musicians, muffin men with their bells and barrel organ players are heard, while from open windows comes the sound of singing practice and a trombone player (p. 285). The social life of the city, like the life of the natural world, is comprehended as sound, its unarticulated complexity given voice.

During the time that Woolf was writing *The Years*, a vigorous campaign was being waged against street noise. The *New Statesman* was unsympathetic to the Anti-Noise League which in 1935 succeeded in outlawing milk-carts during the early morning hours. 'There was a kind of joy-bell gaiety in the clanging of can and bottle,' the writer declares, 'The joy of life expresses itself in a crowded chorus [. . .] With street cries I should never dream of interfering.'[19] In an earlier defence of street musicians against their detractors among the respectable classes, the *New Statesman* notes that some of the noisiest participants on the streets are young boys who seem intuitively to know that 'where there is noise, there is life'.[20] In *The Years*, the sense of the streets as embodying a force of unbounded vitality is reinforced by the omnipresence of children. Whenever the text mentions poorer streets, there are children, playing, skipping, running, always curious and responsive to events. When a barrel organ begins to play, 'the children all rushed in that direction' (p. 7). The contrast of the children of the poor to those, like Rose, kept within the bounds of the proper, is stark. The children, moreover, make chalk marks on the pavement and skip in and out of 'their chalk cages', suggestive of a creative energy with potential to overrun and redraw defined boundaries (p. 9).

What Woolf does not explicitly indicate, but what her first readers would have known, is that most of the children to be seen in city streets would be malnourished. The hungry rapaciousness of the working-class women in the text was only too real in the actual world beyond. There was, indeed, 'nothing to feed their hunger upon' (p. 86). The insufficient diet of the poor was as much in the headlines during the 1930s as was housing. Lack of proper shelter and diet were twin faces of poverty and causally related. While there was general consensus that slum housing needed to be cleared there seemed an unsolvable problem of how to provide new housing at rents the working class could afford. As many experts on the subject pointed out, increases in rent only had the effect of aggravating 'the evils of malnutrition – to shift the incidence of poverty from housing to the food budget'.[21] The problem was exacerbated by the government's policy of promoting private sector provision where the drive for profits also led to jerry building, such as Eleanor is faced with in the novel. In an article on 'The Health of the People' in 1933, the *New Statesman* commented that despite some improvement 'slums, foul milk supply, inadequate medical services' still damage the standard of health for much of the population and 'evidence of malnutrition in children is widespread'.[22]

The government's decision to cut welfare provision to the unemployed resulted in even poorer diets, to protests from the British Medical Association, many individual GPs, nutrition experts and other concerned groups as well as trade unions. In 1934, Eleanor Rathbone set up a Committee for the Children's Minimum to campaign publicly for recognition of the minimum standard of nutrition required by children to maintain health as set out by medical authorities. One ameliorative measure urged by Rathbone's Minimum Committee and by many others, was the provision of free milk to school children.[23] In another of those moves during the era that marked a transition from private to public ethos, the Milk Marketing Board had been set up to regulate the supply, price and quality of the milk produced by the great number of independent farmers. For this reason, milk was also a topic prominent in the news and public debate. The *New Statesman* commended the Milk Marketing Board in 1933 as a 'most important experiment' in what it called 'socialisation', the expansion of public provision and structures for the welfare of the whole population, an implicit recognition of the common life.[24] In 1935, the journal was pointing out that 'cheap milk for schoolchildren could not have been organised on a national scale without the existence of the board'.[25] Even so, in 1936, Sir John Orr revealed shocking evidence that half of the country's population was living on a diet which was below the standard required for the maintenance of perfect health and he warned that the scandal of actual starvation in the country would inevitably result in disease, stunted growth in children, poor physique in adults.[26]

In *The Years*, Colonel Pargiter points to the high seasonal price of milk when Eleanor presents him with the household accounts, a reference to the unstable fluctuation of supply and cost in pre-Milk Marketing Board days. The text also takes repeated note of the undersized bodies of many of the working-class characters. Crosby's insect-like physique is frequently commented upon and her prominent eyes would also indicate childhood malnutrition. When Kitty visits the Robson family she is struck by how short they all are, feeling she has to alter the focus of her eyes to suit their smallness (p. 63). The exception is their son, Jo, who is tall and handsome, a beneficiary of the improved diet the family enjoys due to Mr Robson's rise in status. Eleanor observes the 'little underfed body' of Mr Duffus, the builder (p. 89). He is also bandy-legged, the common result of childhood rickets, a disease caused by ill-nourishment. The exigency of physical need that human beings have in common with all living things shapes the actual bodies as well as identities of the poor.

Woolf is sometimes thought to avoid class issues in her work. *The Years*, nevertheless, is pervasively concerned with the constitution and policing of the boundary, or chalk marks, between working-class and middle-class worlds, a rigorous disavowal of any common life. The text marks a moment of transition in the relations between the respectable and the poor; the beginning of a process of convergence between the two. For the first and second generation of the extended Pargiter family, however, the two worlds remain distinct and separate. In *Comfort, Cleanliness and Convenience: The Social Organization of Normality*, Elizabeth Shove notes that, 'the social order is defined and reproduced through rituals of everyday life; rituals that in turn confer meaning on goods, artefacts, even infrastructures [. . .] they are implicated in the management of boundaries between social groups'.[27] Woolf is always astute in recognising the way artefacts or things provide substance for structures of belief. In *The Years*, Mrs Malone registers her maid's neglect of duties by cushions not shaken sufficiently. Her daughter Kitty responds to a feeling of being snubbed by the Robson family by indicting the inferiority of their things. Everything in their house is ugly, she thinks, reviewing with disgust the cheap curtains, darned tablecloth and 'florid' china (pp. 60–2). Kitty pushes from her mind all the ponderous things in the Lodge that oppress her.

Eleanor has a similar urge to Kitty's desire to extend her relations with the working-class people in her housing project. In particular, she is drawn by the glimpse of Mr Duffus's large family life, always 'hoping they might ask her in' (p. 87). But, suspecting that he is swindling her, she 'adopted the tone of the Colonel's daughter [. . .] She saw him turn sullen before her eyes [. . .] You have to bully them or else they despise you' she thinks (p. 89). Where the two class worlds are in intimate daily contact in the middle-class household even more drastic social strategies are required to maintain the fiction of separateness. Although servants inevitably acquire the most intimate knowledge of the family they serve, conversation is abruptly interrupted in their presence. Celia halts what she is saying to Eleanor when the maid comes in to clear away the coffee, turning to polite trivia and 'adapting her voice to the presence of servants' (p. 186). Crosby colludes in pretence that she is mute, deaf and invisible, stifling her laughter at the Colonel's jokes. Despite her long service for the family she remains, even in retirement, unable to speak for herself in their presence.

The most powerful dividing line between the world of respectability and the world of the poor, however, is that written on the body. This is not surprising since embodiment constitutes the basis for recognition of creaturely communality. Otherness and division must therefore start from the body. Not only are the working-class physically stunted and malformed, they are also deemed unhygienic. The class line cleaves apart what is perceived as clean and proper and what is designated dirty, improper and loathsomely other. In *The Road to Wigan Pier*, published in 1937, George Orwell declared that the smell of those often termed the 'great unwashed' was an insuperable barrier between the classes. Even those working-class people, like family servants, who were known to be clean were 'faintly unappetising'.[28]

In *The Years*, the respectable characters appear almost eager to notice any absence of cleanliness in those perceived as beneath them in social status. As one of her tenants waddles in front of her, Eleanor notices fastidiously that a 'wisp of yellow hair hung down behind her dirty ears', the unhealthy, wispy hair adding somehow to the sense of unwholesomeness (p. 89). Martin describes the caretaker in the basement of the empty house in Browne Street as 'a dirty old woman' (p. 135). Eleanor's repulsed response to the estate agent, who comes to evaluate the family home after her father's death, makes quite explicit the way notions of cleanliness function viscerally at the interface of class antagonism. Eleanor looks at the man's neck, 'washed imperfectly in some sink in Wandsworth'; she was annoyed at the way he had gone round their house, 'sniffing and peering, he had indicted their cleanliness, their humanity [. . .] He was hauling himself up into the class above him, she supposed' (p. 194). Eleanor's class resentment at the man's lack of deference to the middle-class home renders her unaware that she equally indicts *his* humanity as identified with cleanliness. Her disparagement of his need to wash in a sink points also to the way material infrastructure, like plumbing, perpetuates, exacerbates or can erase class boundaries.

Inevitably, the bathroom, as the site of interface between the self as body and the self as individual cultural identity, is a site fraught with potential conflict and tension. For the confined middle-class family the bathroom sanctioned the right to privacy, maintaining a disavowal of bodily being, in contrast to the zinc tub in the common kitchen or backyard which had to serve as washing facility for the working class. Even into the 1940s, whether or not a house or flat had its own bathroom was 'one of the major dividing lines' of social class (Ravetz, *The Place of Home*, p. 134).

For all these reasons, the enforced intimacy of a shared bathroom, and even more so the bodily matter exuded there, was source of deeply-felt fear and revulsion. Sara's account of the detritus of body hair and grease left in the bath by her Jewish neighbour, whom they can hear, while she speaks, coughing and clearing his throat, infects North with revulsion and disgust almost as strong as Sara's. 'North felt a shiver run through him. Hairs in food, hairs on basins, other people's hairs made him feel physically sick' (p. 307). This visceral response to a sense of contamination from the emissions of unhygienic otherness is not confined to middle-class fastidiousness. Far from pointing to the commonness of embodied life, it fuels the abhorrence and hatred directed at any groups or identities deemed unclean and other, whether of race or sexuality or appearance. Crosby calls the Belgium Count who spits in the bath 'a dirty foreigner' and 'a dirty brute', not properly human in his disgusting habits. Earlier in the story, in Oxford, Edward's friend, Gibbs, who is to marry Milly, expresses the disgust he feels for Ashley, a homosexual, by terming him a 'dirty little swine' (p. 49). The scrawled swastika points to the violence implicated in such processes of othering.

Alongside this recognition of social divisions based upon what is deemed the clean and proper body, there is an almost comic reiteration in the text of middle-class rituals of bodily hygiene. Delia admires her father when he comes down for dinner: 'He looked so pink and clean and genial in his dinner jacket' (p. 32). Whenever a middle-class character turns in for the night, the narrative dutifully records the ceremony of teeth-cleaning. After dinner at the lodge, Kitty in her bedroom 'began to brush her teeth', Eleanor decides to put off thinking about the poor families she is helping 'till she was brushing her teeth at night' (pp. 55, 29). Similar attention is given to the hot water left in many bedrooms during the story for a final wash before sleep, as when Eleanor washes herself 'methodically but carefully' due to the water shortage (p. 178). Characters make announcements that they are going to take a bath and the Pargiter children share a memory of being washed by a slimy cloth in their infancy (pp. 29, 140). Eleanor, returning from Spain, notices all the soap in a shop window and thinks 'how thoroughly people wash in England, even the air smells of soap' (p. 175). By the end of the novel, Eleanor is proudly showing off her modern shower (p. 278). There is, indeed, a reference to washing or cleanliness at least once in every ten pages of the story. Whatever else Woolf cut from her original chapters, she clearly did not want to omit these multiple details of hygiene rituals. It is hard to think of any other novel that so highlights the performance of bodily cleanliness. The textual reiteration seems to mimic the habitual everyday practices whereby the proper, hygienic, middle-class body is produced.

If Woolf is having fun at the expense of middle-class mores, there is, nevertheless, more serious irony involved. The cleanliness of the respectable classes is largely dependent upon the labour of the unhygienic unwashed. The 'water-jug [. . .] swaddled up like an old woman' in a guest's bedroom has been lugged all the way up from the basement by a servant and the used, dirty water will be carried down again by a servant (p. 53). The same physical effort is required for all the other water made available in respectable bedrooms throughout the narrative. In addition, the text refers many times to the washing of clothes and linen. The child Rose comes down in a dirty dress because the laundry has not been returned (p. 10). Before the arrival of the national grid, which made electrical goods available, all dirty washing had to be done by hand. Laundering was one of the most gruelling, physically demanding of all women's work, and for that reason only done by the most impoverished. The harsh soap required and the heavy lifting of wet cloth took a quick toll on health. Mrs Levy, confined to bed, speaks of 'when I was left a poor widder woman scrubbing and mangling', and she stretches out her arm 'which was wrung and white like the root of a tree' (p. 27). Her hard labour that has kept the middle-class household clean and proper has rendered her an object of physical disgust.

Yet Woolf does not represent the poor as pitiable victims. Crosby, despite the frailty of her body as she struggles against the weather, 'seemed to express an unconquerable determination; she was not going to give in; she was bent on surviving' (pp. 274–5). Deploying de Certeau's concept of the 'tactic' it is possible to see the various working-class people in the text as actively making use of what possibilities come their way and creatively producing their own possibilities. A tactic, de Certeau explains, exists outside the regime of the proper, the structures and routines of respectability. Those who have to rely upon tactics must always be on the look out for opportunities and must constantly manipulate events to turn them into opportunities (*Practice of Everyday*, p. 37). The exploited, of necessity, have to be able to exploit. Perhaps the clearest example of this in *The Years* is the waiter who seizes the chance of getting a double tip from Martin, a licit and an illicit one (p. 210). Eleanor thinks Mr Duffus has taken advantage of her, 'swindled her', by passing off shoddy workmanship. Eugénie clearly believes Mr Toye has exploited her gullibility, promising that tomorrow she will confront him and declare, 'No, Mr Toye, you have deceived me once too often' (pp. 89, 130). Meanwhile, there is the suggestion that her housemaid manipulates Eugénie's guilt at her untidiness. The maid waltzes around with a hat Eugénie has given her to 'atone for the mess in the drawing room' (p. 104).

Even Crosby seizes upon opportunities that come her way: 'for many years she had been hoarding odds and ends with a view to her retirement. Indian elephants, silver vases, the walrus that she had found in the waste-paper basket' (p. 196). Almost certainly the family would have given her these things had she asked, but this would have underlined her dependence rather than assert a right to ownership as the secret hoarding does. As she slowly clears the table and draws the curtains the prolonged and irritating creaking of her cheap shoes is surely a tactic of self-assertion in defiance of her muted presence in family life. In her early days, Kitty was piqued by the refusal of the Robson family to treat her as one of themselves. As Lady Lasswade, her maid, Baxter's, politely impersonal attendance and 'inscrutable, pursed-up' expression still renders her uncomfortable (p. 241). Baxter is an altogether more modern servant than Crosby, being unafraid to draw her own boundaries of where her responsibilities end and of pursuing a life of her own quite independent of those who employ her. Crosby, herself, comes up against the non-deferential attitude of a new generation of working women. 'It was all take-it-or-leave-it now,' Crosby mutters, addressing in imagination, 'the red-haired servant girl who had flung out of the house without warning. *She* could easily get another job' (p. 274).

In a somewhat reverse direction, sections of the middle class, especially women, were moving towards what could be termed downward class convergence. In *The Years*, Maggie and Renny manage without servants, although Renny admits this necessitates some disregard for middle-class mores: 'we are extremely dirty', he says (p. 255). Eleanor's final home in the novel had previously been a workman's flat, and Sara lives in a lodging-house that North calls a slum (pp. 296, 283). These rooms would have been rented from private landlords whose properties were often inferior to new rented housing offered to working-class tenants by local authorities. A correspondent to the *New Statesman* pointed out that working-class flats being built in Euston were an improvement on middle-class flats available in central London.[29]

Sara's outrage and disgust at the habits of the neighbour with whom she has to share a bathroom suggests that convergence does not necessarily produce community feeling. As electric wiring and indoor plumbing became increasingly standardised features of new or improved working-class housing during the 1930s, the better-off of the working class were able to espouse the complex values of respectability and privacy that modern convenience allowed. As Shove suggests, 'Cleanliness values bore on all who wished to better their lives or felt the sting of invidious class comparisons' (*Comfort*, p. 100). Whereas, into the beginning of the twentieth century, regular washing marked out middle-class status, as it does for the characters in *The Years*, by the 1930s, it had become 'a basic condition of social acceptance' (Shove, *Comfort*, p. 102). A condition of respectability was beginning to be available to the labouring population and with it, perhaps, recognition of a potential common life shared by middle and working classes alike and materialised in the national grid and piped water supply.

Clearly, housing was the central factor driving this transition of life styles and values. The years 1933 to 1938 witnessed a great boom in house building so that by 1939 approximately one-third of all houses were new. As a result, the possibility of home ownership extended down to the lower middle class and to the upper levels of working-class occupations. This mass market in home ownership was facilitated by a concurrent expansion of building societies. In 1910, the amount societies advanced was just over £9 million, while in 1938 it was £137 million. The result, writes John Burnett, was 'a growing convergence of standards between the established members and the new entrants to the class' (*A Social History*, p. 245). Not only was there a growing standardisation of housing, with amenities of running water, electricity and gas, but there was also a convergence of the values and ambitions derived from homeownership. 'Above all,' Burnett claims, for those 'able to buy a house instead of merely renting it, and to luxuriate in the sense of security and achievement which property-buying brought, [was a] [. . .] predominant ambition' (*A Social History*, p. 245).

Woolf's precise notation on types of housing throughout the narrative traces this very material process of transition. The need of embodied beings for shelter produces a social history given substance in houses as well as archives. At the end of the novel, Eleanor thinks, 'Always there were rooms [. . .] Always from the beginning of time' (p. 384). The rooms inhabited by the main characters at the beginning of *The Years*, in Abercorn Terrace, Browne Street and the Lodge, are spacious and the houses themselves imposing private family dwellings. As the story progresses these high-status properties move down the social scale, to become multiply-rented rooms and lodgings. The old houses in Milton Street, where Sara lodges, 'had seen better days' and the doorway and stairs of the lodging house 'had once been [part of] a gentleman's residence' (pp. 280, 281). Meanwhile in Oxford, Dr Malone so dislikes the 'cheap red villas' that characterise the neighbourhood in which the Robson family and Miss Craddock rent housing that 'he would always make a round to avoid them' (p. 56). The Robsons, unlike the very poor, can afford a house that has two ground floor rooms allowing for the status-enhancing, never to be used, front parlour. Dr Malone's dislike of the new cannot hold back the process of time. By the end of the novel, Milly is complaining of 'brand-new villas everywhere' (p. 339). As Eleanor and Peggy drive to Delia's party, the cab takes them down 'mild respectable little streets where every house had its bow window, its strip of garden, its private name' (p. 299). There is suggestion here of both conforming sameness and, paradoxically, of aspiring individualism, as asserted in private names. Nevertheless, the villas seem more part of the current of life than the glimpsed 'pale pompous beauty' of the ghostly stucco columns of Abercorn Terrace that the two women glimpse from the cab window.

What is at stake in this transitional moment materialised in the types of building seen on a drive through London? Is it a movement away from the pale pomposity of the middle-class house with its geography of vertical hierarchy, its life-restricting codes of privacy, properness and individualism? Is it a moment of dissensus, an opening out into possibilities of a more egalitarian sense of life and self as a horizontal continuum with the vitality of the natural world and of the social energies of city streets? This would entail a dismantling of the traditional vertical regime of perceptibility structured by idealist individualist values, to be replaced by an inclusive, comprehensive regime of the perceptible recognising as worthy of notice all domains of human existence – cultural, social and natural. It could be argued that the shared physical necessities of human life were leading, in the 1930s, to ever-greater degrees of commonality as materialised in the infrastructure of utilities and in the movement from private to public provision. These are possibilities and ideas that preoccupy the characters at the end of *The Years*. Eleanor, for example, recognises that identity comes not from private life but from social interaction: 'My life's been other people's lives' (p. 331).

North imagines an extension of self as comprehending a larger reality. He wants 'at the same time [to] spread out, make a new ripple in human consciousness, be the bubble and the stream [. . .] myself and the world together' (p. 369).

On the other hand, does a world of little red villas, each with their private name, suggest rather that the individualism and divisiveness of the private house are coming to dominate an ever larger section of the social world? The Anti-Noise League was campaigning against the vitality and noise of the city streets in the name of decency, privacy and house-owner rights. The house, whatever its size, is pre-eminently a stage for the performance of possessive individualism. There is certainly plenty of egoism on display at Delia's party. Peggy is bored by the 'I, I, I' of a young man's conversation but she compares its heedless persistence to a vacuum cleaner or a telephone bell, suggesting such male assertion is as commonplace in the present day of domestic technology as in earlier decades (p. 325). North wants to shield Maggie from the 'contamination of family life' that Milly represents, only to realise that Maggie is equally ready to talk 'about *her* children now'. None of them is interested in other people's children, he thinks, 'Only in their own; their own property; their own flesh and blood [. . .] How then can we be civilized?' (p. 341). Yet Peggy later thinks that he too 'would produce little Gibbses, more little Gibbses' (p. 357). The estate-agent advertisements and the talk of houses with several bathrooms, moreover, suggest the continued dominance of consumer acquisitiveness, of the quest for privacy and disavowal of physical necessity.

Delia's party itself attempts to stage social convergence. She has invited people who are commoners and those who are noble; there are those in formal evening dress and those who are not; some ignore decorum and drink soup out of mugs, some wait for spoons. 'That had always been her aim;' she thinks, 'to mix people; to do away with the absurd conventions of English life' (p. 359). Eleanor can also be seen to further the movement of convergence when she asks her brother, Edward, to encourage the son of her porter in his desire to go to college. Edward, too, approves of this widening of class opportunity. He points approvingly to one of Delia's guests, Chipperfield, who is a great railway man and son of a railway porter. Yet Chipperfield epitomises the equivocal outcome of class mobility. He has bought himself a 'delightful house' with two or three hundred acres for shooting and 'old masters' upon his walls. During the 1930s, there was public debate, much of it critical, as to the changes in life style and modes of speech by those of working-class origin who had risen to prominence as members of the Labour Party and trade unions as well as in business.

That Delia's husband, the arch conservative, Patrick, calls the property advertisements 'a manifesto' is surely a highly ironic joke. Property was indeed the manifesto, not of class revolution, but of respectability for those anxious to gain a higher social status; it was equally the lynch-pin holding in place vertical social structures and individualist values. North looks at his fellow guests and thinks that for all Delia's pride in her promiscuity, 'where are the Sweeps and the Sewer-men, the Seamstresses and the Stevedores?' (p. 364). Kitty is one of the most robust in insisting that she can drink her soup from a mug in defiance of convention. Much earlier in her life she had been tempted to throw decorum much more radically to the winds in her attraction to working-class young men. Later, as Lady Lasswade, she attends the opera *Siegfried* and as the hero hammers the sword that will destroy the old order, she is reminded of the 'Hammer, hammer, hammer' she heard coming from the garden of the Robsons' house from which a young man, their son, emerged with wood shavings in his hair (p. 165). Yet, ambivalently, in the text, this also echoes the 'Hammer, hammer, hammer' of the drunken working-class man beating at the door.

In the 1930s, there was almost universal recognition that the older order was giving way to new social and material structures. As always, the outcomes of such moments of dissensus were difficult to predict. Many hoped for, and possibly even more feared, the end of class and gender inequality. In addition, by the late 1930s, European war seemed almost inevitable. In this respect the last section of *The Years* strikingly echoes the ending of Chekhov's *The Three Sisters*. In each work, the main characters stand hesitant before the future, fearful yet desirous of change. Chekhov's world was about to be irrevocably transformed by the Russian Revolution and Woolf's by the Second World War. Characters at the end of the novel express yearning for a new order very much in the way Chekhov's characters do. 'To live differently . . . differently', North thinks (p. 381). Nicholas raises his glass to 'The human race [. . .] now in its infancy, may it grow to maturity' (p. 383). 'There must be another life,' Eleanor insists to herself, 'She felt as if she were standing on the edge of a precipice with her hair blown back' (p. 385). As in Chekhov's plays, there are no concrete proposals, no programmes or manifestos for a prescribed new world, only the desire for an opening up of the horizons of the possible, for a redistribution of the perceptible.

Woolf's novels are always highly dialogic, an orchestration of multiple voices within the social continuum. In the final section of *The Years* perspectives and voices change constantly. The novel, however, concludes with two striking images that resonate like alternative possibilities. As dawn comes, Eleanor watches as a young man and woman get out of a cab before a house. The man fits his latch-key to the door, and opens it. They stand for a moment on the threshold and then the door shuts behind them with a little thud (p. 391). If this represents the future, it seems an ominous turning away from the fullness of life, a retreat into the sheltered privacy of the house. This is the limitation of space that Woolf hoped future women writers would escape from. That 'little thud' of domestic enclosure is also the fate that, one hundred years earlier, Jane Austen had resisted for her female protagonists.

Just before Eleanor sees the young couple step out of the cab and enter the house, Delia brings up from the basement, where so many of the servants in the novel have lived invisibly, the children of the caretaker and, like Marie Antoinette, she offers them cake.[30] They eat hungrily but when asked to sing for their supper, they sweep fierce or frightened eyes over the assembled guests and break into a song that is pure sound with no recognisable words. They sing harshly, fiercely and discordantly. 'As they stood there they looked so dignified; yet they made this hideous noise' (p. 387). This, in itself, seems a moment of transition, the mute and invisible newly, shockingly perceptible. It stages an aesthetic and political dissensus, at once hilariously carnivalesque, yet equally tender, hopeful and terrifying.

Are these the voices of the future? Earlier in the novel Woolf had made audible the wider social and physical worlds that are largely rendered mute and unseen in regimes of representation structured upon individualism and idealism. In *The Years*, the common life of the physical world expresses itself as sound as well as visibility. The life of the city streets is also materialised as voices, as street cries, musicians and children singing as they skip over chalk marks. In *The Waves*, Louis desires to draw a steel ring of pure poetry around the physical energies and appetites of common life and thereby discipline it into an abstract universal order. Woolf resists any imposition of meaning upon the children's voices. The moment resonates without any interpretive screen placed upon it. It remains pure possibility.

The Years has been much criticised for its failure to be wholly realist or wholly modernist. Yet Woolf's writing moves well beyond earlier traditions of social and psychological realism. She practises a form of worldly realism that emphasises self, not as individual mind, but as embodied being and part of a material continuum with social structures and processes, with the whole physical universe, and with the potent world of things. From a modernist concern with technology, she produces a radical materialist history. This egalitarian, mobile perspective and aesthetics wholly undercuts the idealist, vertical representative regime still dominant within so many political and cultural domains today.

Notes

1. Virginia Woolf, *A Room of One's Own*, p. 86
2. *New Statesman*, 1935, January–June, p. 625; 1935, July–December, p. 664; 1933, July–September, p. 751; 1933, October–December, p. 480.
3. *New Statesman*, 1933, January–March, pp. 155–6.
4. Virginia Woolf, *The Years*, ed. Anna Snaith, pp. 132, 133.
5. John Burnett, *A Social History of Housing 1815–1970*, p. 107; for contemporary accounts see the *New Statesman*'s detailed articles and correspondence on housing development and debates during the 1930s.
6. *New Statesman*, 1933, April–June, p. 467.
7. See Alison Ravetz with Richard Turkington, *The Place of Home: English Domestic Environments, 1914–2000*, p. 123.
8. Hermione Lee, *Virginia Woolf*, p. 642.
9. *Diary of Virginia Woolf*, 4.172.
10. *Essays of Virginia Woolf*, 6.9.
11. *New Statesman*, 1936, July–December, p. 509.
12. *New Statesman*, 1936, April–June, pp. 858–60.
13. Alex Zwerdling, *Virginia Woolf and the Real World*, p. 47; the quotation is from *Diary of Virginia Woolf*, 5.70.
14. Mitchell A. Leaska, 'Introduction' to Virginia Woolf, *The Pargiters: The Novel-Essay Portion of* The Years, p. xv.
15. Anna Snaith, *Virginia Woolf: Public and Private Negotiations*, p. 99.
16. Linden Peach, *Virginia Woolf*, p. 168.
17. Michel de Certeau, *The Practice of Everyday Life*, p. 117.
18. *New Statesman*, 1935, July–December, p. 211.
19. *New Statesman*, 1935, July–December, p. 275. Woolf also appreciated street musicians: see her essay on 'Street Music', *Essays of Virginia Woolf*, 1.27–32.
20. *New Statesman*, 1933, July–September, p. 68.
21. *New Statesman*, 1936, April–June, p. 247. As with housing, the journal contains frequent articles and correspondence on malnutrition, especially of children.

22. *New Statesman*, 1933, July–September, pp. 344–5.
23. *New Statesman*, 1934, January–June, p. 215; p. 439; pp. 873–4; p. 993.
24. *New Statesman*, 1933, April–June, p. 467.
25. *New Statesman*, 1935, January–June, p. 311.
26. *New Statesman*, 1936, January–March, p. 174.
27. Elizabeth Shove, *Comfort, Cleanliness, and Convenience: The Social Organization of Normality*, p. 13.
28. George Orwell, *The Road to Wigan Pier*, pp. 112–13.
29. *New Statesman*, 1933, April–June, p. 411.
30. A correspondent to *New Statesman*, in a letter advocating more home baking by poorer women, refers to Marie Antoinette's supposedly infamous suggestion, 1936, July–December, p. 122.

Conclusion

> In so many ways, there has been a prising away of life from place, an abstraction of experience into different kinds of touchlessness. We experience, as no historical period has before, disembodiment and dematerialisation [. . .] We have in many ways forgotten what the world feels like [. . .] We have come increasingly to forget that our minds are shaped by the bodily experience of being in the world – its spaces, textures, sounds, smells and habits. (Robert Macfarlane, *The Wild Places*, p. 203)

What Robert Macfarlane describes here can be thought of as a redistribution of the perceptible, a turning away from the tangible experience of physical existence. Macfarlane's concern is the very modern one of the threat posed by this distancing and abstraction of our experience of the world to its ecological survival. Much earlier, at the turn of the eighteenth century, Jane Austen is also writing in reaction to this same redistributive formation, albeit still in process of emergence and consolidation. In *Sense and Sensibility*, the term 'society' retains for her the immediacy of personal interaction and shared feelings, even while its meaning is in process of change as part of the shift towards abstraction and aggregation as a way of knowing the world.

Struggles of representation as to what is noteworthy, what is above or below the horizon of visibility, are equally aesthetic and political. I have argued that both Austen and Woolf come to maturity as writers in periods of radically contested values in the eras respectively of the French Revolution and the First World War. In addition, their materialist understanding of reality and the writing practices they fashion from that understanding draw upon a tradition they share of British Enlightenment scepticism. The thinking of David Hume,

Adam Smith and David Hartley substantiated a position of dissent from what became, increasingly, a consensual aesthetic and political regime, an ideology sustaining the hierarchical ordering of the mental above the material. For both Austen and Woolf what is at stake in this disembodiment of experience is the pushing out of sight of our shared existence as creaturely beings, beings subject to the same physical needs and vulnerabilities. It is recognition of this commonality that underlies the immediacy of Mrs Jenkins's response, in *Sense and Sensibility*, to threat of hardship, 'I must see what I can give them' (p. 241). Yet already, the novel notes, this reactive sympathy is giving way to privatised gentility. In *Persuasion*, the characterisation of Anne Elliot charts the harm endured by those regarded literally as nobodies, rendered physically and socially invisible and unheard.

For Woolf, too, the common life is that felt upon the pulse and not the little individual life of the private drawing room. For Woolf, though, writing a hundred years later, embodiment has become a problem as well as a means to embrace the universe. In *Mrs Dalloway* and *The Waves*, the body is the site of conscription into coercive and regulatory social and cultural systems, systems that utilise idealist rhetoric to render invisible or contemptuous the material lives brought under subjection. In *The Years*, Woolf explores the force of bodily repugnance as a source of hatred and violence to any class or race or gender deemed unclean. Does increase in bodily privacy exemplified in access to bathrooms intensify feelings of distance and abstraction from the bodies of others? Eleanor practises philanthropy at a safe remove, providing housing for the poor, but the life of her servant Crosby who shares the intimacy of her home remains invisible to her. Not until Crosby leaves does Eleanor notice how dark and low the basement is; up to that moment class distribution of the perceptible has ensured the invisibility of Crosby's material existence.

Disembodiment aids the process of abstraction, whereby real lives, in the particularity of their needs, feelings, hopes and fears, become depersonalised. They become aggregates to be used as a means to achieve ideas, mental systems, the greater good. Harriet is exactly the 'something' that Hartfield needs, Emma thinks. Tenant farmers and the poor can be removed from land for its 'improvement', progress and civilisation require the 'working of hands and feet' to one disciplinary will, national well-being is served by the removal of 'superfluous youth' and a heterogeneous world is taught to see through the unitary vision of Western capitalism. From the Olympian perspective of authority, men dying in war are as distanced and disembodied as matchsticks. The process of conversion, as Woolf suggests, renders the flesh invisible, of no account. It is, as Derrida points out, the process of idealisation itself (Derrida, *Margins of Philosophy*, p. 226).

Against the homogenising vision of the scopic drive, Hannah Arendt asserts the multiplicity of viewpoints that constitute a public world (Arendt, *Human Condition*, p. 57). Austen and Woolf do likewise, experimenting constantly with innovative motility of focalisation. Above all, they dethrone human exceptionalism, the sovereign subject of rationality and interiority. It is this lonely being that provides the model for and credence to claims of divine, scientific, or visionary knowledge, elevating that mental totality above any challenge from empirical experience. In all three novels discussed here, Austen opposes the energy and heterogeneity of a shared world of horizontal relationships to the static uniformity and hierarchy of Olympic privilege and exclusion. Hartfield has to be integrated with Highbury if it is to become part of the processes of national change. The class-bound claustrophobia of Kellynch gives way to the variety and energy of Bath. 'So much novelty and beauty!' Anne Elliot cries in appreciation of movement and change (p. 200). She is surely speaking for most other women trapped invisible and unheard within small regulatory domestic worlds.

In Woolf's fiction, moments of shared being lead to dissolution of the competitive and individualistic self. Fleeting experiences of the world without an 'I' in it allow characters like Martin in *The Years* to lose consciousness of the boundaries of self and feel dispersed into the physical world around him. In *The Waves*, Bernard is 'unmoored' from his sense of 'I' to merge into the life of his fellow beings. In some ways, Austen's experimental writing in *Persuasion* most radically undoes the notion of the unitary self. Anne Elliot's consciousness simultaneously comprehends things (doors slamming), other people as voices and bodies, socio-cultural attitudes involved, and subjective feelings and rationalities experienced as bodily sensation. Things, others, culture and embodied self are inseparable within that compound experience. From such a full perspective any notion of privatised subjectivity seems thin and impoverished.

Things, for both novelists, constitute the shared world. Elinor, in *Sense and Sensibility*, recognises the power of ordinary things to challenge with their material tangibility the charm of wishful thinking. In *Mrs Dalloway*, Septimus Warren Smith is released from the grip of visions when he realises that things are not symbols of a hidden, purer reality but simply the stuff of ordinary shared life.

As this suggests, things, imbued with metaphorical meaning, provide a powerful means of giving spurious substance to abstract ideas and value systems, even while these idealist forms of thought disavow the material and fleshly. Thus, guns in *Persuasion* are shown as constitutive of masculine and class identities. Powerful cars, in *Mrs Dalloway*, make tangible, for Peter Walsh, the ideal of Western progress and civilisation. In *The Waves*, the paraphernalia and rituals of cricket constitute a sense of English identity. Even subjective interiority, Austen suggests, depends upon the props of material objects. Harriet needs her 'precious things' to make tangible her romantic dream of Mr Elton; Marianne articulates a broken heart by playing the piano.

At a macro level, things produce the lived reality and infrastructure of national and global existence. Pipes and wires underneath our homes, Woolf suggests in *The Years*, are material testimony to our shared needs as fleshly creatures but equally they facilitate an increase in domestic privacy, consumer competitiveness and hence a disavowal of the shared life that encourages fellowship. Sanitary and toiletry products exported around the world take with them a Western distribution of values, converting global variety and difference into a unitary economic place. More invisibly, technology makes a reality of scopic ambition that Emma Woodhouse could not even have dreamed of. Cables and telephones already provide Louis, in *The Waves*, with the means to abstract himself from a shared world he has always feared as disorderly and perversely fleshly. He becomes disembodied authority, a voice issuing commands, to discipline the heterogeneity of embodied lives into a regulated conformity. By such material means is physical and social existence converted into the ideal of abstract schemes and visions.

Neither Austen nor Woolf is a revolutionary. They do not envisage or seek a redistribution of wealth or of social order. They articulate a redistribution of the perceptible. Sharing a scepticism deriving from British Enlightenment's quarrel with idealism, and from their outsider's view as women, they challenge the pervasive consensual orthodoxy that privileges the mental above the material. In particular, they reject the rhetorical elevation of abstract systems and beliefs that veil over fleshly needs and vulnerability and the shared life such recognition fosters. As such, their critique is not of any one particular vested interest or class or location of power. What they recognise is the danger inherent in one of the most basic impulses shaping human thought: idealism. The capacity to look beyond the restrictive codes of the actual and probable is vital. Without the power to imagine, both writers show, human life would be enclosed and mean. Their fiction is energised by their worldly vision of the wide possibilities of human existence. Yet any vision or system of belief needs the constant challenge of empirical realities lest it convert 'all this fever of living' into a depersonalised abstraction. It is the enduring temptation and danger of rendering the stuff of material existence imperceptible that makes the critiques of Austen and Woolf so continuously relevant and never more so than at present.

The experimental writing practices they develop to convey their oppositional views, I have termed worldly realism. As opposed to the idealist sanctioning of individualism in much psychological realism and the restrictive actualism of social realism, worldly realism evokes horizontal, interactive, mutually determining relationships between embodied people, things, social world and physical universe, an egalitarian writerly space in which potentially nothing is mute or invisible. It is an approach to Austen's fiction that recognises the grounds and the achievement of her artistic radicalness. Am I also suggesting that Woolf is a realist rather than a modernist? These are not mutually exclusive aesthetics. As Brecht said, we do not have to position them as binary oppositions. Literary criticism should perhaps heed Woolf's condemnation of the adversarial mentality of the public school 'where there are "sides", and it is necessary for one side to beat the other' (*Room of One's Own*, p. 80). Far from adversaries, Woolf and Austen share an experimental energy that produces new representational regimes that expand the perceptibility of all aspects – hair, dirt, tides, clouds, laughter and poetry – of material existence. Against coercive orthodoxy, they demonstrate the liberating blasphemy of mocking irreverence.

Bibliography

Abel, Elizabeth, *Virginia Woolf and the Fictions of Psychoanalysis* (Chicago: Chicago University Press, 1989).

Allen, Richard C., *David Hartley on Human Nature* (Albany: State University of New York, 1999).

Alt, Christina, *Virginia Woolf and the Study of Nature* (Cambridge: Cambridge University Press, 2010).

Appadurai, Arjun, ed., *The Social Life of Things: Commodities in Cultural Perspective* (Cambridge: Cambridge University Press, 1986).

Arendt, Hannah, *The Human Condition*, 2nd edn (Chicago: Chicago University Press, 1998).

Armstrong, Nancy, *Desire and Domestic Fiction: A Political History of the Novel* (Oxford: Oxford University Press, 1987).

—*How Novels Think: The Limits of Individualism from 1719–1900* (New York: Columbia University Press, 2005).

Auerbach, Erich, *Mimesis: The Representation of Reality in Western Literature*, trans. Willard R. Trask (Princeton: Princeton University Press, 1953).

Austen, Jane, *Sense and Sensibility*, ed. James Kinsley, with an Introduction. by Margaret Anne Doody (Oxford: Oxford University Press, 1990).

—*Jane Austen's Letters*, new edition, ed. Deirdre Le Faye (Oxford: Oxford University Press, 1995).

—*Northanger Abbey, Lady Susan, The Watsons* and *Sanditon*, ed. James Kinsley and John Davie, with an Introduction by Claudia L. Johnson (Oxford: Oxford University Press, 2003).

—*Emma*, ed. Richard Cronin and Dorothy Macmillan (Cambridge: Cambridge University Press, 2005).

—*Persuasion*, ed. Janet Todd and Antje Blank (Cambridge: Cambridge University Press, 2006).

Austen-Leigh, J. E., *A Memoir of Jane Austen and Other Family Recollections*, ed. Kathryn Sutherland (Oxford: Oxford University Press, 2002).

Banfield, Ann, *The Phantom Table: Woolf, Fry, Russell and the Epistemology of Modernism* (Cambridge: Cambridge University Press, 2000).

Barchas, Janine, *Matters of Fact in Jane Austen: History, Location and Celebrity* (Baltimore: Johns Hopkins University Press, 2012).

Bazin, Nancy Topping, *Virginia Woolf and the Androgynous Vision* (New Brunswick, NJ: Rutgers University Press, 1973).
Becker, Marvin B., *The Emergence of Civil Society in the Eighteenth Century: A Privileged Moment in the History of England, Scotland and France* (Indianapolis: Indianapolis University Press, 1994).
Beer, Gillian, *Virginia Woolf: The Common Ground* (Michigan: University of Michigan Press, 1996).
Bell, Clive, [1928], *Civilization: An Essay* (London: Chatto and Windus, 1932).
Bell, Quentin, *Virginia Woolf: A Biography*, 2 vols (London: Hogarth Press, 1972).
Bennett, Jane, *Vibrant Matter: A Political Ecology of Things* (Durham, NC: Duke University Press, 2010).
Bhaskar, Roy, with Mervyn Hartwig, *The Formation of Critical Realism: A Personal Perspective* (London: Routledge, 2010).
Bloom, Harold, ed., *Romanticism and Consciousness: Essays in Criticism* (New York: W. W. Norton, 1975).
Blyth, Mark, *Austerity: The History of a Dangerous Idea* (Oxford: Oxford University Press, 2013).
Boradkar, Prasad, *Designing Things, A Critical Introduction to the Culture of Objects* (Oxford: Berg, 2010).
Boucher, David, ed., *The British Idealists* (Cambridge: Cambridge University Press, 1990).
Boucher, David and Andrew Vincent, *British Idealism: A Guide for the Perplexed* (London and New York: Continuum International Publishing Group, 2012).
Bourke, Richard, *Empire and Revolution: The Political Life of Edmund Burke* (Princeton: Princeton University Press, 2015).
Bowlby, Rachel, *Feminist Destinations* (Oxford: Oxford, 1988).
—'Waiting for the Dawn to Come', *London Review of Books*, 11 April 2013, vol. 35, pp. 32–4.
Bradley, F. H., *Ethical Studies* [1876], 2nd edn (Oxford: Clarendon, 1927).
Brecht, Bertold, 'Brecht against Georg Lukács', in Robert Taylor, ed., trans. Stuart Hood, *Aesthetics and Politics* (London: Verso, 1977), pp. 68–85.
Brinkley, Douglas, *Wheels for the World: Henry Ford, his Company and a Century of Progress* (Harmondsworth: Penguin, 2004).
Brown, Bill, ed., *Things* (Chicago: Chicago University Press, 2004).
Buchan, James, *Capital of the Mind: How Edinburgh Changed the World* (London: John Murray, 2003).
Burke, Edmund, *Reflections on the Revolution in France* [1790], ed. Conor Cruise O'Brien (Harmondsworth: Penguin, 1969).
Burnett, John, *A Social History of Housing 1815–1970* (London: Methuen, 1978).
Butler, Judith, *Bodies that Matter: On the Discursive Limits of 'Sex'* (London: Routledge, 1993).

Butler, Marilyn, *Jane Austen and the War of Ideas* (Oxford: Oxford University Press, 1987).
Byrne, Sandie, *Jane Austen's Possessions and Dispossessions: The Significance of Objects* (Houndmills: Palgrave Macmillan, 2014).
Campbell-Culver, Maggie, *The Origin of Plants: The People and Plants that have Shaped Britain's Garden History since the Year 1000* (London: Transworld Publishers, 2001).
Caughie, Pamela L., ed., *Virginia Woolf in the Age of Mechanical Reproduction* (New York: Garland Publishing Inc., 2000).
Certeau, Michel de, *The Practice of Everyday Life*, trans. Steven Rendell (Berkeley: University of California Press, 1988).
Clark, Robert and Gerry Dutton, 'Agriculture', in Janet Todd, ed., *Jane Austen in Context*, pp. 185–93.
Clark, Andy, *Supersizing the Mind: Embodiment, Action and Cognitive Extension* (Oxford: Oxford University Press, 2011).
Cuddy-Keane, Melba, *Virginia Woolf, the Intellectual, and the Public Sphere* (Cambridge: Cambridge University Press, 2003).
Czarnecki, Kristin and Carrie Rohman, eds, *Virginia Woolf and the Natural World: Selected Papers from the Twentieth Annual Conference on Virginia Woolf* (Clemson, SC: Clemson University Digital Press, 2011).
Dalgarno, Emily, *Virginia Woolf and the Visible World* (Cambridge: Cambridge University Press, 2007).
Davenport-Hines, Richard, *Universal Man: The Seven Lives of John Maynard Keynes* (London: William Collins, 2015).
Derrida, Jacques, *Margins of Philosophy*, trans., with additional notes by Alan Bass (Brighton: Harvester Press, 1982).
Dick, Susan, 'Literary Realism in *Mrs Dalloway*, *To the Lighthouse* and *The Waves*', in Sue Roe and Susan Sellers, eds, *Cambridge Companion to Virginia Woolf*, pp. 50–71.
Duckworth, Alistair, *The Improvement of the Estate: A Study of Jane Austen's Novels* (Baltimore: Johns Hopkins University Press, 1994).
Dyhouse, Carol, *Feminism and the Family in England 1880–1939* (Oxford: Blackwell, 1989).
Everest, Kelvin, ed., *Revolution in Writing: British Literary Responses to the French Revolution* (Milton Keynes: Open University Press, 1991).
Foucault, Michel, 'Politics and the Study of Discourse' and 'Governmentality', in Graham Burchell, Colin Gordan and Peter Miller, eds, *The Foucault Effect: Studies in Governmentality* (Chicago: University of Chicago Press, 1991), pp. 53–72, 87–104.
Friedman, Thomas L., *The World is Flat: A Brief History of the Twenty-First Century* (New York: Farrar, Straus and Giroux, 2005).
Froula, Christine, *Virginia Woolf and the Bloomsbury Avant-Garde: War, Civilization, Modernity* (New York: Columbia University Press, 2007).
Fry, Roger, *Vision and Design* [1920] (Harmondsworth: Penguin, 1961).

Galperin, William H., *The Historical Austen* (Philadelphia: University of Pennsylvania Press, 2003).

Gilbert, Sandra M. and Susan Gubar, *The Madwoman in the Attic: The Woman Writer and the Nineteenth-Century Literary Imagination* (New Haven, CT: Yale University Press, 1984).

Gillespie, Stuart and Philip Hardie, eds, *The Cambridge Companion to Lucretius* (Cambridge: Cambridge University Press, 2007).

Gleadle, Kathryn, *The Early Feminists: Radical Unitarians and the Emergence of the Women's Rights Movement, 1831–51* (Houndmills: Macmillan, 1998).

—and Sarah Richardson, eds, *Women in British Politics, 1760–1860: The Power of the Petticoat* (Houndmills: Macmillan, 2000).

Greenblatt, Stephen, *The Swerve: How the Renaissance Began* (London: Bodley Head, 2011).

Guiguet, Jean, *Virginia Woolf and her Works*, trans. Jean Stewart (London: Hogarth Press, 1965).

Habakkuk, H. J., *American and British Technology in the Nineteenth Century* (Cambridge: Cambridge University Press, 1962).

Habermas, Jürgen, *The Philosophical Discourse of Modernity: Twelve Lectures*, trans. Frederick G. Lawrence (Oxford: Polity, 1987).

—*The Structural Transformation of the Public Sphere: An Inquiry into a Category of Bourgeois Society*, trans. Thomas Burger with assistance from Frederick Lawrence (Oxford: Polity, 1992).

—*Philosophy in a Time of Terror: Dialogues with Jürgen Habermas and Jacques Derrida*, ed. Giovanna Borradori (Chicago: Chicago University Press, 2003).

Haffley, James, *The Glass Roof: Virginia Woolf as Novelist* (Berkeley: University of California Press, 1954).

Haldane, J. B. S., *Daedalus, or Science and the Future* (London: Kegan Paul, Trench, Trubner and Co., 1924).

Hamilton, Elizabeth, *A Series of Popular Lectures*, 2 vols (London: Longman and Co., 1813).

—*Letters on the Elementary Principles of Education* [1801], rpt in Pam Morris, ed., *Conduct Literature for Women 1770–1830*, 6 vols (London: Pickering and Chatto, 2005).

Hartley, David, *Observations on Man, his Frame, his Duty and his Expectations* [1791], with an Introduction by Jonathan Wordsworth, 2 vols (Poole: Woodstock Books, 1988).

Harvey, David, *The Conditions of Postmodernity: An Enquiry into the Origins of Cultural Change* (Oxford: Blackwell, 1990).

—*A Brief History of Neoliberalism* (Oxford: Oxford University Press, 2007).

—*Cosmopolitanism and the Geographies of Freedom* (New York: Columbia University Press, 2009).

Hume, David, *A Treatise on Human Nature* [1739 and 1740] (London: Penguin, 1969).

—*Essays, Moral, Political and Literary* [1777], revd edn (Indianapolis: Liberty Fund, 1987)

—*An Enquiry Concerning Human Understanding* [1748] (Oxford: Oxford University Press, 2007).

Hussey, Mark, *The Singing of the Real World: The Philosophy of Virginia Woolf's Fiction* (Columbus: Ohio State University Press, 1986).

—*Virginia Woolf and War: Fiction, Reality and Myth* (Syracuse: Syracuse University Press, 1991).

Jaakko, Hintikka, 'Virginia Woolf and Our Knowledge of the External World', *Journal of Aesthetics and Art Criticism*, Fall 1979–80, vol. 38, pp. 5–14.

Johnson, Claudia L., *Women, Politics and the Novel* (Chicago: University of Chicago Press, 1988).

—*Equivocal Beings: Politics, Gender and Sentimentality in the 1790s* (Chicago: Chicago University Press, 1995).

Jones, Chris, 'Landownership', in Janet Todd, ed., *Jane Austen in Context*, pp. 269–77.

Josipovici, Gabriel, *Whatever Happened to Modernism* (New Haven, CT: Yale University Press, 2010).

Kean, Hilda, *Animal Rights, Political and Social Change in Britain since 1800* (London: Reaktion Books, 1998).

Kelly, Gary, *Women, Writing and the Revolution, 1790–1827* (Oxford: Oxford University Press, 1993).

King, Jeannette, *Tragedy in the Victorian Novel: Theory and Practice in the Novels of George Eliot, Thomas Hardy and Henry James* (Cambridge: Cambridge University Press, 1980).

Klemke, E. D., *The Epistemology of G. E. Moore* (Evanston: Northwestern University Press, 1969).

Knox-Shaw, Peter, *Jane Austen and the Enlightenment* (Cambridge: Cambridge University Press, 2004).

Kumar, Shiv K., *Bergson and the Stream of Consciousness Novel* (London and Glasgow: Blackie, 1962).

Lakoff, George, and Mark Johnson, *Metaphors We Live By* (Chicago: Chicago University Press, 1980).

Langford, Paul, *Public Life and the Propertied Englishman 1689–1798* (Oxford: Clarendon Press, 1991).

—*A Polite and Commercial People: England 1727–1783* (Oxford: Clarendon Press, 1998).

—*Englishness Identified: Manners and Character 1650–1850* (Oxford: Oxford University Press, 2001).

Latour, Bruno, 'Why has Critique Run Out of Steam: From Matters of Fact to Matters of Concern' in Bill Brown, ed., *Things* (Chicago: Chicago University Press, 2004), pp. 151–73.

—*Reassembling the Social: An Introduction to Actor-Network Theory* (Oxford: Oxford University Press, 2005).

Lawrence, Karen, ed., *Decolonizing Tradition: New Views of Twentieth-Century 'British' Literary Canons* (Urbana: University of Illinois Press, 1992).

Leaska, Mitchell A., ed., with Introduction, Virginia Woolf, *The Pargiters: The Novel-Essay Portion of* The Years (New York and London: A Harvest/HBK Book, 1977).

Lee, Hermione, *Virginia Woolf* (London: Chatto and Windus, 1996).

Light, Alison, *Mrs Woolf and the Servants* (Harmondsworth: Penguin, 2007).

Littlewood, Ian, ed., *Jane Austen: Critical Assessments*, 4 vols (Mountfield: Helm Information, 1989).

Loesser, Arthur, *Men, Women and Pianos: A Social History* (New York: Dover Publications, 1954).

Lucretius, *De Rerum Natura*, trans. W. H. D. Rouse [1924], revised by Martin Ferguson Smith, Loeb Classic Library (Cambridge, MA: Harvard University Press, 1975).

Lukács, Georg, *Studies in European Realism*, trans. Edith Bone (London: Merlin Press, 1972).

Macfarlane, Robert, *The Wild Places* (London: Granta, 2007).

McLaurin, Allen, *Virginia Woolf: The Echoes Enslaved* (Cambridge: Cambridge University Press, 2010).

Mansbridge, Jane J., ed., *Beyond Self-Interest* (Chicago: Chicago University Press, 1990).

Marçal, Katrine, *Who Cooked Adam Smith's Dinner? A Story about Women and Economics*, trans. Saskia Vogel (London: Portobello Books, 2015).

Marcus, Jane, ed., *New Feminist Essays on Virginia Woolf* (Houndmills: Macmillan, 1981).

—*Virginia Woolf and the Languages of Patriarchy* (Indianapolis: Indiana University Press, 1988).

Miller, D. A., *Jane Austen or the Secret of Style* (Princeton: Princeton University Press, 2005).

Milnes, Tim, *The Truth about Romanticism: Pragmatism and Idealism in Keats, Shelley, Coleridge* (Cambridge: Cambridge University Press, 2013).

Minnow-Pinkney, Makiko, *Virginia Woolf and the Problem of the Subject: Feminine Writing in the Major Novels* (Brighton: Harvester, 1987).

Moi, Toril, *Sexual/Textual Politics: Feminist Literary Theory* (London: Methuen, 1985).

Monaghan, David, *Jane Austen: Structure and Social Vision* (New York: Barnes and Noble, 1980).

Moore, G. E., *Philosophical Studies* (London: Routledge and Kegan Paul, 1922).

More, Hannah, *Strictures on the Modern System of Female Education*, 2 vols, 3rd edn (London: T. Cadell, Jr and W. Davies, 1799).

Morris, Pam, *Realism* (London: Routledge, 2003).

—*Imagining Inclusive Society in Nineteenth-Century Novels: The Code of Sincerity in the Public Sphere* (Baltimore: Johns Hopkins University Press, 2004).

Namier, Lewis, *The Structure of Politics at the Accession of George III*, 2nd edn (Houndmills: Macmillan, 1957).

Neill, Edward, *The Politics of Jane Austen* (Houndmills: Macmillan, 1999).

Nicholson, Peter P., *The Political Philosophy of the British Idealists: Selected Studies* (Cambridge: Cambridge University Press, 1990).

Orwell, George, *The Road to Wigan Pier* [1937] (Harmondsworth: Penguin, 1962).

Parakilas, James et al., *Piano Roles: Three Hundred Years of Life with the Piano* (New Haven, CT: Yale University Press, 1999).

Parrinder, Patrick, Andrew Nash and Nicola Wilson, eds, *New Directions in the History of the Novel* (Houndmills: Palgrave Macmillan, 2014).

Peach, Linden, *Virginia Woolf* (Houndmills: Macmillan Press, 2000).

Phillipson, Nicholas, *Adam Smith: An Enlightened Life* (London: Allen Lane, 2010).

Poovey, Mary, *The Proper Lady and the Woman Writer: Ideology as Style in the Works of Mary Wollstonecraft, Mary Shelley and Jane Austen* (Chicago: University of Chicago Press, 1984).

Porter, Roy, *Enlightenment: Britain and the Creation of the Modern World* (London: Penguin, 2000).

—*Flesh in the Age of Reason* (London: Allen Lane, 2003).

Price, Richard, *British Society 1680–1880: Dynamism, Containment and Change* (Cambridge: Cambridge University Press, 1999).

Rancière, Jacques, *The Aesthetic Unconscious*, trans. Debra Keats and James Swenson (Cambridge: Polity Press, 2009).

—*Dissensus: On Politics and Aesthetics*, ed. and trans. Steven Corcoran (London and New York: Continuum, 2010).

—*The Politics of Literature*, trans. Julie Rose (Cambridge: Polity Press, 2011).

—*Aisthesis: Scenes from the Aesthetic Regime of Art*, trans. Zakir Paul (London: Verso, 2013).

Randall, Bryony and Jane Goldman, eds, *Virginia Woolf in Context* (Cambridge: Cambridge University Press, 2012).

Ravetz, Alison and Richard Turkington, *The Place of Home: English Domestic Environments 1914–2000* (Abingdon: Taylor and Francis, 2011).

Rawson, Claude, 'Introduction' to *Persuasion* (Oxford: Oxford University Prcss, 1990), pp. vii–xxxvii.

Richards, I. A., *The Philosophy of Rhetoric* (Oxford: Oxford University Press, 1936).

Ricoeur, Paul, *The Rule of Metaphor: The Creation of Meaning in Language*, trans. Robert Czerny, with Kathleen McLaughlin and John Costello, SJ (London: Routledge, 2003).

Roe, Nicholas, 'Politics', in Janet Todd, ed., *Jane Austen in Context*, pp. 357–65.
Roe, Sue, *Writing and Gender: Virginia Woolf's Writing Practice* (Hemel Hempstead: Harvester, 1990).
—and Susan Sellers, eds, *Cambridge Companion to Virginia Woolf* (Cambridge: Cambridge University Press, 2000).
Rosenbaum, S. P., ed., *English Literature and British Philosophy* (Chicago: University of Chicago Press, 1971).
Royle, Edward, *Modern Britain: A Social History 1750–1985* (London: Edward Arnold, 1987).
Rupert, Mark, *Producing Hegemony: The Politics of Mass Production and American Global Power* (Cambridge: Cambridge University Press, 1995).
Russell, Bertrand, *The Problems of Philosophy* [1912] (Oxford: Oxford University Press, 1959).
—*Mysticism and Logic* [1918] (Nottingham: Spokesman, 2007).
Ryan, Derek, *Virginia Woolf and the Materiality of Theory: Sex, Animal, Life* (Edinburgh: Edinburgh University Press, 2013).
Sales, Roger, *Jane Austen and Representations of Regency England* (London: Routledge, 1996).
Sen, Amartya, 'Rational Fools: A Critique of the Behavioural Foundations of Economic Theory' in Jane M. Mansbridge, ed., *Beyond Self-Interest* (Chicago: Chicago University Press, 1990), pp. 25–43.
—*The Idea of Justice* (London: Allen Lane, 2009).
Shevelow, Kathryn, *For the Love of Animals: The Rise of the Animal Protection Movement* (New York: Henry Holt and Co., 2008).
Shorter, Edward, *A History of Psychiatry: From the Era of the Asylum to the Age of Prozac* (New York: John Wiley and Sons, 1997).
Shove, Elizabeth, *Comfort, Cleanliness and Convenience: The Social Organization of Normality* (Oxford and New York: Berg, 2003).
Simpson, Kathryn, *Gifts, Markets and Economies of Desire in Virginia Woolf* (Houndmills: Palgrave Macmillan, 2008).
Smith, Adam, *Essays on Philosophical Subjects* [1795], ed. W. P. D. Wightman and J. C. Bryce, with Dugald Stewart's *Account of Adam Smith* (Oxford: Clarendon Press, 1980).
—*An Inquiry into the Nature and Causes of the Wealth of Nations* [1776], ed. Kathryn Sutherland (Oxford: Oxford University Press, 1993).
—*The Theory of Moral Sentiments* [1759], ed. Knud Haakonssen (Cambridge: Cambridge University Press, 2002).
Snaith, Anna, *Virginia Woolf: Public and Private Negotiations* (Houndmills: Palgrave Macmillan, 2000).
—and Michael Whitworth, eds, *Locating Woolf: The Politics of Space and Place* (Cambridge: Cambridge University Press, 2007).
Southam, B. C., ed., *Jane Austen: The Critical Heritage* (London: Routledge and Kegan Paul, 1968).

Spring, David, 'Interpretations of Jane Austen's Social World: Literary Critics and Historians', in Janet Todd, ed., *Jane Austen: New Perspectives, Women and Literature*, pp. 53–72.

Stafford, William, *English Feminists and their Opponents in the 1790s: Unsex'd and Proper Females* (Manchester: Manchester University Press, 2002).

Stewart, Garrett, 'Catching the Stylistic D/rift: Sound Defects in Woolf's *The Waves*', *English Literary History*, 1987, vol. 54, pp. 421–61.

Sutherland, Kathryn, 'Hannah More's Counter-Revolutionary Feminism', in Kelvin Everest, ed., *Revolution in Writing: British Literary Responses to the French Revolution*, pp. 27–63.

Tanner, Tony, *Jane Austen*, reissued edition (Houndmills: Palgrave Macmillan, 2007).

Tate, Douglas, 'British Gunmakers', *The Field*, 3 April 2012, pp. 1–7.

Thompson, E. P., *Whigs and Hunters: The Origin of the Black Act* (Harmondsworth: Peregrine, 1977).

Thompson, F. M. L., *English Landed Society in the Nineteenth Century* (London: Routledge, 1971).

Thomson, Matthew, *The Problem of Mental Deficiency: Eugenics, Democracy, and Social Policy in Britain c. 1870–1959* (Oxford: Clarendon, 1998).

Todd, Janet, ed., *Jane Austen: New Perspectives*, Women and Literature, vol. 3 (new series) (New York: Holmes and Meier, 1983).

—ed., *Jane Austen in Context* (Cambridge: Cambridge University Press, 2005).

Tomalin, Claire, *Jane Austen: A Life* (Harmondsworth: Penguin, 1998).

Tuite, Clara, *Romantic Austen: Sexual Politics and the Literary Canon* (Cambridge: Cambridge University Press, 2008).

Uglow, Jenny, *A Little History of British Gardening* (London: Pimlico, 2005).

Vincent, Andrew and Raymond Plant, *Philosophy, Politics and Citizenship: The Life and Thought of British Idealists* (Oxford: Blackwell, 1984).

Watt, Ian, *The Rise of the Novel: Studies in Defoe, Richardson and Fielding* (London: Chatto and Windus, 1957).

—ed., *Jane Austen: A Collection of Critical Essays* (Upper Saddle River: Prentice Hall, 1963).

Webb, R. K., *Modern England: From the Eighteenth Century to the Present* (London: George Allen and Unwin, 1969).

Whitworth, Michael H., *Virginia Woolf* (Oxford: Oxford University Press, 2005).

Williams, Raymond, *The Country and the City* (St Albans: Paladin, 1975).

Wiltshire, John, *Jane Austen and the Body* (Cambridge: Cambridge University Press, 1992).

Wittgenstein, Ludwig, *Philosophical Investigations*, trans. G. E. M. Anscombe (Oxford: Blackwell, 1972).

Wollstonecraft, Mary, *A Vindication of the Rights of Woman* [1792] and *A Vindication of the Rights of Man* [1790] (Oxford: Oxford University Press, 1993).
Wood, James, *How Fiction Works* (London: Vintage, 2008).
Woods, H., *On the Nature of Things* (London and Bristol: Wright, Simpkin, Marshall, Hamilton, Kent, 1918).
Woolf, Leonard, *Imperialism and Civilization* (London: Hogarth Press, 1928).
Woolf, Virginia, *Collected Essays*, ed. Leonard Woolf, 4 vols (London: Chatto and Windus, 1966).
—*Diary of Virginia Woolf*, ed. Anne Olivier Bell and Andrew MacNeillie, 5 vols (London: Hogarth Press, 1977–84).
—*The Essays of Virginia Woolf*, 6 vols, ed. Andrew McNeillie (vols 1–4); ed. Stuart N. Clarke (vols 5–6) (London: Hogarth Press, 1986–2011).
—*The Waves*, ed. with an Introduction by Gillian Beer (Oxford: Oxford University Press, 1992).
—*Jacob's Room*, ed. with an Introduction by Kate Flint (Oxford: Oxford University Press, 1999).
—*Mrs Dalloway*, ed. with an Introduction by David Bradshaw (Oxford: Oxford University Press, 2000).
—*Moments of Being: Autobiographical Writings*, ed. Jeanne Schulkind, with an Introduction by Hermione Lee, new edn (London: Pimlico, 2002).
—*Roger Fry: A Biography* (London: Vintage, 2003).
—*The Years*, ed. Anna Snaith (Cambridge: Cambridge University Press, 2012).
—*A Room of One's Own and Three Guineas*, ed. with an Introduction by Anna Snaith (Oxford: Oxford University Press, 2015).
Zwerdling, Alex, *Virginia Woolf and the Real World* (Los Angeles and Berkeley: University of California Press, 1986).

Journals

Edinburgh Review
Gentleman's Magazine
London Review of Books
Monthly Review
Morning Chronicle
New Statesman
The Field
The Times

Index